Remembering Paul Beeson

A Tribute From His Students, Residents, and Colleagues

John N. Forrest, Jr.
Lewis Landsberg, Editors

"No contemporary figure has had more influence on the way western-trained doctors practice medicine than Paul Beeson."
– Richard Rapport, *Physician: The Life of Paul Beeson* (2001)

Perspectives in Medical Humanities

Perspectives in Medical Humanities publishes peer reviewed scholarship produced or reviewed under the auspices of the University of California Medical Humanities Consortium, a multi-campus collaborative of faculty, students, and trainees in the humanities, medicine, and health sciences. Our series invites scholars from the humanities and health care professions to share narratives and analysis on health, healing, and the contexts of our beliefs and practices that impact biomedical inquiry.

General Editor

Brian Dolan, PhD, Professor of Social Medicine and Medical Humanities, University of California, San Francisco (UCSF)

Other Titles in this Series

Patient Poets: Illness from Inside Out
Marilyn Chandler McEntyre (Fall 2012) (Pedagogy in Medical Humanities series)

Bioethics and Medical Issues in Literature
Mahala Yates Stripling (Fall 2013) (Pedagogy in Medical Humanities series)

From Bench to Bedside, to Track & Field: The Context of Enhancement and its Ethical Relevance
Silvia Camporesi (Fall 2014)

Heart Murmurs: What Patients Teach Their Doctors
Edited by Sharon Dobie, MD (Fall 2014)

Soul Stories: Voices from the Margins
Josephine Ensign (Fall 2018)

www.UCMedicalHumanitiesPress.com

This series is made possible by the generous support of the Dean of the School of Medicine at UCSF, the Center for Humanities and Health Sciences at UCSF, and a Multicampus Research Program Grant from the University of California Office of the President. Grant ID MR-15-328363.

Remembering Paul Beeson

A Tribute From His Students, Residents, and Colleagues

John N. Forrest, Jr.
Lewis Landsberg, Editors

"No contemporary figure has had more influence on the way western-trained doctors practice medicine than Paul Beeson."
– Richard Rapport, *Physician: The Life of Paul Beeson* (2001)

First published in 2019
by University of California Medical Humanities Press

© 2019 by John N. Forrest, Jr and Lewis Landsberg
University of California
Medical Humanities Consortium
3333 California Street, Suite 485
San Francisco, CA 94143-0850

Cover image used with permission © John N. Forrest, Jr.

Book design by Virtuoso Press.

ISBN: 978-0-9963242-7-4

Printed in USA

Names and affiliations of authors:

Dr. Robert J. Alpern
Dean and Ensign Professor of Medicine
Yale University School of Medicine

Dr. Elisha Atkins
Beeson Professor of Medicine, Emeritus
Yale University School of Medicine

Dr. John N. Forrest, Jr.
Professor of Medicine, Nephrology
Yale University School of Medicine

Dr. William Hollingsworth
Professor of Medicine, Emeritus
University of California, San Diego

Dr. Philip K. Bondy
Ensign Professor of Medicine and
Chair of Medicine, Emeritus
Yale University School of Medicine

Dr.Bernard Lytton
Guthrie Professor of Surgery, Emeritus
Yale University School of Medicine

Dr. Howard M. Spiro
Professor of Medicine, Emeritus, Chief, Section of Gastroenterology
Yale University School of Medicine

Dr. Franklin H. Epstein
Applebaum Professor and Chair of Medicine, Beth Israel Hospital Harvard
Medical School

Dr. Mark Boyer
Associate Professor of Tropical Public Health, Harvard School of Public Health
Professor of Community Health, Tufts University

Dr. Lewis Landsberg
Professor of Medicine and Dean, Emeritus
Northwestern School of Medicine

Dr. Tony Batsen
Professor of Medicine
 and Cell Biology, Emeritus
The University of Sydney School of Medicine

Dr. Thomas P. Duffy
Professor of Medicine, Emeritus
Section of Hematology
Yale University School of Medicine

Dr. Richard V. Lee
Professor of Medicine, Pediatrics and Obstetrics
State University of New York at Buffalo

Gordon N. Gill, MD
Professor of Medicine and of Cell and Molecular Medicine, Emeritus,
University of California San Diego, School of Medicine

Dr. Kenneth G. Johnson
368 Broadway
Kingston, NY

Dr. Jack Levin
Professor of Medicine and Laboratory Medicine, Emeritus
University of California School of Medicine, San Francisco

Dr. Richard Rapport
Department of Neurological Surgery
Group Health Cooperative of Puget
Sound, Seattle, Washington

Dr. Lawrence Freedman
Professor of Medicine, Emeritus
David Geffen School of Medicine at UCLA

Ms. Christine Hines
Former Mayor, Redmond, Washington
The Redmond Historical Society

Dr. Fred S. Kantor
Beeson Professor of Medicine, Emeritus
Yale University School of Medicine
Mr. Peter G. Beeson
Concord, New Hampshire

Contents

Introduction

This book describes the life of one of the great legends of medicine. I was first introduced to Paul Beeson as a medical student when I encountered "Fever of Unknown Origin," a 1961 seminal article that remains a classic. I was just beginning to acquire a knowledge base in medicine and was naively hoping to place every patient into a diagnostic category. When caring for a patient with a fever, it should be relatively easy to identify the cause, or so I believed. But this article asked the critical question: What etiologies should be considered when you cannot easily identify the cause of a fever? The question was brilliantly posed and answered by presenting the cause in 100 sequential patients. While I have read many great papers during my career in medicine, few have remained with me as long as this one has. One of the two authors was Paul Beeson.

When I arrived at Yale as dean of the medical school in 2004, there were a group of faculty who identified themselves as "Beeson interns." I wondered what caused these highly accomplished physicians and scientists to bear such pride about having trained under Beeson. While I did not know Beeson personally, I did benefit from having trained under and worked for a number of his peers, leaders of medicine from the same generation, and the stories are similar. Beeson served as chair of internal medicine at Yale for 13 years. During this time, he trained a cadre of medical students and internal medicine residents who would go on to become leaders in many fields of medicine, and all would ascribe their success to Beeson. The ultimate expression of their gratitude is evidenced by the preparation of this book.

Beeson combined his talent as a clinician with outstanding science. He is best known for asking a fundamental question, "Why do patients develop a fever during an infection?" He demonstrated that the infectious agent did not cause the fever, but rather that the body's defense against the infection was responsible. He identified interleukin-1 as a cytokine that mediated this.

It was a classic example of a question generated at the bedside by a physician who observed many infected patients with fevers, and was sufficiently curious to ask why and sufficiently brilliant to identify the answer. Only a physician scientist educated as a clinician and trained as a researcher could have done this.

This paradigm, and leaders such as Beeson, inspired an entire generation of trainees to commit themselves to becoming physician scientists. What career could be more fulfilling than caring for patients, performing research to address their problems, and educating the next generation to follow in your footsteps? But alas, medicine and biomedical research have changed. The fund of medical knowledge has increased immensely and the techniques and knowledge required to do cutting-edge research have multiplied. Physicians cannot practice medicine competently unless they keep up with a broad body of literature or specialize in a very narrow area of medicine. All who trained with him would ascribe their success to Beeson.

This paradigm, and leaders such as Beeson, inspired an entire generation of trainees to commit themselves to becoming physician scientists. What career could be more fulfilling than caring for patients, performing research to address their problems, and educating the next generation to follow in your footsteps? The fund of medical knowledge has increased immensely and the techniques and knowledge required to do cutting-edge research have multiplied. Physicians cannot practice medicine competently unless they keep up with a broad body of literature or specialize in a very narrow area. Similarly, to perform innovative research, investigators need to spend the vast majority of their time focused on research.

The net result is that patients receive better clinical care and research is able to address questions that were previously unanswerable. All of this is obviously for the good. But Beeson was elected into the National Academy of Sciences (NAS) for his research accomplishments, and it is rare today to see an MD who actively sees patients elected to the NAS. While one cannot help but celebrate the advances in medicine and biomedical research, one is also left with some remorse over the loss of a great tradition. Will there be Paul Beesons in the future? What would Beeson's career have looked like if he was training today? We still have many brilliant people in medicine and research, but can any of them hope to have the impact that Beeson had? I believe so, but it will be in a different form.

So for now, we celebrate the life and career of Paul Beeson, who was an outstanding and compassionate clinician, performed exceptional research, and most importantly, inspired an entire generation to become physician scientists responsible for many of the advances in medical care and research that we have today. Medicine will likely not experience physician scientists such as Beeson again, just as physics will not have another Einstein and music another Mozart.

But there are still great women and men among us and hopefully they will all learn of the life and accomplishments of Paul Beeson. I believe he will inspire them to advance the field of medicine and rejoice in influencing the generations that follow them.

Respectfully and in awe of Paul Beeson,

Robert J. Alpern, MD
Dean and Ensign Professor of Medicine Yale School of Medicine

Chapter 1

Birth, Early Schooling, High School, College and Medical School

William Hollingsworth & John Forrest, Jr.

Paul Bruce Beeson was born on October 28,1908 in Livingston Montana where his father, Dr. John Beeson, practiced medicine and surgery there. Few boys ever entered the world with such debt and bonding to their fathers as did Paul Beeson. Dr. John Beeson, being the most experienced medical practitioner in Livingston, delivered his wife Martha of their second son, Paul, some eight years after the first son, Harold, had been born. From birth, Paul was closely bonded to his somewhat reticent but powerful father and to his equally strong mother. The Certificate of Birth was signed by a friend of his father, Dr. B.I. Pampel. John and Martha Beeson lived for 60 years after Paul's birth, and Paul was a dutiful and devoted son during all those years.

Livingston Montana, with its five thousand citizens in 1908, is located not far from the entrance to Yellowstone National Park. The Lewis and Clark Expedition had camped on the Yellowstone River nearby. When the Northern Pacific Railway built a spur rail line running south to Yellowstone, Livingston became the "Gateway to Yellowstone National Park."

Dr. John Beeson was a general practitioner, practicing mostly surgery and obstetrics in Livingston. He opened his practice in 1904. He and his wife Martha, a grade school teacher, saved the five thousand dollars needed for the construction of their large, comfortable wooden house on Sixth Avenue, down the street from Martha's parents.

By 1915 when Paul Beeson was seven years old, his father decided that he might have a more successful practice in a larger city and moved his

Figure 1. The frame house where Paul Beeson was born on South Sixth Street in Livingston, Montana on October 18, 1908.

family to Seattle. The Beeson family resided in a house on Queen Anne Hill. Paul entered the first grade at the local grammar school in Seattle. Soon, Dr. John Beeson discovered that he was unable to build his practice sufficiently and do the types of surgery that he wished and was skilled at, and in 1916 he moved his family again to the frontier town of Anchorage Alaska when the Alaska Railroad Company appointed him House Surgeon. Paul, now in the second grade, soon made friends in the classroom. He and a friend shared a cigarette-the only cigarette in a lifetime-behind the new hospital across the street. The new hospital, built in 1916, the Beesons' first year in Alaska, was said to be the largest and best equipped in the Territory and could house fifty patients and Dr. John Beeson was the Chief Surgeon.

Martha Beeson did not return to her employment as a grade school teacher. She taught her two sons the Victorian manners of the day. Paul's older brother Harold was also to become a physician and join his father in practice years later. While the sons respected their often absent and somewhat distant father for his commitment to his patients, it was Martha whose steadfastness, gentle but firm disposition, and personal traits, that shaped the boys character and personalities.

Martha Ash and John Beeson had met and married in Livingston, Montana. Both were school teachers who had followed Greely's dictum, "Go west, young man" (and young woman) and ended up in Montana. The teachers married, and in 1889 moved to Chicago so that John could attend Rush Medical School. While in medical school, their son Harold was born. After completing medical school, John and Martha returned to Montana, although John did manage a year of surgical training in New York. So, Dr. John Beeson became, in Livingston, a general practitioner of medicine and surgery.

John and Martha Beeson were a prototype of the young Westerners of the turn of the century. Martha had grown up in Missouri, where Grandfather Ash had fought for the Confederacy, and John's Iowan Grandfather Beeson had fought for the Union forces in that divisive and devastating Civil War. John and Martha each went to college, he to Valparaiso, Indiana and she to Northwestern in Chicago, before being hired for their first teaching jobs in Livingston.

The Hollingsworths (Dorothy and Bill) were planning to drive to California from Kentucky in 1976 and noted that their route would take them through Livingston, Montana. They asked Paul Beeson for the old Beeson street address, and in Livingston they found the little white house that had been the Beeson home. Its plain, unadorned simplicity reminded one of similar houses in the Grant Wood paintings that were featured on

Figure 2 (left): Early childhood in Livingston, Montana, about 1910.
Figure 3 (right): A young Paul Beeson in Anchorage, Alaska.

the covers of Collier's magazine in the 1930's.

John Beeson was not very successful, perhaps because his quiet manner and his surgical interests were more suited to the towns of the frontier than to the niceties of city practice. At that time, the United States was busy opening up Alaska and was building a railway from Fairbanks to Anchorage and Seward. Dr. Beeson applied for the position as Assistant Surgeon for the railway, was accepted, and shortly thereafter became Chief Surgeon. He stayed in Alaska from 1916 to 1935, first as Chief Surgeon on the railway and then as a practitioner in Ketchikan.

At age 63, in 1935, he bought a practice in Wooster, Ohio, joined with son Harold, then a physician and urologist, and established a practice that grew into the Wooster Clinic of today. Dr. John Beeson worked in Wooster until he reached 84 years of age, and then retired to La Jolla, California. His wife said that he had retired too young, and always warned Paul not to do the same thing.

Dr. John Beeson was quite a person. While in Alaska, he became famous for a trip by dog sled from Fairbanks to the little settlement of Iditarod in an attempt to save the life of a banker and gold miner who was thought to have empyema, a chest infection that needed surgical drainage. Dr. Beeson completed the heroic trip, but found the patient dying of tuberculosis. Every year one reads in the newspapers about the famous dog sled race in Alaska from Fairbanks to Ididerod, an adventure that still captures our imagination. Dr. John Beeson was a patient at Yale-New Haven Hospital, having a needed cholecystectomy when he was more than 90 years old. Paul Beeson was shaving him when I (Bill Hollingsworth) walked into the hospital room, and the old gentleman (now quite senile) was rambling on in a confused way. That scene of Paul shaving the prattling old man solidified my feelings that there existed an unusually strong and silent bond between father and son.

Paul Beeson's school years, and his growing up, took place in Anchorage, a town he enjoyed as a youngster. Anchorage was the gateway to the vast territory of Alaska, and its climate was considerably milder than that which we usually associate with Alaska. He enjoyed the countryside, as well as the town, was the outstanding student in Anchorage schools, and age 16 had completed high school and was ready for college.

Dr. John Beeson worked in his medical practice while Mrs. Beeson tended to all things related to house and children. When Harold had reached college age, she literally took him to Seattle for the better part of a year as he enrolled in college, and when Paul was ready, he and his mother similarly went off to college, to the University of Washington in Seattle. Mrs. Beeson took an apartment for the year and saw Paul off to a proper start in life. Paul loved to tell the story of how he entered premedical courses, rather than the business course which had been the plan in Anchorage. Mrs. Beeson took her son to a clothiers to buy a suit and new shoes before starting classes. The sales clerk, a nice personable young man, mentioned that he had just graduated in business from the University last year. After completing her purchases, Mrs. Beeson promptly marched out, with Paul in tow, and presented him to the college dean, saying, "This is my son Paul. He will study medicine." Her son Paul was not destined to fit shoes! Mrs. Beeson was not one to suffer from self-doubt.

Thus it came about that Paul followed his father and his older brother Harold into medicine as a career. After her year in Seattle, Mrs. Beeson took herself back to her husband in Alaska, who by this time had moved his practice to the town of Ketchikan. Paul lived in his fraternity in Seattle and completed the pre-medical curriculum in three years, before enrolling for medical school at McGill University in Montreal, again following Harold's footsteps. He enrolled in McGill's five-year medical course in 1928 and lived with Harold, also a student at McGill, for part of his medical school time.

Paul Beeson described college and medical school, during which he often lived in fraternities in lieu of dormitories', as a monastic life. Obviously he studied hard and effectively. Beeson's early edition of Cecil's Textbook of Medicine (the textbook he was to edit in later years), he owned as student and resident; he had carefully edited his copy by underlining pertinent passages in ink, using a straight-edge ruler to guide the pen. However, the monastic life did not preclude Paul's learning to drink whiskey with appreciation, but with moderation. That same monastic life also provided him with great experience in the game of poker. Both literally and figuratively he has played poker with skill and daring for all of his life.

Chapter 2

Internship, Residency, General Practice, Rockefeller Institute, Chief Residency with Weiss at the Brigham, War Years in Salisbury England, Marriage to Barbara Neal, Chairmanship at Emory

William Hollingsworth & John Forrest, Jr.

Paul Beeson was accepted as an intern by the University of Pennsylvania, which was a highly coveted spot in 1933. It was a two-year program; with the first year spent rotating through specialty programs and the second year split equally between medicine and surgery. This training was excellent for general practice, and a two-year mixed intern program was mandatory for licensure in the State of Pennsylvania until almost 50 years ago. Dr. Beeson always felt Penn was the pre-eminent medical school in the 1930's. The faculty included O.H. Perry Pepper, a respected internist who ran the Department of Medicine.

T. Grier Miller and William Abbott (well known for their tube for deflating the bowel) were Penn's gastroenterologists. Francis Wood (later Chairman) headed cardiology, and Isaac Starr and Eugene Landis were cardiovascular physiologists and scientists. Detlev Bronk, later President of Rockefeller University, was at Penn medical school in 1933. Donald Pillsbury was among the world's premier dermatologists, editor of the comprehensive textbook of dermatology. Beeson's Chief Medical Resident was Ludwig Eichna, later a distinguished physician and professor in New York. After completion of the two-year internship, Paul had received excellent medical training and was prepared to pursue his life's work.

In 1935, Paul joined the family practice in Wooster for two years, but it became clear to him that general practice was not his calling. As an example of his discomfort with surgery, he tells of receiving a call from the hospital while he was on duty. A young woman friend of the family was recovering from a Caesarian section when suddenly the stitches broke loose and her hospital bed was literally filled with her intestines. Paul took one look at this situation, recalled the life-long tremor of his hands, and called his father for help. Dr. Beeson came, immediately replaced her intestines into the abdominal cavity, and sewed up the incision right there in her hospital bed. There were no antibiotics in those days, but she recovered totally and uneventfully. Paul Beeson, however, had been made acutely aware of his own sense of futility during her unnerving episode.

Through a McGill classmate, Frank Horsfall, Beeson learned that the medical service at Cornell in New York had a vacancy for a medical resident, and he decided to apply, with the active support of his mother, who realized that life as a general practitioner in Wooster was not Paul's calling. He was accepted at Cornell and left for New York in the summer of 1937.

Chance again played a major role in his career, changing his focus from medical practice alone to one combining teaching, research, and patient care. He was enjoying his medical residency at Cornell, but was unexpectedly offered a medical residency next door at the Rockefeller Institute Hospital. Paul's friend and class-mate, Frank Horsfall, later to be a distinguished virologist at the Rockefeller, was getting married, and a group of friends gathered for a prenuptial party that became a bit of a brawl. Thomas Rivers, head of the Rockefeller Institute Hospital, was at the party, took a liking to Paul, and in the midst of the revelry offered him a job as a resident. When heads cleared the next day, Paul found that he still had his offer from Dr. Rivers. The residency involved working on the pneumonia service headed by Dr. Colin Macleod; the main activity was to develop pneumococcal-typing vaccines and to treat patients with antisera specific for the type of pneumococcus that had caused the patient's pneumonia. The type of pneumococcus is determined by a complex carbohydrate capsule on the microbe that determines certain aspects of its virulence. Although Beeson viewed himself primarily as a clinical resident at the Rockefeller, he was influenced by the research orientation at the Institute; many of his later research activities stemmed from work he did during his two years at the Rockefeller. He shared a laboratory with Macleod and with a close friend and colleague, Charles Hoagland.

In the lab, Beeson was more successful than he later admitted. He was the first author on a paper, with Hoagland, about the carbohydrate that determines the blood group A of human red cells. He also, with Hoagland, found that infused calcium carbonate could block the muscular shaking of chills brought on by fever-a finding of possible use in treating patients with rheumatoid arthritis. Much of Paul's later work and interest in the mechanisms of fever began at the Rockefeller from these clinical observations. He, with Hoagland and Walter Goebel, wrote three papers which called attention to the similarities of the carbohydrate on the capsule of type 14 pneumococcus to the carbohydrate on human blood group A. Type 14 has the largest capsule of any pneumococcus, and is the most virulent and lethal for humans of the pneumococcal strains.

More important to Beeson than the specific residency experience itself was the excitement he felt at the Rockefeller- a place ablaze with stimulating research. Rene Dubois, a renowned bacteriologist and general biologist, worked across the hall, and he and Selman Waksman were discovering bacteria from soil samples that produced substances that killed other microorganisms. These early experiments laid the conceptual groundwork for the discovery, soon to follow, of penicillin by Alexander Fleming in England and of streptomycin by Waksman. Oswald Avery was discovering the basis of life in nucleic acids; his brilliant experiments established the foundation for much of modern biochemical genetics.

At the Rockefeller at that time, a large volume of clinical research concerned the induction of fever in patients in an attempt to treat diseases, syphilis and rheumatoid arthritis in particular. The rationale for its use in syphilis was clear enough: The spirochete which causes the disease might be killed at temperatures which the body could produce without fatal damage. The rationale in rheumatoid arthritis was less clear. Beeson and the other Rockefeller residents injected killed typhoid bacilli intravenously to the patients to produce the fever and chills. It was well known that each patient required larger and larger daily doses of the killed typhoid organisms to produce fever. The patients became tolerant of the organisms to produce fever and the tolerant patient could accept doses many thousand-fold higher than the initial dose, which induced fever and chills. Much of Beeson's later work concerning the mechanisms of fever and the tolerance to fever induction by portions of the typhoid organism would reflect those early clinical experiments at the Rockefeller.

Soma Weiss, in Boston, had just moved from Boston City Hospital to the Peter Bent Brigham Hospital, and needed a chief Resident. Someone mentioned Beeson to Weiss, who then went to New York to interview him. Beeson was immediately enthralled by Weiss, and presumably Weiss was impressed with Beeson because he offered him his Chief Residency. By 1939, Paul Beeson was an experienced 31-year-old physician; he had had two years of internship at the University of Pennsylvania, a year of residency at Cornell, two years at Rockefeller, plus two years as a general practitioner.

When he arrived at the Brigham, he found, among his assistant residents, people such as Jack Myers, later to be Chairman at Pittsburgh, Gustave Dammin, later Chair of Pathology at the Brigham, and Richard Ebert, later Chair of Medicine at Arkansas and at Minnesota. These alert young physicians kept their chief resident on his mettle. Among Soma Weiss's research fellows and junior faculty were Gene Stead, Charles Janeway, later to be Professor of Pediatrics at Harvard, and John Romano, who became Chairman of Psychiatry at Cincinnati and at Rochester.

Paul learned a great deal under Soma Weiss. He watched Weiss delegate responsibility to his young colleagues at a time when wisdom tended to be equated with age in most other medical institutions. Beeson also noted that Weiss influenced everyone he encountered, perhaps because he was interested in his house-staff as people and thought of them as future colleagues, not as lackeys. It was an exciting period for a young man from Anchorage, associating with highly talented young people under a leader both caring and charismatic.

President James B. Conant of Harvard University wanted to demonstrate Harvard's support for the embattled British nation already caught up in World War II; he established in Salisbury, England the Harvard Field Hospital Unit, associated with the American Red Cross and made up of medical volunteers, to care for military personnel and civilians disrupted by the war. The Salisbury Fever Hospital was a referral hospital for about 200,000 people from the surrounding areas. The emphasis was on infectious diseases, and Paul Beeson was appointed Chief Physician and served in England with that Unit from 1940-1942; the unit disbanded when the bombing by the Japanese at Pearl Harbor thrust the United States into World War II.

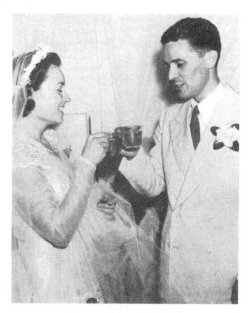

Figure 4. Paul Beeson marries Barbara
Neal in Buffalo, NY on July 10, 1942.

While in England, Beeson had charge of the hospital staffed by four or
five doctors and a group of Red Cross nurses, among whom was a petite,
dynamic young woman from Buffalo, Barbara Neal. Their courtship and
marriage were to instill in them a love of England that would later permit
them to live and work happily in the England of the 1960s and 1970s.

Beeson had a busy time professionally as well as socially in Salisbury.
His unit became involved in an extensive epidemic of trichinosis in
Wolverhampton, which Dr. John Shelton described in *Lancet* in 1941.
Trichinosis is a disease caused by a worm usually found in pigs and can erupt
in man when raw pork is eaten. After being ingested, the worms invade the
intestine and pass into the circulation where they lodge in many organs, but
are found particularly in muscles. As these worms filter out of the bloodstream, the capillaries at the end of the finger nails seem a favorite filter site,
leading to splinter hemorrhages in a line at the end of the nails. Beeson has
a slide of a young Wolverhampton bride whose wedding photo shows the
typical hemorrhagic fingernails of trichinosis.

England in 1941 was unaware of trichinosis because English hogs were
free of the disease. During the war, however, sausage was imported and was
often eaten raw, particularly by young women. Sheldon explains this as an
outcome of the chauvinistic attitudes prevalent at the time. Young women

tended to rush off to work with raw sausage spread on bread, or they nibbled raw sausage as they cooked, while the male of the English species expected, and got, his properly boiled dinner. Paul Beeson was the expert from America and his review of trichinosis in *Lancet* (see publication 12 in Appendix) is a splendid example of his terse, informative, no-nonsense style of writing, and of thinking.

As part of the reaction to trichina worms, as well as to other parasites, the human body mounts a response characterized by eosinophils in the blood, and eosinophils in tissues surround invading worms. These beautiful blood cells had no known purpose in 1940, and they and their function continued to fascinate Beeson. On his return to England in 1965, more than 25 years after the Wolverhampton epidemic, he would do important research on trichinosis in rats, and on the function and control mechanisms of eosinophils.

Beeson also became an expert on meningitis during that brief two years in England when he was given the records of over 3,000 cases. His report was a classic and definitive one, emphasizing that death was a less likely outcome if diagnosis was made quickly and treatment with sulfadiazide initiated promptly. This was important for the care of an army of young men living together in barracks, a situation that rendered them prone to contract infections like meningococcal meningitis.

Perhaps his most important observations in England related to the description and understanding of serum hepatitis, now known as hepatitis B. The military were concerned that so many young inductees living in the closed and crowded society of a military barracks had not had mumps. Beeson and his group collected serum from patients who were convalescing from the mumps, pooled the serum samples, and gave the serum containing mumps antibodies to newly exposed recruits. Although the new recruits developed fewer cases of mumps than would have been expected, many of the soldiers developed hepatitis instead. The English experience with hepatitis following the injections of pooled serum suggested that the serum had contained an agent that caused hepatitis. At that time, however, the only recognized hepatitis (now known as hepatitis A) occurred in epidemics related to food contamination. Such infections were common among troops concentrated in barracks and eating from a common food source. Thus, the association of the serum infections and hepatitis could have been coincidental. When Beeson returned to the United States he encountered six patients at Grady Hospital who had developed hepatitis following blood transfusions, and reported these patients in the *Journal of the American Medical Association* (Publication 17). This was an important clinical observation, since blood transfusions would be used with increasing frequency as elaborate surgical operations were developed. The discovery of serum hepatitis (now known as hepatitis B) was to be the single most important observation attributed to Dr. Beeson. Almost half a century later, the same clinical detective work that Beeson pursued in 1942 would define AIDS, like serum hepatitis, as a highly infectious agent carried in the bloodstream of asymptomatic people.

By the time he left the Harvard Unit in England, Paul Beeson was eminently qualified for a faculty position. His clinical experience had been gained at several prestigious institutions, and the Rockefeller had given him exposure to good laboratory research. The breadth of his interests was reflected in his work, but it was evident that infectious disease problems were his primary interest. His accomplishments in 1942 at age 34 included many attributes that one looks for today in young faculty: diversity of clinical experience, publications reflecting interest in both basic research and clinical observations, ability to take the lead in directing projects as well as to collaborate, and good taste in colleagues and in areas of emphasis.

He was certainly ready to join a faculty, and only Soma Weiss's death kept that first faculty appointment from being at Harvard and the Brigham.

Two assistant professorships in infectious diseases were open in 1942 when Dr. Beeson was considering positions, one at Cornell and the other with Eugene Stead at Emory. Cornell was Beeson's first choice, because he had been there as a resident and would thus work closely with his old colleagues and mentors at the Rockefeller, just adjacent to Cornell-New York Hospital.

He had a firm offer from Stead, however, and had not yet received one from Cornell when Stead, with characteristic forcefulness, insisted that Paul respond to his offer by a specific date. Just before midnight of the deadline, Beeson sent Stead a telegram accepting the position in Atlanta. The next morning, he received an offer from Cornell, but Beeson did not consider breaking the agreement. He said later, "I accepted a position at Emory at midnight, and I could not go back on my word."

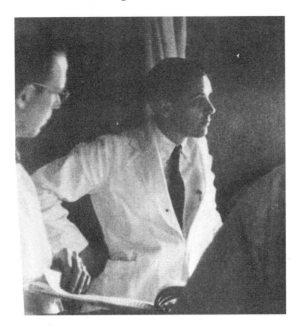

Figure 5. Paul Beeson on rounds at Grady Hospital, Atlanta GA.

With characteristic modesty, Beeson said later that the Emory job was sheer good luck in that he would "never have amounted to anything" in academic medicine had he gone to Cornell which was adjacent to the Rockefeller and full of outstanding young academic physicians. He cites his basic shyness and lack of aggressiveness as reasons he would not have bloomed in New York. But others might fantasize a wholly different history for Cornell had that quiet and unassuming yet tenacious and high-principled young man joined Cornell's faculty at the beginning of World War II. In any event, the game was played out in Atlanta, and within four years Paul Beeson had risen from Assistant Professor to Professor and Chairman.

Beeson would later claim that the Emory experience brought out his abilities because he was the only specialist in infectious diseases within 1,000 miles of Atlanta, and, therefore, was forced to develop his skills. He also pointed out that when he arrived in Atlanta, Gene Stead assigned a laboratory and technician (Liz Roberts) to him. Somehow, until then, Beeson viewed himself as basically a physician making clinical observations. With Gene Stead supplying a laboratory and expecting results, no one would have dared not to become a scientific investigator! Also, as the director of Grady Hospital's microbiology laboratory, Beeson expanded his knowledge of microbiology and acquired a window into the wide spectrum of infections in that crowded Atlanta city hospital known to its devotees as "the Gradys."

Paul Beeson quickly evolved into a classical clinical investigator, using his Grady experience and his research laboratory. His major contribution was to the understanding of how bacteria caused fever, and later how white blood cells from pus cause and sustain fever. He also had an uncanny ability to draw on clinical experience to solve problems. Stead and Warren were beginning to study the heart and circulation, using catheters passed into the heart and needles into the large arteries. Beeson wondered about the differences in the number of bacteria in blood of patients with infected heart valves-was the amount of bacteria higher in the arteries (blood that had passed through the lungs) or in the veins? It turned out that microbes from the heart valve came off evenly into the flowing blood, and the numbers were about equal in artery and vein -in other words, the lung does not sequester bacteria. The surprise came in a purely fortuitous event.

In one patient the heart catheter slipped through the heart and lodged in the large hepatic vein draining the liver; upon investigation, Beeson found that the blood in the liver contained almost no bacteria. Jim Warren became skillful at deliberately catheterizing the hepatic vein, and the same observations were confirmed in six patients. The liver, then, had an enormous capacity to scavenge bacteria from the bloodstream. These classic observations were an exciting by-product of Beeson's questioning mind and the Warren-Stead technology. A few months later, those experiments would never have been performed because penicillin was discovered and was found to cure bacterial endocarditis, a disease until then always fatal. A potentially dangerous heart catheterization would not be condoned after penicillin proved so effective in treatment.

In addition to his classic work on removal of bacteria from the bloodstream and on the mechanism of fever, Beeson was making major clinical observations on many of the diseases common in the clientele of The Gradys – such diseases as rat bite fever, the venereal infections chancroid and lymphogranuloma venereum, and the leptospiroses, an unusual group of infections contracted from rat urine contaminating the human food chain.

In 1947, Gene Stead left for Duke, taking with him his bright young academic team of Jack Myers, John Hickam, and Frank Engel. Beeson was by now quite well known nationally and well-regarded locally, and Emory promptly made him Chairman of the Department. James Warren stayed on at Emory for several years as Professor of Physiology, before joining Stead at Duke as Chief of Medicine at the new Durham Veterans Administration Hospital.

During his six years as Chairman at Emory, Beeson rebuilt the department mostly through the growth and support of local people. Philip Bondy had come to Emory from Boston as resident in medicine as part of the Stead exodus of 1942. He was promptly drafted into the Army, but returned to Emory under Beeson and developed into a first-rate endocrinologist. Bondy would later leave Emory with Beeson, and at Yale University Medical School would take over the renowned endocrinology/ metabolism group headed by the aging and ailing John P. Peters. When Beeson left Yale in 1965, Bondy succeeded him as Chairman. Ivan Bennett was a local Grady resident who worked with Beeson in infectious diseases and rapidly became a highly regarded investigator. He, also, would leave Emory with Beeson in 1952, emerge as a strong teacher and clinical investigator at Yale, and then leave Yale to head the infectious disease group at Hopkins. Later he became Chairman of Pathology at Hopkins and Dean and subsequently Vice Chancellor at New York University.

Paul and Barbara Beeson, despite being Northerners, had adjusted well to the Deep South of Atlanta, and liked it. Sons John and Peter had come along and the Beesons were planning a definitive house in Atlanta, lovingly designed by Barbara. Meantime, Beeson was on one of those annual pilgrimages to the clinical research meetings in Atlantic City, quietly sitting in a stall in the men's room of The Haddon Hall Hotel, when he heard two gentlemen walk in, chatting together as they emptied their bladders in a nearby urinal. One, forever unidentified by Dr. Beeson, said to the other "Oh, we (at Yale) will go down to Emory and get Paul Beeson to replace Francis Blake." Beeson waited for news from Yale, heard nothing, and decided to go ahead and build the house. The house was barely completed when Yale did, indeed, come to Beeson, and it was not until 1985 that Barbara finally designed another house just to suit her, their home in Redmond, Washington.

Chapter 3

Life as Department of Medicine Chairman at Yale University

Philip K. Bondy, Elisha Atkins, Franklin H. Epstein,
Bernard Lytton, & Howard M. Spiro

A Tribute To Paul Bruce Beeson
Philip K. Bondy, M.D.

I first heard Paul Beeson's name when I was an intern at the Peter Bent Brigham hospital in 1942. Paul wasn't there. He was in England with the Harvard-Red Cross Field Hospital, studying infectious disease and epidemics in England's heavily bombed population. It was while he was working in London that he described epidemic wry neck, which is still known in England as "Beeson's Disease." He had been Soma Weiss' chief resident, and set a standard against which all other residents were measured.

I met Paul in person around 1944, when he moved to the Department of Medicine at Emory University, in Atlanta. I was in the army, stationed in Rome, Georgia, but often came to Sunday morning Grand Rounds (known as "Sunday School") at Grady Hospital. Gene Stead and Paul were the stars of a fascinating performance. After I left the army in 1946, I joined the house staff at the Grady. In 1947, Gene Stead left Emory to become the Chairman of Medicine at Duke University, taking many of the strong faculty with him, and Paul became the new Chairman at Emory. He needed a chief resident for 1947, and Stead suggested me, so I fell into the post as Paul' s first Chief Resident. After a year of postdoctoral fellowship at Yale I returned to Emory, where I remained on the faculty until I joined Paul in his Hegira to Yale.

Paul carried out his most outstanding research while he was still at

Emory, in demonstrating the presence of "endogenous pyrogen" as a cause of fever. The work was a wonderful example of using a pair of clinical observations to spark fundamental laboratory research. At that time we were treating many cases of neurosyphilis by inducing high fevers by intravenous injection of typhoid vaccine. In the beginning, a few thousand bacilli would produce a high fever; but with repeated injections the patient developed tolerance for the bacilli and the dose had to be greatly increased with each subsequent injection. We also noted that there was a latent period after the injection before the fever began. Paul used these observations to induce tolerance to typhoid bacilli in rabbits. He then showed that, whereas the tolerant rabbits would not develop fever when they received small doses of bacilli, they would develop a fever if they were injected with plasma drawn when the fever started in fresh rabbits injected with a small dose of bacilli. Although the tolerant rabbits did not respond to small doses of bacilli, they were responsive to the "endogenous pyrogen" generated in other rabbits. Years later, "endogenous pyrogen" was identified as one of the interleukins. Although the experimental design was elegant and simple, its execution was laborious. Paul's laboratory contained 20 rabbits at a time, with thermocouples in their rectums hooked up to continuous recording thermometers. The program required expertise in handling, injecting and bleeding the animals, and was dependent on the skill of Elizabeth Roberts, Paul's technician, who came to Yale with him.

Paul's office ran smoothly, largely because of the dedication and skills of his secretary, Betty Pharr. Like Liz, she came to Yale with Paul.

Paul Beeson was a fine physician, an excellent scientist and an inspiring teacher. His memorial service fully recognized and eulogized these aspects of his life. But the speakers, in honoring these qualities, omitted entirely any reference to an equally important aspect of his excellence – his outstanding ability as an administrator and builder. Without these special talents, his influence would have been much less fruitful, and the Department of Internal Medicine he created would not have achieved international eminence.

To appreciate Paul's achievements, one must understand the challenges he faced when he assumed the Chair of Medicine at Yale. He faced three major problems.

The most immediate was the disorganized state of the Department. For years, Internal Medicine at Yale has been split between the Metabolism Service, headed by Dr. John P. Peters, and everything else, presided over by the Chair, Dr. Francis Blake. Peters claimed for his service the exclusive care of all patients with diabetes, endocrine disease, kidney disease, lipid problems and inborn errors of metabolism. His laboratory provided the only clinical chemistry analytical service available to the Department. He resisted aggressively all of Paul's attempts to integrate the Department into a single coherent whole. From many conversations I had with Paul, I know that he considered Peters to be a major impediment to developing the Department he envisioned. There was no way to persuade Peters to cooperate, so Paul was frustrated until Peters' death, after several years, solved this problem.

The second major difficulty was number of teaching beds. At that time, the most important clinical teaching occurred on the wards, where long-term hospital admissions permitted the students time enough to study patients and participate in diagnostic and therapeutic decisions. The heart of teaching was the daily rounds, when faculty, residents and students examined new patients, discussed progress and took appropriate steps.

In order to carry out this type of teaching, it was necessary to have enough teaching beds to provide a regular supply of newly admitted patients for the students to study. Several years before Paul's arrival, New Haven Hospital decided to construct a new hospital, the Memorial Unit. To avoid competition in fund raising, New Haven Hospital and Grace Hospital agreed to join, forming Grace-New Haven Hospital. When the new hospital opened its doors in January 1953, the staff of Grace Hospital was immediately given privileges to admit and care for patients.

Unfortunately, the Grace New Haven Hospital staff included many general practitioners, naturopathic, homeopathic and osteopathic physicians. Paul felt that he could not expose his house staff and students to their teaching; and the Grace staff were unwilling to allow the academic physicians to teach from their patients. It was many years before the quality of the community staff improved to the point where it became possible to assign medical students to patients in the Memorial Unit.

As a result, at first the Department's teaching beds were limited to two Fitkin Wards, one floor of the Winchester wing and the Howard Building, a small infectious disease isolation unit. In the early days, before the development of polio vaccine, Fitkin 2 was almost entirely devoted to long term care of paralyzed patients requiring mechanical respiratory assistance of an "iron lung." Even with Yale's small class of about 60 students, there were barely enough admissions to permit each student to work up the recommended 2 to 3 patients a week.

Paul needed more teaching beds. He obtained them when the Veterans Hospital in West Haven opened its doors; but the Veterans Administration had appointed a staff which Paul considered inadequate as teachers. It took considerable maneuvering to replace that staff with people to whom he could trust his students.

The third problem was finding space in which to house the new staff he knew was needed and funding to pay them. Some offices and laboratories could be obtained by readjusting space assignments -- closing one of the two student clinical laboratories, turning a redundant elevator into a laboratory, and promoting establishment of a hospital -wide clinical laboratory, so the space previously used by Dr. Peters' clinical laboratory could be turned over to research.

These adjustments were relatively trivial compared with the need. The major push was to promote building a new laboratory building. With the support of Dean Vernon Lippard, the School negotiated closure of the Howard building, which it replaced in 1966 with the 10-story Lippard Laboratory for Clinical Investigation.

There were also plans to build a new home for therapeutic radiology and oncology, which came to be known as the Hunter Building. Beeson, an inspired fund raiser, managed to obtain grants and donations sufficient to cover the cost of two additional floors for the proposed building, one for a badly needed Clinical Research Center and another for one of his major projects, the establishment of a basic science research center for the Department of Medicine.

Paul was inspired to establish this center by the Soviet triumph in launching the satellite, Sputnik. He felt that American science had fallen behind and that new programs were required to bolster our nation's scientific effort. A serious defect, he thought, was the loss of talented clinical physicians from basic medical research. He hoped to help rectify this deficiency by providing a facility in which established basic scientists with medical degrees could introduce selected medical residents to the research laboratory and thus encourage them to become productive vehicles for translating basic science into clinical developments. Although establishment of this group did not occur until after Paul left for England in 1965, it was a great scientific success. Of the four new faculty recruited for this endeavor, two were elected to the National Academy of Science and all developed strong ties with basic science departments. Unfortunately, medical residents never took advantage of the arrangement, so it didn't fulfill Paul's hopes.

Yale University did not provide the funding required for the growing Department. Indeed, the income from endowment assigned to the Department would not have supported half of the full-time faculty. It was necessary to find salary and research support for the new faculty recruits. A considerable part of the expansion was supported by both research and teaching grants from the National Institutes of Health, but Paul was also successful in obtaining endowment for named professorships. However, throughout his tenure at Yale, he was keenly aware of the fact that many of his tenured faculty were supported by "soft" money.

His clear vision of the proper structure of a Department of Internal Medicine, combined with the increasing availability of the necessary funds and space, permitted Paul to recruit powerful new faculty which were able to provide leadership in dermatology, neurology, endocrinology, gastroenterology, and hematology. He also supported faculty already in the Department as leaders in pulmonary disease, cardiology and hepatology and developed new section chiefs from among his students in immunology and rheumatology. In spite of the development of subspecialty divisions, however, Paul expected the entire faculty to be competent to teach general internal medicine. His vision was of an integrated faculty, and not one in which each subspecialty developed its own independent territory. I suspect he might have been disturbed by the degree to which sub-specialization has fragmented modern departments of medicine.

Paul Beeson came to Yale to develop a modern, collegial, effective Department. He encouraged the academic growth of the faculty, and promoted sensitive, caring, expert medical practice. His success is manifest in the high regard in which the Yale Department is held throughout the world. We miss him; but we are fortunate to have known him.

Paul Bruce Beeson-Recollections of His Stay at Yale

By Elisha Atkins, M.D.

PBB is a shy and in many respects a private man. His conversation with his colleagues at Yale was seldom laced with anecdotes and his busy life was not built around occasions for small talk. He had a shrewd ability to judge both problems and people, and like other leaders who inspire those around them, he took a genuine interest in the lives and careers of his associates; he would listen with complete attention to their concerns or plans for the future and his advice was carefully given and individually considered. He always had time, unlike many less busy people, for his house staff as well as for his junior colleagues and especially for students whom he individually counseled for their internships in medicine. All of us valued his advice, coming as it did from years of work and reflection starting as a general practitioner with his father and brother in Ohio. As he once said to me, "The real satisfactions of academic medicine do not lie in the hours and certainly not in the pay but in the opportunities to work with young people."

He could be direct in his criticism of a careless or a thoughtless act but his comments were given in private and were never meant to humiliate or embarrass. At the daily house staff report, held promptly at ninethirty in the morning, the drop of his poised pencil tip on the table was occasionally used to terminate an unproductive or sophistical argument. Similarly, his praise was spare and earnestly sought and when given was always deserved. During the Eisenhower years, he was a beleaguered Republican in a noisy sea of academic Democrats, and his famous Mona Lisa smile often indicated his wry amusement or simply friendly tolerance of contrary opinions about politics and other nonmedical matters.

Even with the increasingly heavy responsibilities of the chairmanship, his door remained open and his quiet sense of humor never deserted him as he made his decisions without flurry or strain. PBB enjoyed challenges of all sorts and characteristically he found time in his crowded life to act as a medical consultant to the Space program, which in its early days fired his imagination as a frontier in Man's continuing exploration of his world.

At a period when medical science was in danger of withdrawing further into the laboratory, he brought it back to the patient by encouraging doctors to start their studies of disease at the bedside-a point of view that was developed in an important Presidential address to the American Association of Physicians in 1967. His imaginative and pioneering studies clarified the causes of fever and of kidney infection, as well as the role of that mysterious cell, the eosinophil.

As a physician, he listened attentively to everything a patient had to say, skillfully asking the important questions at the right moment, whether of the patient or the house officer to clarify a point in making the diagnosis. But his concern for all the aspects of illness never led him to be satisfied with diagnoses merely, as he taught by his example the old dictum that there are no diseases in medicine but only ill patients. As a teacher PBB exemplified beautifully the comments Bertrand Russell made of Alfred North Whitehead: "Whitehead was extraordinarily perfect as a teacher. He would elicit the best of which a pupil was capable. He was never repressive or sarcastic or any of the things that inferior teachers like to be. I think that in all the abler young men with whom he came in contact, he inspired as he did in me, a very real and lasting affection." We all envied his formal presentations of subjects at Grands Rounds or in lectures which were remarkably lucid, concise and free of jargon.

Under his gifted and energetic guidance, the Department of Medicine at Yale grew from about ten members in 1952 to nearly 100 at the time of his resignation in 1965 to become the Nuffield Professor of Medicine at Oxford.

Despite his many honors and achievements, PBB has remained a modest and friendly man whose scientific curiosity, pursuit of excellence, concern for others, and gift for friendship have been his guiding qualities.

Dr. Atkins is professor of medicine, and a former colleague of Dr. Beeson.

Paul Beeson

by Franklin H. Epstein, MD

I returned to Yale in December of 1953 as an Assistant Professor of Internal Medicine, assigned to the Division of Metabolism under Dr. John P. Peters. I had gone to Yale as a medical student and spent two years on the house-staff and was returning after a year and a half in the army medical corps assigned to Alaska. Beeson had been appointed a year and a half earlier as the new Chairman of Internal Medicine at Yale, replacing Francis Blake.

Paul Beeson was a wonderful chairman of medicine. First of all, he was a good doctor. His diagnoses were accurate and logical. He himself was absolutely honest as well as modest. He was always humane, concerned with the patient's welfare as well as with the well-being of his staff. He had a great eye for excellence, particularly in the young people whom he recruited to his department. My wife always said that one of his great assets was his handsomeness. People liked him and did not want to disappoint him. He knew how to use his presence as well as his silence. He never spoke first at a committee meeting but his few words, expressed toward the end of the meeting, always carried great weight. He was a natural leader. When he came to Yale, Beeson was the lone Republican in a sea of Democrats. He is the only person I ever knew whose political views became more liberal as he grew older, so that by the time he returned from Oxford, England, he had become a staunch supporter of government medicine and opposed US involvement in Vietnam.

I have been asked to comment on the relationship between Paul Beeson and John Peters. Peters, then at the end of a brilliant career as a physician-scientist, had a national and world-wide reputation as an expert in the chemical aspects of disease. He fully expected to be appointed as the Chairman of the Department of Internal Medicine at Yale when Francis Blake retired in 1952 at the age of 64, only to die two weeks later. He had, in fact, been appointed acting Chairman of the Department until the appointment of Paul Beeson later that year. At that time, Peters was 65 years old and expected to retire at the mandatory age of 68, three years later. He regarded the anticipated short appointment as Chairman at Yale as the capstone of his career and he was sorely disappointed when that did not occur.

Always forthright and outspoken, John Peters did not deem tact a virtue. He could never understand why, if he demonstrated convincingly that someone was foolish or mistaken, that they should take it personally. It was said that at the Atlantic City meetings of the American Society of Clinical Investigation and the Association of American Physicians, the crowds of academic physicians tilling the boardwalk, parted like the Red Sea when they saw Peters strolling along with a colleague. He was known throughout the country as a vehement and vocal supporter of federal health insurance and federal support for medical research. He had never deferred to authority in his life.

Paul Beeson had worked at the Rockefeller Institute, the Peter Bent Brigham Hospital, and at Emory University Medical School. His clinical chiefs had been Soma Weiss and Eugene Stead. These were great physicians and dominating personalities who expected to be deferred to. When Beeson succeeded Stead as Chairman of Medicine at Emory, it would have been natural for him to expect that he too would have been deferred to. But that was not the personality of Paul Beeson.

The story is told that at one meeting of the American Society for Clinical Investigation and the Association of American Physicians in Atlantic City, George Thorn was in the Chair. When the time came for questions, Peters was called on first. Peters came to the microphone to announce, "What we have heard here is nothing more than a catalogue of ships." He was referring to what has been termed the most boring book of Homer's *Iliad* in which the contents of each Athenian ship was described in excruciating detail. Beeson was shocked but George Thorn shrugged it off.

I have to say that in two years I never heard a derogatory word from Peters about his chief, Paul Beeson. Peters respected Beeson's ability as an expert in infectious disease and was exceptionally pleased by his published strictures against instrumentation of the urinary tract as a cause of pyelonephritis. What Peters regarded as his intellectual disagreements never extended to personal rancor.

Dr. Paul B. Beeson: In Memoriam

By Bernard Lytton
Donald Guthrie Professor of Surgery/Urology, Emeritus
Yale University School of Medicine

Paul Beeson was my first friend in New Haven. I arrived in the United States from England, shortly after the death of my first wife from influenza. I had recently spent 18 months doing cancer research in London and arrived at Yale in March of 1962, a rather unhappy, lonely and newly minted surgeon, to take up a position as an assistant professor in the section of urology. Dr. Lindskog, the Chief of surgery, suggested that I introduce myself to Dr. Beeson. I walked into his office one afternoon, unannounced and in his gracious and quiet way he invited me in, sat me down and asked me to tell him about myself. I clearly remember the suggestion of a wry smile that always played around his lips as he looked at you with those penetrating blue eyes. He listened with a quiet and studied concentration that always made you feel that you were the only person that really mattered; a wonderful quality that endeared him to so many. Hearing of my interest in the role of white cells in the transfer of delayed hypersensitivity, he promptly suggested that I meet with his fellow in the lab, Vince Andriole. He called Vince down right away and we soon agreed that I should work with him. So began an excellent working partnership, which developed into a rewarding friendship that has lasted ever since.

Dr. Beeson had me present my work on immune transfer at one of his research seminars. Subsequently he was kind enough to ask me to join the group, which included Elisha Atkins, Larry Freedman, Fred Kantor and Vince Andriole, that accompanied him to the meetings of the Interplanetary Society, better known as "the pus club." The interactions between members of the group proved to be as entertaining as the meeting itself. Elisha Atkins, a devout democrat, would express his point of view with great vigor and eloquence, laced with literary quotations. His rhetoric, however, would run right off Dr. Beeson's rock like defense of his republican beliefs.

Shortly after I arrived, Dr. Beeson was faced with caring for President Griswold who was dying of cancer. I had mentioned that I had worked at a home for the dying in London where Dr. Cicely Saunders, a remarkable and charismatic physician working for her Ph.D. in pharmacology, had transformed the care of these patients by listening to their fears and concerns and then treating them with various combinations of analgesics and psychotropic drugs so that they remained alert and were free of pain, relieved of their anxiety, and able to sleep at night. They even went home for weekends. I explained Dr. Saunders' methods to Dr. Beeson who immediately suggested that we invite her to speak at Yale. Being unfamiliar with the American system I said that I doubted that Dr. Saunders could afford to travel to America, to which he promptly replied that he would take care of it. Cicely Saunders was pleased to accept the invitation and gave an inspiring talk in Fitkin amphitheater, which though poorly attended, did include in the audience the then Dean of the Nursing School Florence Wald, and so was the Hospice movement born in New Haven.

Dr. Beeson's hospitality also extended to invitations to cookouts at his Woodbridge home given for the residents and faculty in his department. Later my new bride Norma was included. We were pleased and privileged to become part of that "company of physicians" in the department of medicine with its strong feeling of camaraderie that was so successfully fostered by the Beesons.

I will be forever grateful for and never forget his personal warmth and generosity of spirit together with his many acts of kindness and hospitality extended to me when I joined the junior faculty at the Yale medical school.

Paul Beeson

By Howard Spiro

I first met Paul Beeson in the late spring of 1954 when, with the sponsorship of Dr. George Thorn at the old Peter Bent Brigham Hospital, Marian and I drove from Boston down to New Haven to see him about the possibility of setting up a gastrointestinal section at Yale Medical School. Paul was very cordial, we talked for a half hour or so, shook hands, and in December 1954 shortly after Christmas, we moved to New Haven on the strength of that handshake. There were no contracts, no long list of requirements, I simply switched sides at Harvard-Yale football games and my laboratory work moved from the Massachusetts General Hospital to the Howard Building, auspiciously named, at the Grace-New Haven Community Hospital.

Things were a little less happy the next time I met Paul shortly after January 1, 1955. At that time he told me that he could pay me only $6,000 a year rather than the $6500 he had promised. We were a young couple with three children and a new mortgage, so I demurred. Paul reassured me that I could go to the VA hospital in West Haven to earn some extra money there as an attending physician. That proved to be a very important turn of events because I established there the first of many long-lasting relationships with hospitals other than The New Haven Hospital.

It may seem ungracious to begin with that story, but I bring it up because several others have told much the same tale, which suggests a certain parsimonious wrinkle in Beeson's character. Of course, it might have been part of an uncharacteristically byzantine plan of his to plant "settlers" in a hospital without much Yale representation. That may well have been true because others have suggested that Paul was eager to establish some kind of hegemony at the West Haven VA Hospital, in part because of the difficulties with the sainted John Peters that Phil Bondy has so frankly described in the October 2010 issue of *Connecticut Medicine.*

In support, Mike Kashgarian told me that as a fourth-year student he asked Paul Beeson for advice about interning at Johns Hopkins. But Paul told him that he had not sent anybody out to Washington University and suggested that Mike go out there to see what things were like. When he returned, he told Paul that he really would prefer Baltimore, but Beeson responded, "We really need to send someone to St. Louis!" And so Mike dutifully went there, but hurried back to New Haven the next year to do pathology. That adds another dimension to what might have seemed simply building relations by sending students where you want contacts.

"Dr. Beeson" as we all called him, gave us new young section heads freedom to do whatever we wanted. I had been working on pepsin secretion in gastric juice and its reflection in urine, hoping to study gastric secretion without putting a tube into the stomach, and I continued that tack when I came to New Haven. I also set up the makings of a clinical section in the feeling that we could do anything we wanted. Not that Paul was an absentee landlord, he was busy setting up a new department and parrying the displeasure of the older inhabitants like Peters.

Several decades later, I wrote a piece which gave Paul credit for bringing Jews to a Yale which had been something between suspicious and disdainful of Jewish candidates. Paul wrote to me that my praising him for changing Yale cultural prejudices had brought about many dinner invitations that greatly decreased the isolation Barbara and he had felt after retiring to Seattle! To be fair, I also credited John Peters with increasing "diversity;" and his equally beady-eyed grand-daughter, a later medical student at Yale, assured me that Peters had overcome the cultural anti-Semitism of his class.

Paul Beeson had an enormous influence for the good on those who worked with him. It could have been calculated, but I am sure that it was inherent. He so personified goodness and virtue that we all felt obligated to work toward the vision that we felt Paul Beeson had of us. It was a form of charisma, I guess.

For some years in the 1950's, before air-conditioning closed our office doors, and when my office had moved next door to Paul's, colleagues who left his office would come into mine and some would ask me something like, "Howard, what you think Dr. Beeson thinks of me?" Some people very close to him asked that self-same question, telling of an uncertainty that led me to wonder whether, like many other leaders, he kept his distance from all but his family. Certainly I felt that I should do my thing, and bother him only when it seemed absolutely necessary.

This unusual ability to get people to work for the image they felt he had of them, the heights they could reach, seemed unique. He seemed intuitively to understand what we all worried about, and he used that to urge, almost to goad, us on. That unique ability verged on charisma, a kind of God-given ability that I have seen in few if any other medical leaders.

Dr Beeson was not above the kind of paternalism that makes chairmen, oops "chairs," shape the destiny of those who work for them. It was done with a good heart, to benefit those whose careers he guided. They have flourished, but I often wondered whether they had followed their star—or his!

I acquired a far more spare style of writing than I had brought down from Boston. Dr. Beeson took the time to go over – word for word – each paper that I wrote, and helped me to phrase them in a less euphuistic style than I had been taught at Harvard College. To be sure, we were a small department, everyone knew everyone else, and sociability was widespread. Nevertheless Paul saw his duty and did it. He left when things were growing too big, and he left the department better, much better, and able to flourish in his absence.

When Beeson came to Yale, he seemed quite conservative, more than a little wary of the left-leaning liberals he would bring to New Haven. Over the years Paul shed his conservative background to sponsor many progressive ideas, but that was not what he looked or sounded like when I first came to Yale. When the federal government so advised, he built a bomb shelter in his basement, used in later years by others as a wine cellar, and insisted on a certain degree of propriety. Occasionally his proclivity for civility led him to make the wrong choice of people, but when it was brought to his attention, he changed.

Paul grew angry at the Duff and Hollingshead book that exposed faults with the hospital and medical school. I believe he never forgave those two loyal Yalies for the bad repute that he felt they had brought to the medical school.

While he was Chairman of Medicine for about 13 years, he remade that department just about completely, bringing in a number of young men to establish various sections of several subspecialties. It is a measure of his enduring influence that Yale Medical School, after his death, held a memorial service for the man who had left about 40 years before and only a few years ago put up his portrait in the Fitkin Amphitheater.

In his much admired comparison of Paul Beeson with William Osler, Dr. Thomas Duffy makes the point – one I had never considered before – that at least during his academic life Beeson did not take care of patients on a one-to-one basis, unlike the sainted Canadian with the large private practice. That observation seems important, because on reflection, I have the feeling that Sir Galahad of King Arthur's Round Table provides the proper metaphor/comparison for Paul Beeson. Sir Galahad was virginal, had no close friends, and embodied god-like purity unlike all the other knights. He left the sword in the stone, and legend has it Galahad was taken up to heaven in an Assumption.

Tempering such high flown imagination, the report by Bill Hollingsworth states that, "Beeson accepted occasional personal private patients whom he and his Chief Resident managed, together with the housestaff ... it was evident that he took care of patients because he liked caring for them," but there cannot have been a great many of them.

Paul was known for his compassionate clinical teaching, for sitting down at the patient's bed, to get patients to talk about themselves. I know that he had been in practice with his father and brother, but he left after a few years. Yet that apparent unwillingness to take care of patients one-on-one could buttress a comparison with Galahad. Paul was a consummate teacher and a wonderful leader, but no one could think of becoming just like him – that was beyond our ability. You could do what Paul thought was proper, but no one – so far as I know- was ever presumptuous enough to think that they could become a second Beeson. In that sense it was really God-given and beyond man's choosing. Paul was so pure that it is hard to imagine, Barbara and the children aside, his engaging in the kind of I-and-Thou relationship that Martin Buber has so vividly described.

I throw this out simply as another dimension to the man who gave me my chance in academic life and put me on the path I have followed into old age. It is useful to let the weaknesses – better, foibles, if such they are – of our leaders be known. They make following them so much more comfortable.

I have never met anyone like Paul Beeson.

November 14, 2010
New Haven, CT

Chapter 4

Receiving the Association of American Physicians (AAP) Kober Medal

Petersdorf Introduction and Beeson's Reply

By Robert G. Petersdorf
Seattle, Washlngton

D r. Ebert, Professor Beeson, Barbara, Judy, Peter and John, Members of The Association, And Guests:

Today, I am going to tell you an adventure story. It is a story that has in it a bit of Marco Polo, Don Quixote, John Glenn and perhaps even Walter Mitty. It has something in common with all of these because it describes how men's actions, dreams and aspirations affect their environment and how the environment, in turn, determines the actions of men within it. It differs largely because our hero does not overcome the environment through physical prowess or mechanical derring-do but conquers by an inquisitive mind, an extraordinary degree of understanding of his fellow man, an uncanny knack for playing the odds, and a smart wife. It also differs because the environment is not an uncharted part of the universe or even space, but the world of academic medicine.

Like all adventure stories, this one must have a beginning and ours is in Livingston, Montana. If ever there was a picture of a two-year old saying "Look out world-ready or not, here I come," this is it. He also learned early that every adventure story has its ups and downs and that even heroes end up on the short end of the stick once in a while.

From Livingston, the scene changes to Anchorage where our hero received an early Arctic survival course that was to prepare him for the cold English winters of later years, and also provided him with his first competitive experience as an American abroad, a role in which he was to be cast many times in subsequent years. His decision to go into medicine was based on thorough analysis and careful thought. When he was being graduated from high school, he was undecided as to whether he should pursue a career in medicine or business. When the clerk who sold him his graduation suit told him that he was a graduate in business administration, our hero decided on medicine. This was the first time he gambled for higher stakes and won, but it was by no means to be the last.

He pursued his medical studies at McGill. Whether he learned any medicine is not quite clear, particularly since he spent most of his time becoming expert at poker, learning the odds at roulette and making the acquaintance of les jeunes filles de Montreal. In this setting, he showed his first dash of investigative talent. The story has it that he and his fraternity brothers spent a good deal of time playing poker on the roof of their house. It was too much trouble to traipse down the stairs to get the beer so our hero devised a hoist whereby a bucket could be lowered, filled with beer, and lifted to the roof without spilling a drop or disrupting the game.

Following internship he went into general practice in Ohio where his father had started a group clinic-one of the earliest in the United States. In a sense, he is the only legitimate Professor of Medicine who came out of general practice, quite a contrast to the present climate in which a lot of ille-gitimate Professors of Family Practice have come out of internal medicine. More importantly, this experience provided him with a sense of importance of the elementals of medicine-the history and physical examination- and gave him a "feel" for the patient which he has retained and which he has passed on to his students.

However, in the long term, general practice did not satisfy him, and he made his bed in medical science. Here at the Rockefeller Institute, it was for him, as for all his contemporaries, the pneumococcus. But it was also just the beginning. What it really did was to teach him how to calculate the odds in the laboratory as well as in life.

This promising career as an investigative shill was interrupted by more house-staff training at the Brigham and by the Great War. He joined the Harvard Red Cross Unit which was stationed in Salisbury, England and wrote some papers on typhoid and trichinosis. Here, life taught him another lesson: that is, that partnership practice is better than soloing and that two heads are better (and much prettier) than one. Barbara will make her appearance subtly, but strongly, throughout his adventures. The war over, he returned to the Brigham only to fall under the spell of academe's pied piper, Gene Stead, who blew his fife and tooted him to Atlanta.

There in the basement of an old building which was even too decrepit for Sherman to burn, steeped among rabbit pellets, he began his career as an independent investigator. And here his talents as a gambler really came to the fore. The first hand he played dealt with fever. Common theories for the cause of fever at that time included dehydration, electrolyte shifts, adrenal and thyroid overactivity, and a primary fault in central thermal regulation. He postulated that fever may well be related to a product of tissue injury. This had been suggested by Menkin who claimed that he had discovered some thermogenic substances but these were contaminated by endotoxin. These negative data did not deter him and, although fever did not seem like a very fast horse in the 1940's, he bet on it and in a classic series of studies produced and characterized leukocytic pyrogen. Virtually all subsequent studies have been based on this early work. He probably showed his greatest talent as a gambler by cashing in his chips after the first discovery because since that time the fever horse has not run too fast, as those of us with less foresight have learned. But like the consummate gambler that he is, Beeson emerged the big winner.

It is interesting that in the early days of the Public Health Service, his grant application to study the mechanism of fever was turned down. This should raise the spirits of all of the bright young men whose investigative plans have been circumcised by Cap the Knife this spring. Although we should probably stop to sing "We Shall Overcome" at this point, we'll dispense with it for the sake of time.

Equally important to our hero's progress in Atlanta was that he really gained his spurs as a clinician. Rounding became second nature to him and he excelled at it, not so much because he dropped an avalanche of pearls but because he asked the right questions. For example, one day he was examining a patient with unexplained fever who had had a series of studies which had not been useful. The patient was a poor historian, but during one of his few lucid moments Paul asked him what made him sick. He answered, "I'se got the rabbit fever" and so he had. On another occasion, there was a patient at Grady who had a remarkably regular fever and in whom all studies were negative. He finally elected to go home, only to return in three weeks with the same course. Once again all studies were negative, but this time PB took a careful history and found out that one of the nursing supervisors at

Grady—half-crazy old lady that she was—had given the patient a handful of sulfa tablets on discharge, saying that they were good for fever. Armed with this information, he went to the laboratory and cultured meningococci from the blood.

In 1947 Gene left for greener pastures, and Paul became Chairman of the Department at Emory. Life was not easy. As befits a Chairman of a Department of Medicine, he was assigned an office in the basement which flooded every time it rained; but he was active in the laboratory and on the wards, and he was happy. However, the meeting in Atlantic City in 1951 changed his fate. While he was performing at one of the booths in the men's room (delicacy prevents me from showing a picture of this), he overheard two unidentified men talking. "I hear Beeson is going to Yale," one said. "That's right," the second replied. With its usual precise attention to administrative detail, Yale had neglected to ask him to visit before disseminating the information that he was their choice to become Head of the Department. But everything came out all right and the following spring he was ensconced in New Haven.

One of his early impressions at Yale was the industry and dedication of the house-staff. He believed that getting to know them was very important, so on his first morning in New Haven he went to the dining room at 7:15 to join them for breakfast. To his surprise none of the house officers were there. That impressed him a great deal because he figured that they were

Figure 6. Dr. Beeson's Department of Medicine Faculty at Yale in 1952-53.

already on the ward, so the next morning he came in at 7:00 and again failed to find the house-staff. On the third day he came at 6:45, only to find the dining room closed. He eventually learned that the usual breakfast time for the Yale house officers was closer to 8:15 than 7:15. In fact, the first year at Yale must have been a psychic trauma to him. The chief resident-not his own appointee-invariably staggered into morning report 15 minutes late, tieless, hair unkempt and shoe laces untied. He was soon replaced by the more traditional Beeson chief resident-short-cropped hair, white button-down shirt and striped tie.

Beeson was close to his house-staff because he basically believed that the future of medicine belonged in the hands of young men. He helped them professionally and came to know them and their families socially. At his annual house-staff picnics he let his hair down (his hair has always been pretty short so that he couldn't let it down too far) but he made the boys and girls feel like he was one of them. He even engaged in some semblance of intramural sports which usually was confined to poker.

He could also be a strict disciplinarian. When he first made the affiliation between the New Haven and the West Haven VA Hospital, some of the house-staff were less than enchanted with VA rules and regulations. This resulted in a rather lengthy although fairly innocuous-by present house-staff standards-gripe session. Somehow this was reported back to him, and at the next residents' report he told us in no uncertain terms that our job was to learn medicine and to take care of sick people and not to bitch like common soldiers. Then there was the time that a somewhat flamboyant assistant resident, having successfully managed a patient with a difficult cardiac arrhythmia, proceeded to festoon the residents' office with reams of EKG paper that had been expended in the management of his patient. When PB saw this, he roundly chewed the resident, indicating that he considered his action less than dignified and not befitting a physician and that, furthermore, he saw no reason to use so much EKG paper in the management of any arrhythmia in the first place.

We never knew whether he was serious because he ruled by reason and he put his stamp on the service in New Haven, not as a disciplinarian but as a doctor and a teacher. He was never too busy to see a patient—day or night—and he took exquisite pains to show younger physicians the importance of a sensitive patient-doctor relationship. For example, he always chose a patient with a fatal disease as his subject for the first lecture he gave to the freshman medical students. Once such a patient would be selected by the resident, he would spend several hours with him each day so he could grasp the nuances that characterize the fragile bond between a dying patient and his physician. He always went to great lengths to point out how poorly the house-staff did in ministering to this type of patient's complaints—not only his pain but his insomnia, his diet and even his constipation.

And there was the time that the chief resident took him around to see three or four patients with complex febrile illness. Each of these patients was receiving multiple antibiotics and none was getting better. His advice in each instance was the same—stop the drugs. At the conclusion of the rounds, the resident commented that they really had not done much that day. That enigmatic, Mona Lisa smile that we have come to know so well crossed Beeson's face and he agreed that they probably had not, but we all knew differently. It was his teaching by example that left a lasting impression on students and house-staff.

The early years in New Haven were not all roses, primarily because in 1954 he had to undergo a series of difficult and unpleasant operations. He lost a good deal of weight and became unhappy and depressed. It was then that he turned to the laboratory for psychotherapy. Again, holding true to his pattern of betting a then seemingly slow horse, he focused his attention on pyelonephritis. In the early 1950's there was a mass of misinformation concerning this disease. In a beautiful article in the Yale Journal in 1955, he systematically reviewed some of the important issues dealing with pyelonephritis. He quickly laid to rest the lymphatic and hematogenous pathways as major routes by which bacteria reach the kidney and emphasized the importance of the ascending route. In the laboratory he and his colleagues conducted a classic series of studies that emphasized the role of obstruction in the pathogenesis of urinary tract infection (4-6). Always keeping his investigative eye on the patient and his problem, he became convinced that the urethral catheter was an important source of urinary tract infections, and in an eloquent but simple experiment he and Guze set out to prove this thesis (7). In patients undergoing gynecologic surgery they showed that the anterior urethra was not sterile even after the most assiduous external preparation, and by aspirating the bladder they demonstrated that in a significant number of cases the simple passage of a sterile catheter through the urethra introduced bacteria into the bladder. Armed with this information and data obtained by others, he rose to the attack and in a carefully reasoned, no-nonsense editorial in the Green Journal he argued the "case against the catheter" (8). The urologic fraternity rose up and the verbal contents of their urinals cascaded about him, but his views prevailed. Routine catheterization became the exception rather than the rule, the urologist's objections have long been washed down the drain, and in all the controversy the patient emerged the winner.

During his early Yale days, he also became engaged in his favorite avocation, editing textbooks. He received his early lessons from two of the old masters. They were a lot younger then and these lessons enabled him to graduate from the best to the second-best textbook in the world. Then there was the first long meeting of the Harrison Editorial Board in Wyoming. Subsequently they graduated to the Virgin Islands, Sicily and Madeira. I don't think Beeson made a very good bet here—the editors of the other book never seem to get out of mid-town New York.

After he had been at Yale six years Beeson's department had grown in both size and stature, and as the administrative chores grew heavier he decided that the time was ripe for an intellectual and physical rejuvenation. He did an unprecedented thing for Yale—he took a sabbatical and went to the Wright-Fleming Institute in London. This interlude enabled him to

Figure 7. Dr. Beeson with his faculty and Yale house-staff in 1964. Beeson (front row, 9th from left) is flanked by his chief residents, Dr. Jack Levin to Beeson's left, and Dr. George Thorton to Beeson's right.

accomplish three things: firstly, it permitted him to work in the laboratory with his own hands and he and Rowley demonstrated very clearly the effect of ammonia on the kidney's susceptibility to infection (9). Secondly, it gave him a chance to become reacquainted with his family—a luxury that even department chairmen should be permitted to enjoy from time to time; and, thirdly, it afforded him another taste of merry Old England including the cold and coal scuttle and some of the pomp and circumstance. It was, in a way, the forerunner of things to come.

He returned to New Haven rejuvenated and ready to enter the chairmanly rat race once again, but he was more relaxed and it seemed that he had found a home. In 1962 his faculty and former house-staff joined in giving him a surprise party to thank him for the ten good years he had given them at Yale. He turned to breeding department chairmen and during those years chairmanships at Vermont, Washington, Kentucky and Rutgers, to mention just a few, were populated by his trainees.

These were Beeson's Eisenhower years, so to speak, but during this apparent era of serenity he figured that it was time to reshuffle the deck once again. With all the stealth befitting a CIA operation, he went to a small town in Canada, obtained a Canadian license which permitted reciprocity in England, and one fine day announced to his department that he had accepted the Nuffield Professorship of Medicine at Oxford and was leaving Yale shortly. Nobody knows what motivated this move. Perhaps he was tired or wanted a new challenge, but a more plausible reason is that he had to leave the country because he had bankrupted at least three department chairmen during their weekly poker sessions. There were tears all around but these tears turned to smiles as his friends and colleagues realized how happy he was with the prospect of this new adventure so he, Barbara and Judy were off to Oxford.

During his first year at Oxford it seemed that he might have drawn a bad hand. He learned that running a British firm was far different from being head of a teaching service at an American university hospital. He was dissatisfied with his rounds, the residents report didn't swing, and he lived in a huge unfriendly apartment on the High that was cold even in July when I visited him and must have been frigid in the winter. It was during that Siberian winter of 1966, when things seemed not to be going well, that he again turned to the laboratory to help him cope and he bet on yet another seemingly barren area, the eosinophil. His interest in this cell stemmed from an epidemic of trichinosis that he had described when stationed in England in 1940 (10). Ever since that time, he had wondered what made the eosinophils appear and what the role of these cells was. Most of us have too dull a memory to remember the bright ideas of our youthful years and even if we remember them, by the time we reach our mid-50's, we are too fat, affluent and lazy to do anything about them. But not PB. He took this idea, which had been germinating for 25 years, to the laboratory and he and his colleagues produced a Trichinella infection in rats, showed that it was immunologically mediated and, more specifically, that the T lymphocytes were primarily involved in the induction of the eosinophil response by the bone marrow and in the mobilization and distribution of non dividing cells in other tissues (11). These studies are certain to be of fundamental importance in cellular immunology.

By the end of 1966 he had adapted to the English life-style; he watered the flowers in his office, learned to take two hours for lunch at Magdalen and generally, but not always, observed the inviolate morning and afternoon tea breaks. He bought a typical English country house, which looked very English from the outside but was, by Barbara's dictates, all-American on the inside, and which became the American embassy in England for so many of his friends and former colleagues. He became a gentleman farmer and appeared to enjoy it even though his main job was clearing the horse dung out of the stables. He, who kept three secretaries hopping at Yale, never ceased to be embarrassed by his inability to keep one busy at Oxford. The present incumbent spends at least some of her time ministering to a dachshund who shares the office with her, making this the only professorial office in England with a live mascot.

Professionally his impact on Oxford was subtle but inexorable. He completely revamped the introductory course for medical students using pathology, microbiology, and pharmacology as appropriate bridges between the pre-clinical curriculum and the clinical years. He built a small but unique department of eager young investigators who were able to apply sophisticated techniques to the solution of clinical problems. He attempted to forge the separate British medical firms, which are traditionally autonomous, into a team that shared facilities, teaching duties and consultants, and he asserted himself in British biomedical politics by telling the Ministry of Health what was wrong with their long-range plans for medical education. He even voted to permit women to become members of Magdalen College.

Having been spared the Blitz of 1945, Oxford was subjected to one in 1971. No fewer than four members of your Association invaded the Radcliffe Infirmary. You can immediately spot the difference between the Ivy League professors and the rugged frontiersman from the West, can't you? The year culminated with a meeting of a group, euphemistically called the Interplanetary Society but realistically the Pus Club, which he, Barry Wood and Walsh McDermott had founded nearly 20 years ago. The ostensible purpose of this group was to have young men present their work in progress but it really is an extension of Mory's and specializes in Green Cups, fine wines and monumental mornings after. The meeting in Oxford last spring ended with a magnificent banquet in the hall at Magdalen; and as the toasts were drunk and the odor of fine port pervaded the hall, it suddenly became clear to the more than 100 people there that the man at the center table was the reason that most of them were there and that in one way or another he had played a vital and positive part in their lives.

This might be a good place to end this story, but it is not the end of his adventure, by any means. As many of you know, PB has resigned his post in Oxford and will be returning to the States sometime next year. Characteristic for him, he is leaving several years early so that his successor might be chosen in time to plan the new Radcliffe Infirmary. But we know that it is not the end of his adventure—we are looking forward to the next chapter because it surely will be as exciting, varied and challenging as the past.

Why is the Association giving the Kober Medal to Beeson? Is it because of his investigative triumphs—it has been said that Beeson has more "firsts" than anyone else in infectious diseases? Is it because he is a good doctor, clinician and teacher who has been an inspiration to many young men? Is it because he has served as American academe's ambassador with courtesy, grace and friendliness? Or because he is the recipient of many honors? Is it because he has, as President of this Association, shown remarkable clairvoyance by warning us five years ago that we had better turn our attention to true clinical investigation? Or is it because he is a wise counsellor and warm friend who has helped countless young men attain their place in the academic world? All of these accomplishments are contributory, but in my view not any of them is the reason. Beeson deserves the Kober Medal because he has taught us, probably more than anyone else in academic medicine, how to live the academic adventure fully, how to live it with humility and humor, with style and graciousness, and to live it with an understanding and kindness for his patients, his students and his colleagues, in a spirit of giving to all of them more than he has received. In short, he has been the example of what the best in academic medicine is all about.

Some years ago Beeson received a gold medal. He was immensely proud of it and showed it to Barbara. With her true Republican Yankee eye, she thought it looked a little funny and had it appraised and it turned out to be bronze. I don't know whether the Kober Medal is gold or bronze, but it is the highest honor the Association can bestow on one of its members, and bronze or gold, Paul and Barbara, it wants you both to have it with all of the admiration, gratitude and love that you so richly deserve.

1. Bennett, I. L., Jr., and Beeson, P. B.: Studies on the pathogenesis of fever. I. The effect of injection of extracts and suspensions of uninfected rabbit tissues upon the body temperature of normal rabbits. J. Exp. Med., 98: 477, 1953.

2. Bennett, I. L., Jr., and Beeson, P. B.: Studies on the pathogenesis of fever. II. Characterization of fever-producing substances from polymorphonuclear leukocytes and from the fluid of sterile exudates. J. Exp. Med., 98: 493, 1953.

3. Beeson, P. B.: Factors in the pathogenesis of pyelonephritis. Yale J. Biol. Med.,28 : 81, 1955.

4. Guze, L. B., and Beeson, P. B.: Experimental pyelonephritis. I. Effect of ureteral ligation on the course of bacterial infection in the kidney of the rat. J. Exp. Med. 104: 803, 1956.

5. Guze, L. B., and Beeson, P. B.: Experimental pyelonephritis. II. Effect of partial ureteral obstruction on the course of bacterial infection in the kidney of the rat and the rabbit. Yale J. Biol. Med., 30: 315, 1958.

6. Freedman, L. R., Kminskas, E., and Beeson, P. B.: Experimental pyelonephritis. VII. Evidence on the mechanisms by which obstruction of urine flow enhances susceptibility to pyelonephritis.

Yale J. Biol. Med., 33: 65, 1960.

7. Guze, L. B., and Beeson, P. B.: Observations on the reliability and safety of bladder catheterization for bacteriologic study of the urine. N. Engl. J. Med 1956; 255:474-475.

8. Beeson, P. B.: The case against the catheter (editorial). Am. J. Med., 24: 1, 1958.

9. Beeson, P. B., and Rowley, D.: The anti-complementary effect of kidney tissue. Its association with ammonia production. J. Exp. Med., 110: 685, 1959.

10. Beeson, P. B.: Factors influencing the prevalence of trichinosis in man. Proc. R. Soc. Med. 34: 585, 1941.

11. Walls, R. S., and Beeson, P. B.: Mechanism of eosinophilia. VIII. Importance of local cellular reactions in stimulating eosinophil production. Clin. Exp. Immunol.,12: 111, 1972.

Beeson's reply
ACCEPTANCE OF THE KOBER MEDAL FOR 1973

This is a great occasion in my life. I am enormously pleased and also greatly surprised to find that my name will be added to the list of distinguished people who have received this award since 1925.

The event has in fact caused me to make a statistical analysis of the previous Kober medalists in an effort to uncover any threads that may link us. An obvious one is having held the office of President of the Association, as had 20 of the 46 before me. On looking over their fields of interest I note that no more than 16, beginning with the first two, Noguchi and Theobald Smith, had worked in the area of infectious disease. And what was specifically intriguing was to see that three of them- Welch, DuBois and Wood had also investigated the pathogenesis of fever. It may be that a few eyebrows will lift when I claim Welch in this connection but I think I can justify it if you will allow a brief historical note. In 1888 Welch gave the Cartwright lectures in New York on the subject of "The General Pathology of Fever." In four lectures he sifted through much evidence, good and bad, considered several hypotheses, and then came to some firm conclusions:

(1) that there is excessive heat production during fever, though not as much as would be generated by vigorous exercise,

(2) that there is something wrong with the dissipation of heat from the body,

(3) that the fault must lie in central regulation of heat exchange,

(4) that extraneous substances such as bacterial products could not be the agents that directly upset thermoregulation; and

(5) and to me this is the most remarkable- the disturbance in thermoregulation must be mediated by some product of the host's own tissues. Even now, 85 years later, these lectures make astonishingly good reading. They were frequently cited during the early part of this century and they undoubtedly influenced the thinking of later workers. They certainly had something to do with my decision to look for a fever producing substance in the neutrophil.

The meetings of this Association have always been a great pleasure to me. I first attended as a guest in 1938 and have missed very few since then. I like the traditions. The Association resists change, its programs are slanted toward clinical subjects, the pace is a little slower, and the discussions are as informal as can be managed in a large assembly. A feature that I have particularly enjoyed has been this Kober Medal ceremony. When I first began to come the recipients were far senior to me; nevertheless it was nice to see the men, to learn something about their backgrounds and to find out just what it was they had done. I would like to recall a few snatches of my memories of them.

The first that stands out was 1945 when O. T. Avery received the medal. It was the custom then for the recipient to stand on the platform during the address of presentation. Inasmuch as I had previously worked in the same institution I knew Avery to be a very shy man and could imagine what an ordeal it was for him to stand there and be talked about. But he did, and gave a charming little response, saying quite characteristically that in selecting him the "court had been packed" in his favor because nearly all the officers and councilors had formerly been colleagues at the Rockefeller Institute.

A few years later the medal went to E. C. Kendall shortly after his Nobel Prize for cortisone. The presentation was made by his clinical colleague,

Philip Rensch, who in closing assured Kendall that the medal was made of gold and begged him not to tinker with it! Kendall replied rather briefly but used the occasion to express his gratitude to the Mayo Foundation for continuing to support his research during 19 years in which there had been little evidence of accomplishment. He questioned whether any other institution would have been so tolerant.

The next occasion I'll mention was Arnold Rich's in 1958. In that I was struck by his description of the leisure of academic life in the 20s and 30s. He spoke of "leisure for trying to know one's field well, leisure to associate with fresh young minds, leisure for communion with one's colleagues."

In 1961 the award went to O. H. Robertson, and Peyton Rous gave a delightful account of Robertson's achievements, including his happy retirement studying the ecology of fish. Rous related that Robertson had recognized an endocrine disturbance in spawning salmon, which had features of the Cushing's syndrome.

So much for memories of former Kober ceremonies. Turning now to the practical subject of academic opportunities, I find on looking back that members of this Association have been responsible for each one of the succession of jobs I have held.

In 1937 when my plans for the future were quite formless, I chanced to meet Tom Rivers at a dinner party. He was just about to take over the directorship of the hospital of the Rockefeller Institute and had an unfilled residency. He offered it to me that evening and I accepted immediately. Until that occasion the possibility of an academic career had never entered my mind.

Two years later another member needed a resident. This time it was Soma Weiss, who was moving to the Peter Bent Brigham Hospital. A friend recommended me to him, we met in New York, and I signed on. Weiss died only four years later at age 43. This was a catastrophe for medicine. Beyond doubt he was a great man, in terms of capacity to inspire others and his remarkable effectiveness in teaching. To be with him on ward rounds was an enthralling experience. Everyone there would become intensely involved in the discussion he was leading. I came to realize that Weiss didn't achieve that kind of effect without effort. He remarked one day as we were walking back to his office that his whole body ached after a ward round session.

My enlistment to work in a Harvard hospital unit in England during the

Figure 8. Dr. Soma Weiss, Departmental Chair of Medicine at the Peter Bent Brigham Hospital. Weiss is in the front (bottom) row; Dr. Beeson is in the second row from the top, next to Dr. Jack Myers.

early years of World War II was effected by Sidney Burwell who was Dean at Harvard then. Next, Gene Stead gave me my first job in academic medicine when he invited me to go with him to Emory as Assistant Professor. Gene then kindly arranged for me to become Professor and Chairman at Emory, simply by moving to Duke and taking everybody else in the department along with him. My move to Yale was, I am sure, largely due to the backing of Hugh Long who was Dean. We had been acquainted since my medical school days at McGill. The most recent transplantation, from Yale to Oxford, was organized by one of our honorary members, George Pickering, and I am glad he's here today to celebrate with me.

I'd like now to touch on the pleasure and profit I have had from working with young doctors. I cannot possibly express the gratitude I feel to a long series of interns and residents who have made clinical work so stimulating and rewarding. I am thinking not only of their interest and their questions, which are so essential to the success of bedside teaching, but also of the fact that our teaching sessions have been two-way exchanges. These young doctors have managed -their part with so much grace: casually mentioning a diagnosis I had not thought of or seeming to let slip some bit of information about a normal value or a special property of a drug.

Similarly, one of my great privileges has been to have a series of exceptional young men as research fellows. It is an exciting adventure to go along with one of them, talk over results, and plan the next experiment. While touching on the subject of research training I would like to make another brief digression to say how much I like Oxford's arrangement for work leading to the Doctor of Philosophy degree. Candidates must devote full time to their research. There are no formal courses to be taken. The one requirement is that new knowledge be produced. The necessity to write a thesis, and to defend it, provides just the right goad. In this country I think we err sometimes by trying to combine research training with clinical responsibility or some other distracting activity.

I have saved for the end my words about someone who is not medical – merely married to a doctor. She has been widowed by these meetings each May of our life. She has had to create a new home each time I've wanted to take another job. She's here now and is just as pleased as I am that we're receiving the Kober Medal.

1. Welch, W. H.: On the general pathology of fever. Medical News, 52: 365, 393, 539, 565, 1888.

Chapter 5

Leaving Yale, Nuffield Professorship at Oxford and Knighthood

Lewis Landsberg, Mark Boyer & Tony Batsen

Lewis Landsberg

Paul Beeson led the department of medicine at Yale for 13 years, from 1952 to 1965. Over this period of time the faculty experienced a 10-fold increase in size and the department was widely recognized as one of the best in the country. These were halcyon years for academic medicine; support for research from the National Institutes of Health, and the emergence of research-intensive subspecialties fueled the growth of departments of medicine. I was a medical student at Yale from 1960 to 1964 and both fortunate and proud to be a member of his last group of Yale interns.

Many of the essays in this book address the special qualities of Paul Beeson; the reverence that he engendered throughout the department was legendary and was mirrored in his national and international prominence. And so when he left Yale for Oxford in 1965 there was a palpable sense of loss and sorrow that reverberated throughout the department and the medical school. We all wished him well and hoped that we could live up to the legacy that he had established at Yale.

His reasons for leaving Yale for Oxford were widely appreciated: he did not enjoy the administrative burden necessitated by the growth of the department; this imposed limitations on his interactions with students and residents and on the time he had for research. It seems likely that his fondness for England, dating from his participation in the Harvard-Red Cross hospital in Salisbury during the war and his recent sabbatical in Oxford, contributed as well. Leaving at the peak of his department's success and his own personal and professional eminence, fulfilled as well, the old adage "leave while they still want you to stay."

THE FITKIN IRON 'TERNS (JUNE, 1965)

Figure 9. Dr. Beeson playing softball with the Fitkin Iron 'Terns at a picnic at his house in Woodbridge CT in June 1965. Beeson is on the far right. From left to right (standing) Federman, Dear, Levin, Fischer, Tilson, Ross, Burke, Landsberg, Silverstein, Beeson; kneeling: Forrest, Viola, Knight; laying in front: Lee.

Beeson's last group of Yale interns, informally dubbed "the Fitkin iron terns" by his last Yale chief resident, Jack Levin, were instrumental in preserving his legacy at Yale. This group formed a "Beeson Society" that sponsored colloquia, advocated for naming the medical service at Yale in his honor, and commissioned and funded a portrait of Professor Beeson that hangs in the Fitkin amphitheater to this day.

And so he moved to Oxford to become the Nuffield professor. It was a move that paralleled that of Osler, who left Hopkins to become the Regius professor some 60 years previously. It was a remarkable honor befitting his status and accomplishments in American medicine.

Despite the large differences in organization as compared to American medical schools, Beeson's innate charm, dignity, and goodness won out. He was able to centralize services for the firms constituting the Nuffield department while personally running his own firm.

The move also allowed Beeson to spend more time on research. He had a longstanding interest in eosinophilia, stemming in part from his experience with trichinosis in Salisbury during the war. Working with post-doctoral students, he was able to demonstrate that a factor from lymphocytes, now identified as IL 5, was responsible for stimulation of eosinophil differentiation in bone marrow. This project also demonstrated Beeson's long-standing belief that research by physician investigators should be rooted in clinical observation.

At the pre-doctoral level he advocated for and developed a "bridge course," an introduction to clinical medicine that would better prepare students for their time on the medical wards.

During his time at Oxford Beeson hosted many Yale colleagues and trainees who paid homage to the professor when visiting the U.K. Such a visit might include a tour of the magnificent Magdalen College and lunch at high table or at a neighboring pub "the Trout." A steady stream of people from Yale Medical School did sabbatical years at Oxford as well.

In recognition of Beeson's outstanding contributions at Oxford he was made a "Knight Commander of the British Empire" in a ceremony at Admiralty House on December 12th, 1973. This was an exceptional honor granted to very few Americans and testifies to the important and enduring impact he had in the U.K.

Figure 10. Dr. Beeson in formal dress on December 12th 1973, the day that he was made Knight Commander of the British Empire in a ceremony at Admiralty House.

Paul Beeson as the Nuffield Professor of Medicine, Oxford
Mark Boyer

Many people who knew Paul Beeson from his years at Emory and Yale lost track of his medical career when he left New Haven for the Nuffield Professorship at Oxford. They understood, of course, that he had accepted one of the premier medical positions in the UK but did not appreciate the quality and depth of the Oxford experience for The Prof. The years in England allowed Dr. Beeson the luxury of a superb, though somewhat lower keyed milieu in which to bring his talents to bear on all kinds of challenges related to the practice of medicine.

What is also forgotten is that Oxford gave Dr. Beeson opportunities to explore in the laboratory those medical phenomena which exited his extraordinarily curious mind. Peers, students and colleagues have remarked on his interest in all matters pertaining to humans and their health. Whether it was the mechanism of eosinophilia or questions surrounding infective endocarditis, work in the laboratory complimented his amazing range of clinical interests.

I don't really remember how I ended up in Oxford in 1967. I had just completed a residency in internal medicine at Western Reserve, and some-one (now unknown but I am eternally his debtor) mentioned that some doctor from Yale had taken a position in England and was looking for a couple of young physicians to join him. Not being part of the Yale/Emory medical cabal, I knew virtually nothing about Paul Beeson nor his reputation. A pleasant correspondence with the Prof followed my enquiry, money was pulled together and I shortly appeared at his office at the Radcliffe Infirmary. I knew somehow that I would be working with eosinophils (see Tony Basten's contribution), cells about which I knew nothing except their association with trichinosis and certain allergic phenomena. I had worked in Haiti; there - because of endemic parasitism in the population, eosinophilia was taken for granted but I knew nothing about how and why these mysteri-ous cells appeared in the bloodstream.

Dr. Beeson's work was largely clinical, but he had a small laboratory (on the floor just below Sir Hans Krebs); Tony Basten from Australia was already immersed in the mysteries surrounding the mechanism of eosinophilia and the Prof, knowing of my interest in chemotherapeutic drugs, assigned me to find out whether these agents might affect the production of these peculiar cells and whether—through manipulation of the timing and dosage, some information on the causes of eosinophilia might be found.

The work – both Tony Basten's and mine – went extraordinarily well. I met weekly with the Prof. There was no demand for immediate progress, no assigning of directions, no deadlines, no pressure. Always astute questions - often based on clinical observations. Dr. Beeson was amazingly accessible, concerned for the welfare and career of young physicians and each meeting gave new avenues to be followed. He would come occasionally to the lab and I remember very clearly his peering through the microscope and exclaiming – almost like a little boy – at the wonderful spectacle of the mysterious eosinophil. Occasionally Tony and I were invited to Magdalen College for dinner or to his house on Boar's Hill where Barbara made us feel extraordinarily welcomed. I remember long conversations about the pros and cons of keeping a horse in Oxford.

Although I did weekly clinics and was a House Officer, I primarily worked in the laboratory but had no specific research standing. One day the Prof – after about a year of exiting revelations – asked me, quite casually, if l had ever considered writing a dissertation for the DPhil. (For those brought up in the US, a DPhil is Oxford' s PhD. To qualify for the degree one only has to write a dissertation – comparable in quality to the US PhD – and defend it before two examiners. The good news is that theoretically you can complete the degree in a relatively short time; the bad news is that - not having taken the preparatory courses required for a US PhD, some of the basic scientific groundwork can be little sketchy) The idea had never crossed my mind but Dr. Beeson clearly appreciated the work, understood well the discipline of completing the DPhil, and with nurturing and constant encouragement by the Prof, the dissertation became a reality. A neophyte in the intricacies of British academics, Dr. Beeson was able to see and guide work within that system and to understand how his direction could help someone embarking on an academic career.

After I had written the dissertation and returned to the States awaiting a time to re-appear in Oxford and defend it, I heard through the grapevine that one of my examiners – a world renowned but crusty and difficult academic from the north of England – had read the dissertation and apparently expressed the opinion that it "was pretty thin stuff." I panicked. Constant transatlantic telephone handholding by Dr. Beeson not withstanding I returned to Oxford for the examination with off-the-wall trepidation.

Now, I am well aware of the personal and clinical strengths of Dr. Beeson and his ability to motivate and touch those with whom he came in contact. The world has recognized his caring and concerned manner with patients and colleagues. His personal virtues are legendary and he has been rightfully recognized worldwide for his talents. But when I stepped into his office and he told me that the crusty old practitioner who was to be my examiner had fallen, broken a leg, would not be able to examine me and that he had been replaced by a local luminary who knew me, knew the work, and knew the Prof, I was convinced that Paul Beeson was about as close to God as one could get. My examination was a total success. Amazing accolades have rightfully followed Dr. Beeson's medical and personal career but how or even whether he engineered my successful DPhil defense, he has a rightful place where good men go.

I have thought over the years about the qualities that made the Prof such a superb physician, colleague and mentor. While I can easily list his virtues, it is impossible to create for others an explanation of the man's qualities and his influence on people in the field of medicine. My experience as his trainee at Oxford was an amazing one and I join the group who were privileged to be influenced by Paul Beeson.

The Beeson Days in Oxford
Tony Basten

The Nuffield chair of Medicine which he took up in 1965 was Dr Beeson's third Professorial appointment and Chairmanship of Department. When I arrived from Australia as his first Oxford graduate (D.Phil) student in early 1966, I remember him showing me in some puzzlement his letter of appointment in which he was addressed as 'Mr' Beeson- this I explained was simply due to the fact that he was not an Oxford graduate; his reply "in that case I should hope not!"

"The Prof." as we used to call him, offered me eosinophilia or iodides in granulomas as a D.Phil. project and when I chose the former he effectively launched me on my career as an immunologist. Both projects, however, reflected his firm conviction that the laboratory was there to sort out unresolved clinical problems- hence the importance for the researcher to remain in touch with clinical medicine. He was, I recall some years later, very concerned at the comment of a previous Director of NIH who referred to the inevitable 'dwindling bedside connection' for the researcher.

During my doctorate I had a meeting with him every Monday morning (American not British time) to report on the past week's progress. His patience was limitless as I did battle with parasite infested rats and familiarized myself with the then alien world of research.

Later on, when it was time to write up and present at meetings, he read (and corrected) every word and rehearsed me at least three times for each talk- that sort of attention from my perspective set the standards of good mentorship for the rest of my research career.

Having completed the doctorate, I spent my fourth year in Oxford as a senior resident on the Professorial clinical service. There I found a very different Beeson. Needless to say he always did a round on 'take' nights to see new admissions at 11pm which kept us all on our toes. However, during regular rounds he expected everything to be in 'apple pie' order.

Two episodes I recall only too vividly because they led to my being summonsed to his office afterwards. The first was related to the fact that one of the patients had a rash—classical rose spots he told me that I should be ashamed of myself for failing to diagnose such an obvious case of typhoid. On the second occasion he was even more concerned. "Boy," he said, "the intern tweaked the buttock of one of the nurses and it is your responsibility to ensure that it never happens again even though he may be another Australian."

His contributions to the Oxford Medical School where he initiated highly significant changes in the curriculum and to British Medicine in general were substantial. In recognition of these services he was given a knighthood - at the time if I recall correctly he was one of only three US citizens to be honored in this way, the others being Alastair Cook and Douglas Fairbanks Junior.

Like all his former trainees in the lab and the clinic, I admired him enormously for his unique talents and approach to medicine and medical science. Now that he has gone, there is no doubt that his legend will live on both sides of the Atlantic.

Emeritus Tony Basten, Sydney, Australia.

Chapter 6

Sir Paul Beeson and Sir William Osler Were Stewards of Internal Medicine in the 20th Century: Similarities and Striking Differences

Thomas Duffy

William Osler and Paul Beeson were the preeminent and most highly esteemed academic internists of the 20th century; a period that saw extraordinary advances in medicine and science. Their careers literally bookended the century with their reputations generated in their positions as chiefs of medicine; Osler at Johns Hopkins at the beginning of the century from 1899 to 1905 and Beeson at Yale at mid-century from 1952 to 1965. Osler's fame is perpetuated by numerous Osler Societies throughout the world, an Osler Library at McGill University, an Osler Building and Medical Service at Hopkins. Beeson has been likewise honored in the medical service at Yale, Beeson Chairs of Medicine at Yale, a Beeson Ward at the Radcliffe Infirmary in Oxford, a Beeson Award for excellence in clinical medicine at University of Washington, and scholarships in aging research bear his name. Both men created textbooks of medicine which further enhanced their reputations and kept them in the public eye of medical practitioners; Osler's text was in active circulation from the first edition in 1893 through 1938. Beeson initially served as an editor of Harrison's Text before transferring his highly touted editing skills and knowledge to Cecil's Textbook of Medicine. Both men found great fulfillment later in their careers as Professors at Oxford and were knighted by British Royalty for their work on behalf of the nation. The many parallels in their lives and their comparable achievements contribute to the description of Beeson as the Osler of his period, the heir to his mantle.

Some naysayers decry the magnitude of Osler's accomplishments, believing his greatness has been over exaggerated (1). Boston-trained physicians worship elsewhere at the altar of Soma Weiss, the Harvard chief of medicine, whose eminence was aborted by his premature death at 42 years of age. Osler has been portrayed as the father of cool detachment, an enemy of empathic caring, possessing the public tone of the academic snob (2). Although he bears the title of the great clinician, some suspected he was more interested in autopsies than in living patients. It is rumored that the major reason for his eager acceptance of the Regius Professorship at Oxford was the too great burden of caring for patients in his busy but very profitable consulting practice in Baltimore (3).

Still, most others, a legion of others, have been kinder and more respectful and adoring of the man; the adulation has continued up to the present. Annual meetings of the Osler Society are held with pilgrimages to his shrine at the Osler Library where his ashes are interred. An Osler Newsletter keeps his image alive for modern physicians. Former Osler house officers sport their Osler ties bearing Osler's maxim of equanimitas. His biography (4), for which Harvey Cushing received the Pulitzer Prize in 1926 has profited from a recent, more spirited and better balanced interpretation by Michael Bliss in 2007 (5). He departed from America for England over a 100 years ago but many of his most ardent admirers believed sainthood was now the more proper destination, his death was almost nine decades ago and still the sobriquet, Oslerian, conveys the master clinician, the doctors' doctor, the model to which all physicians once aspired.

During his clinics he displayed his vaunted skills of observation and inspection but he also emphasized any laboratory analysis that would aid in solving a patient's problems. He founded the Interurban Clinical Club whose objectives were to stimulate the study of internal medicine and to promote the scientific investigation of disease. Osler recognized and nurtured the vital links between the practicing physician and the basic scientist in the person of the clinical scientist. The club was strongly influential in the development of the scientific basis of medicine throughout the 20th century and up to the present (6). He was no Luddite resisting advances in the field- he was a critical presence in making it all happen. He established the foundation that permitted the later wondrous achievements of modern medicine, the field in which one of his heirs, Paul Beeson, was to play an equally important role. Although separated in time by half a century, the parallels in their lives, the trajectories of their lives were remarkably similar.

Both men had comparable family backdrops and educational pathways. Osler's father, Featherstone Lake Osler, ministered to a congregation on the Canadian frontier. Beeson was born in 1908 in Livingston, Montana, a cowboy town on the edge of Yellowstone, but his father, a general practitioner and surgeon, soon moved his family and practice to Anchorage, Alaska where Paul attended high school. His father's way of life influenced him and his brother in their choice of a profession and their devotion to the profession. Osler and Beeson both attended McGill Medical School and spent time at the University of Pennsylvania. Osler underwent two years of post-graduate continental seasoning, a common practice in his era, when he visited European clinics and laboratories where he was greatly influenced by individuals such as Virchow in the scientific approach to clinical medicine that he imported to the JHMS. Beeson's scientific orientation was born of his experience as a house officer at Rockefeller University Hospital where Oswald Avery was making the revolutionary discovery of DNA as the genetic engine of life. His work at Rockefeller brought him to the attention of the fabled Soma Weiss at Harvard who chose him as his Chief Medical Resident and where Soma daily imparted to him his total commitment to the study of general medical problems in individual patients. Soma's stardom was in daily evidence as he presided over morning report with his residents, an exercise that constituted then and at the present time, a ritualized handing on of the oral tradition of medicine, an exercise that Dr Beeson zealously conducted with all his trainees.

Osler and Beeson shared other experience in common; they both served abroad with the military during the World Wars. It was during his military service that Beeson fell in love with his future wife, Barbara, a nurse, and their long lasting marriage witnessed Barbara's acceptance and facilitation of medicine as Beeson's demanding mistress. Osler's marriage had the same loving arrangement. His wife unburdened her husband of all need of attending to the details of domestic life. She was so committed to his career that a requirement she imposed before consenting to marriage was that he completes his *Textbook of Medicine*—pre-nuptial agreements had a different collateral in that period. Both men reached the acme of their lives, Osler at Hopkins and Beeson at Yale, after they had had previous experiences as chiefs at other institutions- Osler at McGill and Penn, Beeson at Emory. They both left their parent institutions in America, Beeson after 13 years at Yale and Osler after 16 years in Baltimore to become respectively the Nuffield and Regius Professors at Oxford.

In the post-War years, Osler's otherwise idyllic life, was sundered by the tragic death of his only child, Revere, who died in the closing months of WW I as an infantry soldier in France. This was a tragedy which set in motion a decline that ended in his death in 1919; he lived out his life in a house in Norham Gardens, Oxford, christened "Open Arms," a sanctuary for all his students and colleagues whom he and Grace so warmly welcomed (7). Beeson returned to America to live out another wonderful chapter in his life—he became a Veteran's Administration Distinguished Professor at the University of Washington where he voluntarily requested the privilege of attending on the medical wards for six months of the year. It was during this period that he became impassioned with and championed the cause of the nascent field of geriatrics in America. His role as a catalyst in the field was crowned by the establishment of the Paul Beeson Physician Faculty Scholars in Aging Research, an initiative that has fueled the field of geriatric research throughout America. He cast his net even farther in his later years- he and his wife confronted the threat of nuclear war by playing prominent roles in Physicians for Social Responsibility. His concern for patients and the world in which they lived their lives never waned- he grew bolder as he grew older. He died in 2006 at age 97 with no hiatus in his ongoing interactions with his large coterie of reverent acolytes.

Beeson's life and impact replicated in fashion and content the events and accomplishments of Osler's life. And if his achievements in praxis, litterae and scientiae in medicine are compared to Osler (8), the total assessment is more or less the same although the emphasis on each is different. He was, like Osler, mainly a transmitter and transmutor but he was also a more creative transformer in medicine. He recognized the link between hepatitis and blood transfusions; he studied the eosinophil and the pathogenesis of pyelonephritis and endocarditis. He discovered with colleagues endogenous pyrogen, IL-1, which initiated the identification of the cascade of cytokines that play such an important role in health and disease. His scientific accomplishments dwarf those of Osler; he was the model physician-scientist of his era, carrying out his adage that in order to be successful in academic medicine, it was necessary to get one's hands dirty in the laboratory. Litterae was also a prominent part of his life. He did not possess the remarkable breadth of classical literature and history that Osler commanded; he had not received the classical education that Osler's Canadian/English schooling had provided him. However, Beeson thought and wrote widely on medical subjects and medical education His name has remained known to students and house staff because of his classic article on FUO which is a reference that is still read and quoted even now, years after its publication (9).

His life was the subject of a biography published in 2001 by the neurosurgeon, Richard Rapport (10), recalling the neurosurgeon Harvey Cushing's biography of Osler. Praxis, the practice of medicine, was never a large part of his life—all of his other responsibilities and involvements precluded his assuming responsibility for patients other than as an attending on the wards. There is no suggestion that patients sought out his consultative services like many Americans who crossed the Atlantic to be seen by Osler when he was the Regius Professor at Oxford. He created an outstanding Department of Medicine surrounded by seminal individuals such as Gerald Klatskin, Howard Spiro, Gerry Burrow, Fred Kantor, and his last group of Fitkin iron interns that included John Forrest and Lew Landsberg. He was a founding member of the Interplanetary Club, better known as the Pus Club in Infectious Disease circles. All of his accomplishments were crowned in a similar fashion to Osler by doctrine or teaching of medicine, a realm in which he excelled. House staff teaching was literally his playground and he sought out opportunities throughout his career to be so engaged.

There was another very important aspect in which their vision for medicine overlapped and which provides important insights regarding their conception of internists in the twentieth century; it is an aspect that represents the only apparent controversy or kink in their otherwise seamless careers in medicine. For Osler, the full-time system in academic medicine first introduced in the aftermath of the Flexner Report was an innovation to be resisted. Osler was strongly critical of this requirement and what he believed might be its potential consequences. Osler's opposition to the full-time system was based on his belief that all teachers of medicine should assume some daily responsibility to care for their own patients in order to continue to be grounded in the real details of their patients' lives. He believed that the full-time system would create a generation of so-called clinical prigs who were more comfortable in the laboratory and classroom than at the bedside. He was apprehensive that the medical student who was admitted to the ward would find an impoverished clinical encounter there.

The controversy involving the full-time system was played out in the early part of the century when Academic Medicine in America was still a fledgling enterprise. Ironically, over the subsequent decades Osler's vision for Internal Medicine as scientific medicine was realized because of the full time system that he initially resisted. Internal Medicine in Osler's era had been the oxymoronic specialty of general medicine but this gave way to sub-specialty medicine as the knowledge base of medicine literally exploded. For Beeson, the progressive erosion of the general field of Internal Medicine by its fragmentation into specialties, was something of which he disapproved but could not prevent. The medical texts that both created were dramatic testimonies to the extent of such a transformation.

Osler's Text was a single authored text (11); one individual could command the entire corpus of medicine at the time and create a text that was the bible of Internal Medicine for nearly five decades. The Cecil and Harrison texts which were edited by Beeson were very different—they were 120-130 authored texts. The advances in medicine were made by full time physicians who narrowed their fields of investigation as the depth of knowledge in each area deepened. Beeson was dismayed by the effect that this fragmentation of the broad specialty of Internal Medicine had upon the teaching and learning of medicine. He questioned how the growing clinical specialization could fail to have a detrimental effect on our competence as physicians and as teachers of clinical medicine. He was apprehensive regarding the increasing tendency of academic physicians to devote most of their time and thought to laboratory medicine. He thought it difficult for physicians to have a relationship with mitochondria. Hospitals were in need of specialists; medical schools required a larger perspective of the patient. It was this philosophy that made geriatrics such an appealing field for him, allowing a better balance between an exaltation of high technology and a focus on the broad problems of growing old, of comforting and caring for whole people instead of intracellular components.

In reviewing the papers of Dr. Beeson in the Archives and Manuscript Collection at Yale, one discovers that it was this focus, this concentration, by Beeson upon the patient that was a major source of inspiration for his students and colleagues. Beeson's first principle in medicine was the centrality of the patient in the care of patients. He is often described as sitting on a chair at the side of a patient's bed with quiet attention to each individual patient. He evoked, according to one of his trainees, a "quality of mercy" in all his interactions with patients. And this strongly admired man—students spontaneously stood as he entered a room-was shy, almost diffident, without the burden of ego. By the example of his life, he characterized the ideal academic physician, an ideal to which all who were his students aspired. He was, in simple terms, a good and dedicated and fortunate man of unquestioned integrity. He was, in his mother's description of him, a perfect person and he brought that perfection to his life in medicine.

Osler by contrast was a more magical presence at the patient's bedside with his dazzling display and fireworks of solving the patient's problem; Beeson was different- he was a listener, inspiring by silent presence more than his command of medicine. Osler's kindness to patients was also memorable, especially his ability to enchant little children. Both men extended to their patients the same kindness that characterized their interactions with students and fellows. Letters of congratulation were frequently sent to colleagues upon their promotions and publications, births and deaths. Spouses and children were always included in warm and tender greetings. There is no record of an incident in which they spoke badly of a colleague; in fact, Osler believed it was unprofessional to do so. He reprimanded his closest associate, Harvey Cushing, for such behavior and pointed out the negative consequences of such a practice. They rarely had to discipline anyone; their example inspired others to strive for lives beyond the ordinary. No one wanted to appear unworthy of them. One of his Fitkin 'terns reflected that his group was able to enjoy true affection for one other because Dr. Beeson gave them permission to be that way.

There still remains the question as to why Osler and Beeson endure as legendary role models in Medicine, even at the present time when all of the achievements in molecular biology have shifted the axis of Internal Medicine more and more from the bedside. The question is made more difficult because both men challenged the alterations in medicine that made Internal Medicine scientific medicine and the intellectual core of all of medicine. Osler rejected the full-time system and Beeson was troubled by the rise of medical specialization. They also both retreated to sinecures at Oxford where they were no longer in positions to direct the subsequent course of American Medicine. And yet the legends continue after almost a century since Osler's death and close to four decades since Beeson's reign at Yale ended. They continue to be recognized and invested in as the leading actors in the great drama of internal medicine in the last century, they were and remain spiritual fathers to all who have succeeded them in the medical profession. Their persona and accomplishments were always on display in their very public and influential positions at several major medical institutions in America and England.

Osler and Beeson both embodied those qualities of great leaders; they were catalysts, inspirers and consciences for their generation and subsequent generations of physicians. Their accomplishments in medicine, linked to and outdistanced by their personal qualities, explain the image of greatness attached to their person. They were stewards of Internal Medicine in the 20th century. Both deserve to receive the honor and grace that are promised to those who fulfill the Hippocratic oath, who lived a Way of Life that continues to inspire all of their descendants in Medicine. Their Way of Life is one to which physicians aspire even in the 21st Century.

1. Bondy, Philip. What's So Special About Osler? Yale Journal of Biology and Medicine 1980, 53, 213-17

2. Weissmann, Gerald. Against Aequanimitas. Hosp Pract 1984, 19: 159-69

3. Fye, WB. William Osler's Departure from North America. The Price of Success. N Eng J Med 1989 May 25; 320: 1425-31

4. Cushing, Harvey. The life of Sir William Osler. Oxford University Press, London

5. Bliss, Michael. William Osler: a life in medicine. Oxford University Press, New York, 1999

6. Harvey, A. McGehee. The Interurban Clinical Club (1905-1976): a record of achievement in clinical science. Philadelphia, 1978.

7. Duffy, Thomas. The Osler- Cushing Covenant. Persp. Bio. Med 48.4,

2005:592-602

8. Spector, Bernard. Osler: An Example of litterae, scientiae, praxis and doctrina. Bull Hist Med 23-1949; 378-86

9. Petersdorf R, Beeson P. Fever of unexplained origin: report on 100 cases. Medicine 1961;40:1-30. 2.

10. Rapport, Richard. Physician: the life of Paul Beeson. Fort Lee, NJ. Barricade Books, 2001

11. Osler, William. The Principles and Practice of Medicine 1892. New York, D.Appleton and Company

Chapter 7

The Beeson Symposia

The Rule of Thumb*: Taking Care of Real Patients

Richard V. Lee, M.D. *Professor of Medicine and Pediatrics and Obstetrics, Adjunct Professor of Anthropology and Social and Preventive Medicine, Director, Division of Maternal & Adolescent Medicine Director, Division of Geographic Medicine Department of Medicine. State University of New York at Buffalo*

*RULE OF THUMB: A rough, guesswork measure, practice, or experience, as distinguished from theory, in allusion to the use of the thumb for rough measurements. The first joint of the adult thumb measures almost exactly one inch (2.5 cm). *Brewer's Dictionary of Phrase and Fable*, 15th edition.

Sometime during my internship (1964-1965) I went to see Dr. Beeson about a letter of support for my application to the Indian Health Service. He agreed, reluctantly, after describing the NIH laboratories, the CDC's Epidemic Intelligence Service and the Atomic Bomb Casualty Commission, as better career choices. I was not dissuaded by his concern that I might not have a future in academic medicine.

In 1967, after two years of internal medicine house-staff training, I wrote to Alvan Feinstein about the remarkable prevalence of and problems with acute rheumatic fever on the Fort Peck Indian Reservation in north-eastern Montana. I have savored his reply, along with the reprints of his Irvington House papers on rheumatic fever which he sent to me, because his opening sentences went sort of like this:

"Dear Dick, Thank you for your letter which astounded me. I was surprised that Yale had actually trained doctors who take care of real patients and worry about science."

Twenty years ago, Howard Spiro and Harvey Mandell published an essay in the *New England Journal of Medicine*, "Leaders and the Swan " in which they argued that high tech procedures were the proper domain of clear sighted, steady handed, highly coordinated youth. They had the temerity to imply that the mundane realities of continuous caring for real patients were possibly more difficult, more challenging, than the repetitive performance of procedures and protocols. Nevertheless, ten years later Howard advised me that the kind of homespun medicine I wrote about in my Jaundiced View essays in the American Journal of Medicine was outmoded, and impossible; "hopelessly romantic" was his diagnosis.

So much for my Yale professors!

There has always been a disparity between the academy and the practice of medicine and a need for periodic reminders that the object of the academy and the practice is the care of the patient. Now there seems to be a growing disparity between the medical trenches and the commercial and legislative concepts of taking care of patients. Like the blind men and the elephant, the medicine espoused in the groves of academe, in the corridors of political power, and in the board rooms of the health care industry are each different and none of them has a complete notion of the patient and the care of the patient. It is the notion of medicine, of doctors caring for and caring about patients, after all, which is the subject of our colloquium today and the target of the current economic and educational changes that seem to be running amok with the profession.

Notions of medicine and the activities of medicine are shaped by language; by the way we speak. The foundation of medical education is instructing our students in the medical vocabulary and medical speech. One of the crucial elements of successful medical practice is the capacity to translate medical language into the common tongue of patients and to comprehend and to translate the common tongue of patients into a professional and advocacy vocabulary.

I look at medicine as an amalgam, a hybrid: composed of natural history, experimental, theoretical and social science. I do not believe Manichean divisions between science and humanism, molecular biology and epidemiology, generalism and specialism, serve medicine well. However, we create fences to segregate these entities into different tribes or specialties because of their different languages, and segregation breeds prejudice. So that the clinical epidemiologist denigrates the molecular biologist and vice versa, because they speak differently and they do not want to be bothered to understand each other. There is a certain jingoistic ambition to see that one's language is the true and only language of medicine.

Nowadays, we have popular vocabularies of "evidence based medicine," "population based medicine," "outcomes research," "practice guidelines," and "managed care." The proliferation of neologisms indicates a possible resurgence of syphilitic general paresis. In order to practice medicine, new physicians must, in addition, understand the legal language of contracts and torts and corporate operations.

I worry that as we learn so many different ways of speaking, new languages if you will, that we will forget the language of our patients: the speech of the sick, the worried well, and the healthy skeptics. I worry that we are losing the capacity to translate the language of medicine for our patients and for our public.

Physicians need to be linguists: masters of the vocabularies of clinical epidemiology, managed care, natural history, computers, molecular biology, and the legalities of contracts. Physicians must retain, nevertheless, the proto-language of medicine, the root as it were, which comes from the earthy, ribald, emotions of mucking about a biologic barn filled with sick fellow human beings. The polyphony of medicine is as old as the art. We have not yet excised astrology, alchemy, and folklore from our patients' vocabulary. We must not forget about them, because our patients still believe and use them. There is not a huge symbolic leap from astrologic birth predisposition to genetic predisposition.

One feature of the currently popular medical language is a deceptive aura of precision and exactitude: an aura created by the abstract elegance of a large number of numbers that can be mathematically manipulated and of sharply drawn graphic representations of complex clinical circumstances. It has no patience for the colorful, oftentimes crude descriptions by patients of their illnesses, and it does not tolerate deviations from proscribed legal or statistical pathways. With respect to Alvan I call this the Venn Diagram Dogma.

There is something seductive about the ethereal symmetry and logic of the Venn Diagram. It has such discrete, distinct boundaries. The contents within the circles can be considered identical and interchangeable, except where they intersect. Here, art, or graphic illustration, shapes our thinking

Figure 11. Dr. Ralph Horwitz, Dr. Beeson and Dr. Alvan Feinstein at a black tie dinner in New Haven after the Beeson Symposium.

and our language. Its Manichean pole is "the rule of thumb; " the vulgar reality of real patients, who don't fit neatly into a discrete, statistically significant symmetry.

The Venn Diagram Dogma dominates medical language and thinking in the construction of the decision analysis algorithms, malpractice litigation, and the commercialization and industrialization of medical practice. Establishing identical, symmetrical, interchangeable parts was the essence of the Ford assembly line revolution a century ago. We are doing the same in medicine by creating categories of interchangeable parts (diagnoses, procedures, outcomes, and so on) and assembly line pathways. The individual and the exceptional are lost in the Venn Diagram Dogma. One anterior myocardial infarction with second degree block is the same as any other. Just as it is with spark plugs.

The Venn Diagram Dogma leads to language usage that establishes discrete, often artificial, boundaries, like algorithms and contracts. The rule of thumb uses language to explore and to depict the natural history of illness and wellness. The rule of thumb is essential to the doctor-patient relationship. The Venn Diagram is essential for the business of health care.

The danger is that we expect the precision of its elegant simplicity and lose our ability to understand and to describe with words, adjectives if you will, the clinical setting and events that surround each patient interaction. Doctors must understand what patients tell us and doctors must describe that experience for the profession and for the public. The specter of managed care, the industrialization of medicine, is a product in part of the way doctors describe it. If we talk only about epidemiology and evidence based medicine, as opposed to case reports and individual patients, then population-oriented medicine, the assembly line, becomes the dominant model for practice, and for research and education.

Contemporary medical economics is chiefly concerned with regulating the use of resources and with increasing cost effectiveness, both of which rely heavily on the statistics derived from large numbers of patients, procedures, tests, and so on. There is a passion for collecting large series for statistical evaluation and manipulation. I think this has produced a decline in curiosity about and interest in the singular. Careful attention to the individual and the commonplace, previously the hallmark of excellent clinicians, is now considered old fashioned, "hopelessly romantic." Doctors, legislators, insurance executives are suspicious of small numbers or singular cases. Descriptions of single patients are condescendingly called anecdotes,

Figure 12 (left): Dr. Fred Kantor and Dr. Beeson; Figure 13 (right): Dr. John Forrest and Dr. Beeson.

Figure 14. From left to right: Dr. Beeson, Mrs Barbara Beeson, Dr. John Forrest, Catherine Forrest, Dr. James Fischer.

stories concocted by well meaning but scientifically naive clinicians.

My medical life has been a long sequence of anecdotes, of individual stories. These narratives · become trite if they are poorly recorded or if they are compressed into the anonymity of numbers. They lose meaning and become irrelevant if they are never told in a chart, on rounds, or in a paper. Parables have not lost their hold on the minds of patients and pupils. They continue to be potent tools for teaching. Yesterday's dedication ceremony was a grand illustration: every speaker told stories. The chief resident used several patient anecdotes to convey her message. The New England Journal still publishes a Cabot case every issue. I think we should remember that William Beaumont made his important contributions to gastrointestinal disease by the careful study of a singular event, a gastric fistula following a gunshot wound, in a single patient, Alex St. Martin.

I have two episodes from the past two months to tell you about by way of illustration. One of my patients from Yale-New Haven days, a woman I cared for during my residency and then in the Dana Clinic, called me after a hiatus of 20 years. She was concerned that her daughter with newly diagnosed Graves' disease was in mom's eyes not being properly cared for. Yes, she was on PTU, and was advised about risks, surgery, radiation, and reproduction. But she just wasn't confident that the consultant had told her everything she should know, because she wasn't sure what she should do. Mom knew all the numbers given to her daughter but neither mom nor daughter had a sense of how to proceed. They wanted some advice and direction. As mom said, after relating her indecisiveness during a recent bout with angina, angioplasty, and coronary artery bypass, "the statistics weren't much of a road map." What was wanted was my directions, which way would I go.

Last month one of my old patients, a lady almost 90, daughter of an old-fashioned Virginia GP, mother of a modem pediatrician, died after a protracted battle with congestive heart failure, which came on after a long life with rather mild mitral valve stenosis. She had a cardiologist and a gastroenterologist for her at times dreadful gastroesophageal reflux. She had been house bound for a year so I would make monthly house calls and we would talk at least once a week by telephone. She died quietly in acute renal failure after 18 hours in the ICU with her son and I fending off a nephrologist wanting to dialyze, something she had specifically opposed in her written instructions.

What was engaging about Mrs. X was her response to bilateral mastectomy, for Paget's disease on one side and intraductal carcinoma on the other. This had taken place before she moved to Buffalo at age 69. On her first few visits she made it clear that she didn't feel right about herself without a bosom. It had nothing to do with sexual behavior: she and her husband slept in different rooms and had a distant relationship. It had a lot to do with her notion of her womanhood. So we began the surprisingly difficult process of finding a plastic surgeon willing to insert breast implants in a 70-year-old lady. Money wasn't an issue, she had saved up and would not do this under Medicare because "it was none of their business." After several months and considerable arm twisting, a surgeon was found, the prostheses placed, and the patient put in a much better frame of mind.

The everyday language of the vast majority of our patients is not the statistical risk of serum cholesterol of 385 mg/dl. Nor are my patients really interested in a numerical explanation as to why admission to the hospital is not allowed for their particular misery. That so many of our patients (a third or more) use alternative therapies, indicates their general apathy for randomized efficacy studies and outcomes research. My anecdotal experience with patients is that their notion of statistics and outcomes is a lot different from contemporary medical orthodoxy. There is a certain self-centeredness which makes them attentive to Jimmy the Greek kinds of statistics: What are my odds, or my risks, or my gains? Not what are the odds, the risks, or the gains. Where do I put my money? Where do I put my body? Not where does the insurance company put its money. Not where does the HMO put my body. Many patients see contemporary medicine's view of them as a cubist Picasso painting. Their own view is simpler, more prosaic. The implied altruism and anonymity of randomized controlled trials and outcomes research is not a concern for people caught up in the aches and anxieties of real or perceived sickness. In fact, Alvan Feinstein wrote in 1994 that "The great appeal of randomized trials was that investigative clinicians could do scientifically credible research without having to discuss clinical phenomena."

I am impressed at how rapidly the gaps between patient and doctor and the health care establishment are growing. The more we talk in the Venn Dogma and the less we speak the vernacular of real patients, the greater will be our decline in credibility and ability to be our patients' confidante and advisor and advocate. Sure, we can tell them about procedures and costs and outcomes, but will we understand their turmoil dealing with a daughter's divorce, a grandchild's delinquency, a cousin's passing. Will we be part of their life or merely an unpleasant intrusion?

I remember one of Dr. Beeson's professors' rounds in the Memorial Unit when, after discussing a moribund women with pulmonary sarcoidosis, he commented to the intern, me, that she needed special attention because she was "pretty sick." We, and the patient, knew what he meant without calculating an APACHE score.

I think we need both the rule of thumb and Venn diagrams: neither speaks for the whole of medicine. More importantly I think medicine needs colorful language usage that will protect the profession from the depredation of colorless, constricting bureaucrats and their jargon, and provide the stimulus for clinical and basic science. Only a mathematician could love the sterile numeracy of statistics, but physicians must learn to use numbers as potent adjectives in the care of their patients and the management of the profession. Poets delight in creative manipulation of words. Physicians must learn to use the common tongue of patients and illness in the care of their patients and in the management of the profession. The art of medicine includes the capability to blend many tongues, to create an anthem from the polyphony of medicine, to tell a story.

I wrote an essay for the American Journal of Medicine last year, which attempted to look at the generalist-specialist dichotomy from a different perspective. I came up with some non-task, non-training categories which describe these species of doctor. As I prepared this talk it became painfully obvious I had missed the mark and had left out language, the capacity to communicate. How we speak. What we hear. To whom do we talk. And what parables do we tell.

I guess what has me most concerned is that the profession is increasingly populated by people who do not converse with patients. We have plenty of people who speak about patients but do not speak with them. Conversing with patients, using their tongue, is the common, unifying foundation of medicine. Only those who can and do are, in my mind, physicians.

Chapter 8

A Correspondence With Beeson: Differing Views of Clinical Science

Gordon Gill

In this essay Gordon Gill, former Yale resident and current academic endocrinologist, describes his correspondence with Paul Beeson concerning the conduct of research within departments of medicine. Beeson's strongly held point of view was that research in departments of medicine should be related to clinically relevant aspects of disease, focusing on patients and disease. Gill, a molecular endocrinologist, argued that the techniques of molecular biology had rendered descriptive research in departments of medicine obsolete. The resolution of this conflict, as foreseen by Beeson, was the eventual use of the techniques of molecular biology to investigate clinical problems in departments of medicine.

This colloquy demonstrates, moreover, Beeson's willingness to engage with former residents and younger colleagues despite his esteemed position as a preeminent leader in academic medicine. It also provides, in Beeson's own words, a fascinating description of his important research. Gill writes:

i) The Beginning of a Dialogue

In 1984 I published an essay in *The American Scholar* on "The End of the Physician Scientist?" Attending the "triple society" (AAP/ASCI/AFCR) meeting in 1983 I had a deep uneasiness that something was wrong; this essay resulted from my exploration of the source of that unease. My unease arose from my sense that the material presented by serious younger (and older) physician scientists were descriptive, esoteric and unoriginal and that few there recognized this. I contrasted this with the original research presented and intensely discussed at Cold Spring Harbor conferences. My concern was that Clinical Investigators were no longer at the forefront of acquiring knowledge; the mantle had passed to the Molecular and Cellular Biologists. Two questions were unanswered: what were the origins of relevant scientific questions and what were the future prospects for original research in Academic Departments of Medicine.

Not long after this essay was published, I met with Paul Beeson when he was in San Diego and was delighted to subsequently receive a thoughtful letter from him that initiated a correspondence centered on those two questions with which he had long been concerned. Our debate centered on the origins of biomedical scientific questions although I expanded it to include other topics. Paul thought that physicians were uniquely positioned to initiate scientific enquiry because they had direct contact with patients. This could be considered a variation of Alexander Pope's "The Proper Study of Mankind is Man" although Paul's position was subtler than that. I took the position that studies of any form of life or biological processes would reveal fundamental principles and mechanisms that would then be extrapolated to humans and their diseases.

In his first letter Paul stated the end game: "My hope would be that in a couple of decades the techniques will have become established, and the body of molecular biology sufficiently understood, that the medical investigator can make use of them, and apply them to patients' problems."

My generation of scientists trained in the 1960s and 1970s were of necessity reductionists; the tools of molecular, cellular and structural biology were not directly applicable to clinical investigation but were uniquely suited to basic science questions of development, cell growth and division, gene transcription and signaling networks. Only now with the human genome, the "Omics" (genomic, proteomics, metabolomics), large scale computing capable of handling megabytes of data, high throughput DNA sequencing, etc., can humans again become subjects for cutting edge scientific inquiry.

In the same letter Paul also staked out his position.

"I think I would quibble with you about the term Physician Scientist. To you a scientist seems to be a molecular biologist. I would argue that science should be pursued at several levels, and of course with regard to physician scientists I would stand by my point in the presidential address that the physician has one of the great advantages of access to man and to experiments of nature - things the molecular biologist cannot work on."

In response I staked out my position. "I agree fully that the best role for a physician is as a scientist concerned with altered physiology and development, that is human disease, but I believe that in these present times that physicians who wish to contribute in a major way to human diseases processes such as atherosclerosis, cancer or viral diseases such as AIDS, can be optimally effective only if they use the best tools available for investigations. It is my belief that these are at the present time the tools of molecular and cellular biology, though there will be other tools in the future."

I also raised the question of how physicians can be both physicians and scientists and, if separate functions, how the bridges between the two can be built. These were questions Paul had raised before me.

ii) The Origin of Medically Relevant Questions

The next letter from Paul was 4 pages, typed single space, obviously by him, on both sides of the paper. I had challenged him and he was responding much more firmly. I'll return to his rebuttal below but the treasure to me was his review of some of his own research and how it arose. Some excerpts from this very long epistle:

> I was elected to the National Academy of Sciences in 1969 and let me tell you a few examples of how that happened.

> In Atlanta in about 1943 I saw a patient with "toxic hepatitis," a man who had suffered a severe burn three months previously, and had had transfusions. Shortly before that I knew that a lot of American soldiers had developed hepatitis after having received yellow fever vaccine, containing human serum. I got to looking through records of Grady Hospital patients with "toxic hepatitis," "catarrhal jaundice," etc., and quickly came on five other instances of jaundice occurring 2 to 4 months after transfusion. I wrote them up and published them, and that was the first report of serum hepatitis following blood transfusions. (This was due to the subsequently discovered Hepatitis B virus, a continuing world wide scourge despite there now being an effective vaccine).

Paul then described his studies of tolerance to typhoid vaccine. Before Penicillin, patients with general paresis were managed with fever therapy. Body temperatures were raised by infusions of typhoid vaccine in the hope of killing the spirochete. Increasing doses of typhoid vaccine were required to generate equivalent elevations in temperature. To study the mechanism of this tolerance, he used rabbits and found that tolerance required the reticulo-endothelial system; blockade of this resulted in loss of tolerance and death of the animals. These studies were, I suspect, the beginning of his lifelong interest in the causes of fever.

I was asked to write an article on fever for the McBride book on patho-physiology of clinical manifestations. I did, and collected a lot of isolated observations of causes of elevations of temperature in a great variety of clinical states. The only thing I could see to link these together was tissue injury, and I became convinced that some product of tissue injury must be disturbing thermoregulation. I tried a number of kinds of cells, and organ suspensions and eventually got positive responses when I injected rabbits intravenously with suspensions of neutrophils, obtained by irrigating the peritoneal cavity with sterile saline. This was the origin of the concept of endogenous pyrogen, followed by much other work, including that of Barry Wood and Elisha Atkins. For 35 years it was repeated in textbooks that a product of the neutrophil was the endogenous pyrogen. Within the past few years that has been refuted, and it appears that our results were due to the presence in our cell suspensions of small numbers of macrophages, and these cells are the main source of endogenous pyrogen. I don't feel particularly guilty about that. People got PhD degrees doing dose response curves on suspensions of polys. When we did our work the techniques of cell separation were crude, and we couldn't separate out the few macrophages which were apparently responsible for the febrile response. The concept of an endogenous product was right, and it led eventually to a more accurate answer." (There is now an enormous litera-ture on cytokines and other inflammatory mediators, produced primarily but not exclusively by macrophages).

Paul next described his work on the proclivity for increased tissue pressure to favor bacterial infection, especially in the urinary tract.

I was always curious about the way measures to reduce local pressure would favorably affect the outcome of localized infections – incising a carbuncle, draining an empyema, relieving urinary or biliary obstruction – all these would suffice to let the natural defense mechanisms clear up the infectious process. So at Yale we began a long series of studies on the pathogenesis of E coli renal infections, using as an obstructive mechanism either tying of a ureter or scarring the collecting tubules of the kidney with a small cautery needle. Then when the bacteria were inoculated intravenously, infection would develop in the obstructed kidney, or the obstructed portion of a kidney. I still don't know just what the mechanism of the increased tissue pressure blocking host defenses is, but it is real, and we added a lot of experimental substance to that clinical observation.

In the course of the kidney work we became impressed by the fact that you can inject E coli into many organs and tissues of rabbits, and no infection results. Only the kidney that is obstructed develops an infection. Yet there should be no difficulty with humoral factors such as antibody or complement reaching these obstructed areas, and it became pretty obvious that some chemical factor in the renal tissue must favor the survival of E. coli there. I went on sabbatical to England to work in Derek Rowley's lab at St. Mary's. I started out to see whether there might be something in renal tissue that inhibits the lysis of E. coli in the test tube, from lysis by antibody and complement, and hit the jackpot right away. Kidney homogenates prevented bacteriolysis, whereas homogenates from many other tissues had no such effect. It was then easy, with a red cell lysis assay, to show that kidney tissue inactivates complement, probably by glutaminase and ammonia production.

His final description of his research concerned factors that enhanced eosinophil production. This interest arose from his studies on trichinosis when he headed the Harvard Field Hospital Unit, a volunteer unit associated with the Red Cross, in Salisbury, England before the US entered World War II. The trichinella worm encysted in striated muscle elicits eosinophilia. Paul reasoned that some signal from striated muscle to the bone marrow must exist.

And after I went to Oxford, where I had far less clinical and administrative responsibilities, with a small department and a small patient service, I enlisted Tony Basten, a bright young Australian who came to work with me on a fellowship, and we undertook to try to learn what that factor in blood might be. We were inclined to think it must be a humoral substance, and so we tried to produce eosinophilia in rats by giving them large doses of plasma from litter mates with trichinosis. No success at all. We attended a lecture by Peter Medawar at the Dunn School, and he was talking about the effect of neonatal thymectomy on immune responses. This seemed a good way of testing whether the message to the bone marrow was being carried by lymphocytes. And yes, the thymectomized rats got little or no eosinophilia when we gave them trichinosis. Then Tony learned the technique of thoracic duct cannulation, to get lymphocytes from rats with trichinosis, and we found that these lymphocytes did indeed produce an eosinophil response. We then tried various immunosuppressive agents, such as prednisone and chloramphenicol, and again found we could prevent the eosinophil response. We worked a lot of combinations with that system, showing that we could block the enhanced, secondary eosinophil response to a second injection of dead trichinella larvae, etc., etc. And there is still no question that the mechanism of eosinophilia is mediated by T lymphocytes.

The development of the hematopoietic-lymphoid system remains the best understood program of stem cell development and has resulted in bone marrow stem cell transplantation and the use of developmental regulators: erythropoietin, granulocyte-macrophage colony stimulating factor, thrombopoietin-so Paul's inquiry into development of eosinophil precursors was relevant to this major line of inquiry of medical importance.

Having elegantly defended his position, Paul became a bit testy.

I cite that work, and some of the others before it, as the kind of extension of knowledge that clinicians can make, based on questions that confront him at the bedside, and which the molecular biologist would never get a handle on. This is what I meant in my AAP address in advocating that you can tunnel into our mountain of ignorance by working at it from both sides … Those bright young guys at Cold Spring Harbor can never come up with approaches like that, no matter how many genes they splice. And I don't agree with you that the clinician who wants to advance knowledge

of human biology must always use the brightest and best branches of new science. I fully agree that molecular biology in the 20th century is just as spectacular and will lead to just as much important fall-out as did the discovery of the microbial origin of infectious disease in the 19th c. ...
The research of the clinical investigator, in my opinion, should have some relation to his clinical work. Otherwise he will end up presenting second class stuff at the Washington meeting, as you described. I too have been aware of the quality of much of the stuff presented there. The thing that proves it to me, is the nature of the comments from the audience. All day long the only audience contribution is for somebody to get up, always beginning by saying that this is "elegant work," and then asking a question about the methodology. This, to me, appears to be simply a personal advertisement, to demonstrate the questioner understood some of the scientific methods employed in the research. I don't question for a minute that this is second-rate stuff.

I will stop now. I just had to respond and say I do not agree with you that you ought to be entitled to use that "best and brightest" kind of science in your own scholarly work, or life won't be worthwhile. I think there is a level at which clinicians can contribute importantly, if they take advantage of their access to human phenomena. Things will be apparent there that would never be observed in laboratory animals because of infrequent occurrence. It is the infrequent occurrence that clinical medicine is tooled up to disclose, and there is a lot of gold there, which the molecular biologist would never be stimulated to dig for.

Before I turn to subsequent correspondence with Paul, I need to state my position, which of necessity, is a present one, since I saved few copies of letters I sent in the 1980s and not all of those I received. Acquisition of new knowledge is always dependent on what is already known (as Isaac Newton wrote to Robert Hooke "if I have seen farther it is by standing on the shoulders of Giants") and on available technologies; the position of the acquirer is irrelevant. I quite agree with Paul that physicians should be uniquely interested in, and fine-tuned to, discoveries relevant to human disease. We differ, I think in part, because of different technologies and available tools. In Beeson's time clinical observations could be taken into animal models; in my era of molecular biology and genetic manipulation, discoveries often arose from studies of organisms such as Drosophila or from molecular dissection of regulatory mechanisms that led from the bench to bedside. I predict the present era too will differ because of large data sets derived from "Omics" and computational methods to use these to acquire a new level of understanding of the complexities of living systems especially humans and their environment including our microflora.

The big discoveries of course belong to others such as Joe Goldstein and Mike Brown (cholesterol metabolism), Mike Bishop and Harold Varmus (oncogenes), John Gurdon and Shinya Yamanaka (pluripotent stem cells); the list goes on. Because this chapter focuses on the correspondence between Paul Beeson and me, I will only describe some of my own modest work to defend my view of how scientific inquiry arises.

After residency and clinical fellowship in Endocrinology and Metabolism at Yale, I began my research training in 1967 with Len Garren whose laboratory was located on the 5th floor of the Hunter building. Because I had no significant research experience, Len reluctantly gave me a little bench space in a sort of closet across the hall from his laboratory and made several suggestions for research projects unrelated to the major focus of his lab. He suggested I "look into Cyclic AMP" as a possible topic. Earl Sutherland, one of my Pharmacology professors at Vanderbilt, had discovered this "second messenger" of hormone action, the enzyme that produced it, and the enzyme that degraded it; he would consequently receive the Nobel Prize for this work. Unsure how to "look at Cyclic AMP," I audited some courses on the Yale campus taught by Alan Garren, Dieter Soll and Joe Gall and decided a way to begin was to ask how Cyclic AMP worked. Following the reasoning of Walter Gilbert's identification of the bacterial lac repressor, I decided to try and isolate a receptor or protein that specifically bound Cyclic AMP. This work used biochemistry, not molecular biology. I devised a method to separate protein-bound (3H) Cyclic AMP from the free nucleotide and used this assay to purify a specific binding protein. I continued this work when I moved from Yale to San Diego in late 1968 to the newly formed Division of Endocrinology in the newly formed Medical School of the University of California system (UCSD). Having identified a receptor for Cyclic AMP, the next question was how this receptor functioned. Subsequent studies at UCSD showed the Cyclic AMP receptor was the regulatory subunit of

Cyclic AMP-dependent protein kinase (A-kinase). Binding of Cyclic AMP induced one of the most striking allosteric changes in biology, releasing the inhibitory regulatory subunit and freeing the catalytic kinase subunit to phosphorylate proteins and to migrate around the cell to do so.

Throughout my career, I maintained an interest in protein kinases that placed phosphate groups on proteins and on phosphatases that removed these phosphate groups. I did use molecular biology to study the Epidermal Growth Factor Receptor (EGFR). Another of my Vanderbilt professors, Stanley Cohen, had discovered EGF, its cell surface receptor and the fact that EGFR was a kinase that phosphorylated tyrosine residues on proteins; this work led to his receiving the Nobel Prize. In my lab we cloned EGFR, mutated residues and regions of the protein to dissect its linkage to down-stream signaling pathways and to identify sequence "codes" that directed its intracellular trafficking and thus the ability of extracellular EGF to signal growth and migration. We isolated the first sorting nexin (SNX1) involved in vesicular trafficking of cell surface receptors (there were, at last count, 17 members of the sorting nexin family).

Using cloning methods, we identified a family of phosphatases, 3 that, were part of the molecular complex that suppresses transcription of neuro-nal genes and thus maintains neural stem cells. These are down-regulated as part of the process of neural stem cell development into mature neurons. In other studies we isolated, using molecular biology techniques, an adap-tor protein, the nuclear LIM Interactor (NLI) that brings together in the nucleus, the DNA-binding LIM Homeodomain proteins in a combinatorial transcriptional code that specifies developmental processes. The case I most intensively studied, was development of vertebrate motor neurons.

I would argue that none of these experiments arose from clinical observations; all arose from basic science observations. It would be hard to deny that signal transduction involving Cyclic AMP, Growth Factors and their signaling, development of the nervous system are all not highly relevant to human biology and disease. A-kinase was the first kinase whose molecular structure was determined and has served as a paradigm for all the subsequent kinase structures. Kinases, especially tyrosine kinases, are a major target of anti-cancer drugs. Gleevac, that targets the abl kinase that is mutant in chronic myelogenous leukemia, was the first successful kinase inhibitor. Small molecule inhibitors of EGFR and monoclonal anti-EGFR antibodies are both used in cancer therapy. Downstream targets of EGFR are prominent targets for drug design. Understanding nervous system development and the possibility that Scp phosphatase inhibitors might activate endogenous neural stem cells for replacement or aid in producing neurons from neural stem cells for replacement are surely relevant to human disease. The major point is that molecular biology approaches generate scientific questions that have relevance to clinical medicine.

iii) Research by Physicians in Academic Departments

After two years in Oxford as Nuffield Professor, Paul became President of the Association of American Physicians. In his Presidential address in 1967 and in a subsequent article in *Daedalus* he raised the questions we dealt with in our correspondence. It was not a coincidence Paul left New Haven for Oxford. As he wrote to me in 1986:

> Yes, I was becoming unhappy, with far less urgent crises around me, when I gave up the chairmanship at Yale in 1965. I was delighted with the prospect of taking a job with a ward service of 40 beds, with six full-time people, and six house officers. I was even able to get back to some investigative work, on experimental endocarditis and the mechanism of eosinophilia. What had been dawning on me at Yale was that I was sitting in the office all day long, seeing somebody about his or her problem, every half hour. And then, a week or so later, after turning from one problem to another, I couldn't be sure sometimes just what I had committed myself to. I did once ask half a dozen good friends, like Bondy, Lerner, Atkins and Amatruda, to come over to my house for an evening and talk about what I ought to be doing. The result was nothing helpful. Every time I raised a subject that I might turn over to somebody else the answer was that it would be better for me to keep on doing it.

In his Presidential address Paul reviewed the growth of academic departments of medicine fueled by the growth in NIH research dollars following WWII. He follows a similar theme in his *Daedalus* article by comparing the work and role of former great chairs of medicine with the job of a hypothetical chair in 1986. He takes the same position as that in our correspondence.

I question the desirability of having substantial numbers of our potentially ablest clinical investigators dashing into competition with scientists
in, say biochemistry departments. If one looks at this as if we were simply
participating in a science contest, the odds strongly favor the biochemist.

Furthermore I should think any doctor would have difficulty in accepting
the thesis that an understanding of man's afflictions awaits only a thorough
knowledge of the physio-chemical events taking place in his cells. Surely
we are aware that the genesis, the expression, and even the treatment of
human illness must involve social, psychological and environmental factors not likely to be disclosed by laboratory research.

I feel that the present overwhelming emphasis on certain fashions of
investigative activity is causing us to sacrifice some of our real advantages.
The clinician may have his best opportunity to take a giant step by perceiving some previously unrecognized association.

Paul did recognize, long before me, that there were problems but his diagnosis differed from mine. He wrote:

The lowly status of clinical investigation is, I am sorry to admit, to a large
extent deserved. We don't often quantify historical facts and physical
findings or check for observer error, or divide our subjects into comparable groups, in the way we do when conducting a laboratory experiment.
Today's academic doctors, despite better scientific schooling than most of
his predecessors, often seems to lose his objectivity when he sets foot on
the ward.

My diagnosis almost 20 years later was that the ability to ask relevant
questions depends on both the state of knowledge at the time and on the
technologies available to the investigator. For the years in question such were
much more relevant to reductionist biology than to clinical investigation and
that was what the brightest and best academic physicians were of necessity
drawn to. Neither the knowledge base nor the technology were available to
do cutting edge clinical research. Now with advances in imaging technology
such as fMRI, PET scans, ultrasound and in the ability to sequence genomes

and measure with increasing precision metabolic products that can be interpreted based on systems biology and the computer technology to handle and analyze these large data sets, clinical investigation is again moving to the cutting edge and drawing the best into clinical investigation.

I don't for a moment think we have solved any of these issues that so engaged us in the past. My most recent issue of the *New England Journal* arrived today (issue of June 13, 2013) with an editorial about how the NIH is trying once again to "nurture" the development of clinical scientists. I applaud their efforts but am not optimistic. Knowledge will advance and our ability to better care for patients will continue to improve as knowledge and technologies continue to advance. In his 1967 Presidential address Paul made an apt summary.

> Regarding the research effort in clinical departments, it seems likely that we shall sooner reach the goal we all seek if we give emphasis not only to molecular events but also to a serious and scientific study of patients. In making a tunnel through a mountain the usual practice is to dig from both sides. Wouldn't we be wise to follow the same policy, and work away at our mountain of ignorance from more than one side?

Postscript

I first met Paul Beeson in less than auspicious circumstances. I began my residency at Yale on a Friday in charge of the Winchester ward. As I made rounds with my team of interns and medical students on Saturday morning, I never considered that "The Professor" would have his usual morning meeting with the ward and chief residents on the weekend. Jack Levin, the chief resident, frantically summoned me to this meeting that indeed occurred on weekends as on weekdays. I arrived late sans Paul's tea and, after the meeting, was carefully coached by Jack on the proper way of preparing the Professor's tea that was the responsibility of the Winchester resident. As you saw patients on one side of the hall, you stopped in the kitchen to put on water to boil and laid out cups and pot. As you returned down the hall seeing patients on the opposite side, you popped in the kitchen to pour boiling water into the cups and pot. After finishing rounds you discarded the hot water and then made tea in a properly pre-heated pot to be served to the professor in properly hot cups.

These intimate morning meetings consisting only of Paul with his three ward and one chief resident were unique; they differ greatly from morning report at my institution where the chair is rarely present and residents, interns, medical students, hospitalists and teaching attending physicians fill a large room. The information transfer may be similar but the personal relationship with the professor is lost; in fact the Chair of Departments of Medicine in present times is rarely thought of as "The Professor."

My second less than auspicious encounter with Paul was when he hosted Dame Cecily Saunders, the founder of the Hospice movement in England at Yale. At morning report Paul urged each of us to bring our entire team to her talk scheduled for that afternoon. In the business of acute care medicine, none of us attended. At our meeting the next morning Paul was in tears; his residents had let him down. Our sense of failure was acute; one of Paul's great leadership skills was the sense of personal loyalty he inspired in his faculty and house staff. I do not think to this day, Beeson's leadership in bringing Hospice care to the US is fully appreciated. The first Hospice unit in America was in Connecticut. As for me I served on the board of directors of the San Diego Hospice for a half dozen years and grew to more and more appreciate the role of Hospice in the spectrum of Medical care.

Our correspondence extended beyond the issues discussed in this chapter. At one point in my career I considered a job offer to become chair of a department of medicine at another institution. Paul wrote:

> From what you have written, and in your manuscripts, I have a feeling you wouldn't be very happy worrying about how to keep a teaching hospital afloat, etc." Good advice that I happily took. I sent him an essay I had written for the American Scholar on "Fraud in Science." This arose from my chairing an investigation of a fraudulent Biology professor and what had become a high profile national issue at the time. Paul wrote: "I think the real villains are the big shots you refer to…who put pressure on their young associates to produce.

Paul and I never really came to an agreement on the two major questions of our correspondence. Once, in obvious frustration, he wrote, "I don't think you and I are listening to one another in our exchanges of views. Fine, let Goldstein and Brown get on with their excellent work, but don't kid them or the students or the house staff (or the patients) by having them make attending rounds one month a year. I think one of the real mistakes we make in clinical departments is to insist that everybody give the impression of being a triple-threat person. Some are good at investigation, some at clinical medicine, and others at teaching. But it is unusual to find all three qualities combined in the same person any more. Why not recognize that, and give academic support to people for doing what they do best?" One can only agree with this. In fact, Joe Goldstein told me that he quit attending on the general medical service when he was no longer able to oppose consultant specialists since, while his judgement remained correct, his knowledge of subspecialties had decreased.

The other side to the argument that Paul was making, is how to educate medical students and house staff in the basic sciences underlying the diagnoses they must make and the therapies they must choose. Nowadays everyone carries a pocket computer that gives diagnoses for symptoms, a paragraph summary of all they need to know about an illness, the available medications, dosage and side effects; like a pre-Flexerian apprenticeship with a computer. I would argue, not that Joe Goldstein should be a primary care physician, but he should go to the bedside and show the underlying scientific rationale for caring for that patient. Physicians should be scholars and, as medicine incorporates more and more sophisticated imaging, metabolomics and genomics, they must make decisions based on a more complex knowledge base and on subtle thinking that exceeds the simplistic algorithms in their pocket computer.

From my own career I can appreciate Paul Beeson's viewpoint, although not agreeing with it. Would I have been a better scientist if I hadn't been a practitioner of medicine? Probably, but the joy to me of academic medicine was to discover something that had not been previously known, to follow your own original observations. The satisfaction and joy of that is indescribable. This, in my time, required the best available methods and those were molecular and cellular biology. Would I have been a better doctor if I had devoted full time to this? Undoubtedly, but I think I brought something to the bedside that enriched the thinking of my students, residents and fellows. Although I continued to attend on the general medical wards, my generalist skills were admittedly less and less each year. I was, however, able to stay abreast of my subspecialty of Endocrinology and Metabolism, seeing patients each week in a teaching clinic and in a private setting. I led the Division for 25 years and participated in twice a week conferences. In fact I followed Paul in working on Cecil's textbook of Medicine. Beeson and Walsh McDermott of Cornell edited this major textbook of Medicine. Later I was associate editor for three editions (20th-22nd) of the 50 chapters that encompassed Endocrinology, Metabolism, Bone Disease, Women's Health and Nutrition. After trying to retire I continued at UCSD for an additional 7 years, serving as Dean of Translational Medicine and then as Dean of Science. During those years I did take a back seat from both my own research and medicine although I continued to participate from the rear.

I consider myself fortunate to have had this prolonged correspondence with Paul Beeson who had strongly defended views that he followed in his own career, making the transition from Yale to Oxford where he could work at what he considered the correct level. His leadership at every position he held was exemplary and I have always been grateful to have trained in medicine at Yale while he was there. We were products of different times and with different technologies at our disposal. In fact, it was at Yale during my fellowship that I was introduced to the then wonders of Molecular Biology that are now routine and rapidly being supplanted by computational-based science. The times are always changing but open and engaged communication with your mentors will always be treasured.

Chapter 9

Dr. Beeson Honorary Degree from Yale, Naming of the Beeson Medical Service at Yale New Haven Hospital and Hanging of the Beeson Portrait in Fitkin Amphitheater

John Forrest, Jr.

When he was back from Oxford and living in Seattle, Paul Beeson received an honorary degree from Yale. To receive this degree from Yale and in particular from President Kingman Brewster, was a great honor. In his lifetime Beeson would receive many honorary degrees but this one from Yale was his favorite. A photograph and the words of the inscription of the degree follow:

Figure 15: Paul B. Beeson, Distinguished Physician, U.S. Veterans Administration, and Professor of Medicine, University of Washington

You have found the balance between science and humanity in the pursuit of academic medicine. At Yale and later at Oxford you brought new depths of scientific sophistication to clinical investigation and clinical practice. Rigor and compassion have marked your teaching, your research, your practice and your academic leadership. Yale takes pride in honoring a former leader of its medical faculty as it confers upon you the degree of Doctor of Science.

One winter day Dr. Ralph Horwitz, then the Chairman of Internal Medicine at Yale, and I went down to the office of Joseph Zaccagnino, the CEO of Yale-New Haven Hospital, to see if he would agree to name the Medical Service at Yale "The Beeson Service" and hang the portrait of Dr. Beeson in the Fitkin Amphitheater. Mr. Zaccagnino had the reputation of a controlling person. The single object in the Atrium of Yale-New Haven Hospital was a fountain dedicated to his parents. There were no portraits of prominent MDs and leaders of Departments there. Mr. Zaccagnino graciously said "yes" to both requests.

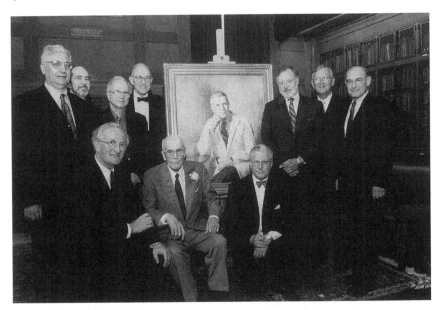

Figure 16: The Fitkin "Iron Terns" and Dr. Beeson. From left to right, (back row) Michael Viola MD, Peter Gross MD, Harold Federman MD, James Fischer MD, the Beeson portrait, Richard Lee MD, Larry Knight MD, John Burke MD, (front row) John Forrest MD, Dr. Beeson, and Lewis Landsberg MD.

Earlier that year, in a ceremony in the Historical Cushing Medical Library the Fitkin "Iron Terns" had gathered for the unveiling of the portrait of Dr. Beeson painted by Richard Whitney.

The portrait hangs in the Fitkin Amphitheater of the medical service where Medical Grand Rounds are held weekly. The plaque is shown in the photograph below.

Dr. Beeson, who met regularly with the "Iron Terns" and followed their careers and families closely, told the group that the naming of the medical service at Yale meant the most to him and was the greatest honor he had received.

Paul B. Beeson, M.D.
1908-2006
Ensign Professor of Medicine
Chairman, Dept. of Medicine 1952-1965

This portrait was commissioned by
Paul Beeson's last Yale Interns,
The Fitkin Iron 'Terns

John Burke, M.D.	Lewis Landsberg, M.D.
Dave Dear, M.D.	Richard Lee, M.D.
Harold Federman, M.D.	Stephen Ross, M.D.
James Fisher, M.D.	Ira Silverstein, M.D.
John Forrest, M.D.	Thomas Spackman, M.D.
Peter Gross, M.D.	Hugh Tilson, M.D.
Larry Knight, M.D.	Michael Viola, M.D.

Jack Levin, M.D.
Chief Resident

Portrait by Richard Whitney in 2003

Chapter 10

Paul Beeson's Uncommon Leadership Style

William Hollingsworth

Paul Beeson was a medical resident at Rockefeller Institute in New York City when, unexpectedly, he was invited by Soma Weiss to become his first Chief Resident at the Brigham. Later, he was to join Eugene Stead in Atlanta as his second full-time faculty member, and to succeed Stead as Chairman at Emory five years later. He was Chairman at Yale for 13 years, and from there went to Oxford for almost a decade.

Paul Beeson has an entirely different personality and leadership style from those of Soma Weiss and Gene Stead, far more subtle and complex. Mrs. Louise Castle described Soma Weiss as exuding energy when he entered a room. When Gene Stead entered a room, his self-confidence, which was not quite arrogance, dominated his environment. When Paul Beeson entered a room, slowly a feeling of warmth suffused the area, elevating the mood and the conversation. I have a lithograph by the Mexican artist, Francisco Zuniga, showing an Indian woman holding a candle in her lap, her head and face encircled by a glow; it reminds me of the subtle Beeson aura. I wonder if Mrs. Castle would concur that Paul Beeson exudes kindness and universal warmth?

Leadership ability is a personality trait usually attributed to Soma Weiss and Gene Stead, and is evident in their actions. Charismatic is another word often used to describe them. Paul Beeson's stature as a leader is more difficult to explain. It is as enigmatic as his smile. Some important leadership traits are obvious. He was a true gentleman at times and in all circumstances, but was not stuffy. His sense of fairness, and the honorable nature of his decisions, are a trait we all admire. Judgement is a difficult personality trait to quantitate, but all of us agree that his judgement of people and issues was remarkably fine. But these features of his personality, alone, do not truly explain why all of us who worked under him loved and respected him to the extent that we overachieved greatly in order to meet the standards we thought would please him. I believe that the magic ingredient in Beeson's leadership was his concern and interest in all of us, personally, in his students, in his colleagues, and particularly in his interns and residents. He is still concerned about us, about our health and about our achievements.

Paul Beeson began to save and send me letters that he received from former students or colleagues. He was interested in defining leadership because he had been asked to participate in a symposium on leadership in medicine. He and his colleagues were curious to learn more about why we felt his leadership. I (the author of this chapter) wrote some of our mutual colleagues, asking them to write me about their impressions of whether Paul Beeson had succeeded as a leader. Excerpts from the letters that Dr. Beeson had received spontaneously and that I solicited are quoted verbatim to give a flavor of his unique leadership qualities.

Excerpts from unsolicited letters to Beeson from former medical students or residents:

"I was reading the Pharos of A.O.A. when I saw a book review by you. I was delighted to be able to find your whereabouts. I'm sure you do not remember me as one of your still scared and wet behind the ears medical interns at Grady in 1948-49. I will always be grateful for your gentlemanly patience and kindness to me as a medical student. At one time in my junior year I seriously considered that perhaps I had no place in medicine as the result of the teaching practices of one particular member of the Dept. of Medicine, but you caused me to think otherwise. There are three men in my life who have made a difference for me. They are my father, Heinz Weens (a Professor of Radiology), and you. Thank you."

"I hope the address I have for you is valid and that this letter finds you in good health. You may not remember me from Yale Medical School, but I was in the class of '58. The reason I am writing is to thank you for the years in which you provided a positive example for me (and many others) and for your kind counseling when I was a sometimes angry and/or confused young man. The example you set had been of great help to me over the year."

"Sitting alone at my desk on this Sunday evening, I just took a break to eat some soda crackers ad a glass of pineapple juice. That combination brought back memories of the Fitkin and Winchester wards when I would keep myself going at 3:00 in the morning as a house officer by raiding the refrigerator for that combination of pineapple juice and soda crackers. I can't let that wonderful memory fade this afternoon without dropping you a brief note to thank you may never have done entirely, for the wonderful years of training you provided at Yale for this bright fellow from Utah by way of Harvard. I think we had all had the rigor that has been associated with the Spartan house officer-ships of a Robert Loeb and a Max Wintrobe. But without sacrificing standards, we also had the dignified gentle warmth and good humor of a Paul Beeson."

The following are excerpts from letters that were solicited from our mutual friends and colleagues:

"We have all speculated from time to time on wherein lies Beeson's greatness and I am sure that the words to follow will not add a great deal of illumination. First there is the shining integrity. One always had the impression one was dealing with a straight person; no guile, no hidden agenda, no political maneuvering. Second, Beeson could focus on you in a way that made you think you were the sole object of his preoccupation at that moment. He projected a sense of caring about the individual and that was manifested in many ways. Even today, he knows the names of wives and children of many of the people who passed through his departments throughout his career, because he made it a point to learn them. Whenever one of our children was born, a hot plate or some other small gift appeared to punctuate the happy occasion. His handwritten invitations to Christmas parties; Barbara and his decoration with shrubs gotten from the Yale golf course for those parties; all contributed to the self embodiment on our part of his ideals. He created a sense of worth in an individual by caring about that individual and making the individual feel that he or she was important to Beeson and therefore should perform at a level commensurate with that importance. In doing this, he created an atmosphere in which individuals tried to do better than they might otherwise do, just because they didn't want to fail this high opinion that Beeson projected of them to them.

Lastly, in addition to the integrity and the focus, we all recognized in Beeson a person who practiced the ideals of medicine in which we had only remotely conceived when we became interested in medicine. By this I mean he cared about patients; he was a good example. When he had patients in the hospital he would come in to see them whether it was a weekend or a holiday, not because the patient was sick and needed his expert advice, but because he said many times that the patient in a hospital really looks forward to seeing his doctor and he thought it important that the doctor appear. He cared about his patients. He didn't lecture about it; he just showed it. That struck a cord in all of us who would like to think that doctors should care about their patients and that we should be like that. He also cared about science. And getting it right. Somehow, he conveyed the notion that science was not the glitter or the sparks of a new finding but rather the substance and the durability of the finding that mattered. His idealism was mature, self practiced and not the sophomoric kind projected on the rest of the world."

"I have always felt that Paul Beeson was a unique leader and an extremely effective one. Paul did not have charisma. He was not forceful in an overt way. He did not rule through fear. Instead he was the only truly effective leader with whom I have had personal contact who led successfully because almost everyone respected him, liked him. and even loved him. Paul Beeson always came through as a compassionate, fine human being who sincerely cared about people. He was in many ways a humble man who had his insecurities and never fully appreciated his own enormous talent. He had the ability to project himself into a situation and see not only through his own eyes but with the eyes of the participants at the lowest levels. There are a number of anecdotes that stand out in my memory of him because they illustrated so well his humanity and his fairness. On one occasion, a patient with pneumococcal meningitis who was receiving 10,000 units of intrathecal penicillin daily in addition to systemic penicillin therapy, suddenly went into status epilepticus and died. It turned out that the nurse who was preparing the penicillin dose for the resident who was injecting it intrathecally made an arithmetic error and gave him 1,000,000 units of penicillin. As soon as Paul heard about this terrible tragedy, he went to the patient floor and sat down with the young nurse and resident to comfort them. In the process he told them that we are all members of a team and that we all shared the successes and the failures. He told them that since he advocated intrathecal penicillin therapy, he had played as much a part in the therapy of that individual patient as they had. His actions meant a great deal to them and helped them recover from their terrible feelings of sorrow and guilt."

"His strength of presence in combination with a gentlemanly reticence represents a unique set of attributes that I have never seen duplicated in academic medicine over the past twenty eight years. In fact, I sometimes wonder if our current milieu would recognize and reward such a person should he appear on the scene. This is brief and to the point. Dr. Beeson might approve."

"As I look back, it seems to me that in many ways Paul was a psychological father to me; his influence remains paramount within me. I know that I modeled myself after him as a physician always learning, reaching for the highest level of creativity and commitment of which I was capable, combining teaching with patient care, and above all, pursuing the highest level of personal and professional integrity. Paul combined genuine modesty with a tenacious pursuit of learning and creativity - a very rare combination (in a profession which accommodates/invites very narcissistic personalities). Paul believed in traditions which served to unite people and make them feel at home -and he was willing to fill the role of tradition-maker and keeper."

"My first experience with Paul B. Beeson was as a third year student on Pitkin I when I was selected to present a case of viral hepatitis to him on student rounds. It was clear from the resident that this was a unique opportunity to impress the Professor so I read widely on all aspects of hepatitis and presented all the pertinent positive and negative findings. Paul Beeson complimented me on the presentation, and from that moment on I became an intense admirer of the man and began to appreciate some of the awe in which his residents held him."

"The call to be Paul Beeson's Chief Medical Resident was completely unexpected, and perhaps in many ways unwanted. However, the fact that he had selected me over my contemporaries was such an enormous vote of confidence, that I knew at that moment that an academic career was my future. I suppose few Paul Beeson Chief Residents would dispute that that year was the most rewarding of their professional life. During that year, not only was the amazing and encyclopedic clinical acumen of Paul Beeson evident, but his great humanity as well. Whenever he saw a ward patient on consultation, he would seek out a family member to explain his findings and offer some encouragement."

Clearly Paul Beeson was a giant in the academic community of his time. He influenced a generation of academicians who became successful in their own right but who were always proudest of being 'Beeson Men' (there were no 'Beeson Women' at that time - what a shame). Paul Beeson was unique in a time of unique and powerful chairs. Those who worked with him strove their professional lives to measure up to his standards. I doubt whether Professors of Medicine will ever have that unique role in molding the careers of a generation of academicians again."

Let us let Paul Beeson have the last word, in a letter to me on January 14, 1989:

"I can understand that you are having difficulty getting anyone to describe me in terms of leadership. I never felt that I was a leader. I felt I had responsibility, and realized that I had power (in such matters as promotions, space allocation and salary). But my only intent was to get good people, and create conditions that would allow them to achieve whatever they wanted, at whatever level they happened to be. The one principle I followed was that the success of the department depended on getting good house-staff. They teach the students, take care of the patients, and are the best pool from which to draw future members of the department."

Chapter 11

Retirement in Redmond, Washington and Exeter, New Hampshire

Lewis Landsberg

After a decade in Oxford the Beesons returned home to the U.S. The decision to leave Oxford was predicated on several considerations: most importantly, a new Oxford university hospital was being developed and Beeson, with characteristic generosity, did not want his successor, Dr. David Weatherall, to live with decisions about the new facility that he had made. Family considerations, with the relocation of his grown children to the U.S. also played a role. In addition, he had been asked about potential interest in a new Veteran's administration position entitled "Distinguished Physician" which provided salary and ancillary support for outstanding academic physicians a the end of their careers. Those so identified could select an academic VA location of their choice. This program seemed tailor made for someone of Beeson's stature. He chose the Seattle VA in large part because his former chief resident and colleague, Bob Petersdorf, was chairman of the department of medicine at the University of Washington. He made the move back in 1974. At the Seattle VA he attended on the medical wards, took morning report, and worked on editing the Cecil-Loeb textbook of medicine.

Members of his last Yale internship group, "the Fitkin Iron terns," visited him in Seattle to discuss plans for upcoming Beeson Society meetings which would focus on the importance of the doctor-patient relationship. After a productive meeting in Seattle he entertained the group at his new home in Redmond WA outside the city. Settling in Redmond, a rural town some 16 miles east of Seattle, permitted Barbara to easily maintain her equestrian activities and allowed easy access to riding trails.

At this phase in his life Beeson developed several new interests: the environment; nuclear disarmament; and aging. Barbara Beeson in particular became a leader in the effort to preserve the unique character of Redmond, advocating for the preservation of farmlands, open spaces and parks. Redmond received a presidential award and became a "Preserve America Community". After he retired from his Distinguished Physician position in the VA Paul Beeson began to consider the horrors that nuclear war would bring. He became an important speaker for the emerging organization "Physicians for Social Responsibility" thereby capitalizing on his prominence by advocating for a sane nuclear policy. At the end of his career he turned his attention to aging, which he saw as a province of general internal medicine. In 1995 the "Paul Beeson Physician Faculty Scholars in Aging" was developed and funded by three national foundations.

The Beeson's final move was to a retirement community in Exeter New Hampshire, in order to be near his son Peter's home in Concord. Through the years our intern group had met with the Professor to discuss issues related to medicine and society and to inform him of our various activities. The last such meeting was held in Portsmouth New Hampshire, near his home in neighboring Exeter. It was arranged by our chief resident Jack Levin. On this occasion we all made a brief presentation about our careers and personal lives. He seemed to really enjoy this and professed to some that this was one of the best days of his life.

We will always remember his life as a shining beacon, a demonstration of what our profession can and should be.

Chapter 12

Reminiscences of Beeson's First and Last Chief Resident at Yale

Kenneth Johnson and Jack Levin

Kenneth G. Johnson, M.D., House-staff 1950-54

I first met Paul Beeson in April 1952 when he came alone, without his family, to the New Haven Hospital. He lived as a monk within the hospital, inspecting and interviewing, jotting notes in a bound composition book. The book filled with a great deal of discordant information, and one week later waiting in his outer office. I saw him drop it into a wastebasket!

Covering for the vacationing Chief Resident at the time, I met with him each morning to make rounds to see the sickest and most challenging patients on the floors. A process that rarely exceeded 30 minutes and called for terse but comprehensive " thumb nail" sketches (his words) while walking or climbing stairs. He was smart, lean and handsome - the gold standard of the academic clinician scientist, transforming scientific knowledge to bedside care. He was obsessive in this pursuit, quietly charismatic and ascetic (I remember that his annual salary was a Yale high $15,000). He also projected a genuine interest in and support for the aspirations of house-staff about their future careers.

He selected me in 1953 as his first Chief Resident, and although I disappointed him by opting for private practice, we remained close, and in 1964 I quit New Haven to go on a Yale assignment as Chief of Medicine at the Atomic Bomb Casualty Commission 1964-67. Shortly, after arriving in Japan, I received a letter from him stating that our agreement for me to work full-time in the Department was superseded by his decision to go to Oxford. He told me that the Yale Department had grown to the point that he had become a virtual Dean and Chief of administration. At Oxford, he looked forward to recapturing the satisfaction of the academic clinical scientist and educator.

On my several visits to the Radcliffe Infirmary, I found him " in his element", much appreciated and highly respected. With some un-ease he accepted a knighthood, but severely discouraged a political attempt to waive the centuries old requirement of British citizenship for appointment as the Regius Professor. Our mutual friend, Sir Richard Doll, was appointment the Regius. After his return to the U.S. - to Bob Petersdorf's department - I included in a piece on the growing promotion of managed care his published paper that was sharply critical of the transition of humanistic medical care in the U.S. to " big business". Interestingly, I once again became his chief resident in his editorship of the American Journal of Geriatrics. At that point, geriatric long term care was not a big business item.

In his time, a modifier applied to Moses in the Rabbinical sayings, Paul Beeson was a great man. It was a time in American medicine when academic clinical scientists were heroes, and we sought to be close to them, and they influenced our future careers. We owe much to Paul Beeson.

My Year with Paul Beeson

Jack Levin, M.D.
Departments of Laboratory Medicine & Medicine
University of California, San Francisco, School of Medicine

At the end of June 1964, I walked up the stairs to the back entrance of the hospital at 330 Cedar Street, where Tom Ferris, who was completing his year as the Chief Resident in Medicine, greeted me. He immediately informed me that a member of the new group of interns had been electrocuted while sailing a C scow sailboat. The aluminum mast of his sailboat had come in contact with a power line. Thus started my year as Paul Beeson's last Chief Resident at Yale.

Being Paul Beeson's Chief Resident was both a heady and humbling experience. Readers who experienced life at an academic medical center in the era which included the 1960s will recall that the Chief Resident represented the Chairman. Therefore, being the Chief Resident for a physician of Dr. Beeson's stature added to the responsibility of the position.

The readers of this volume are almost certainly aware of Paul Beeson's many accomplishments. However, very few will know what it was like to meet with him on a daily basis for essentially 365 consecutive days, and be the beneficiary of his quiet thoughtfulness. He demanded truthfulness. Collegiality with the other clinical services was highly important to him. Although reserved, he was always available to me or any member of the house staff who required his advice. However, although rarely visibly angry, the slightest suggestion that a patient had not been treated with thoughtfulness and consideration would bring forth his formidable fixed gaze and unequivocal expression of disapproval.

Timeliness was expected, and I remember his Sphinxlike smile when we unveiled a sign under the prominent clock in the room in which he received morning report. The sign read: "Beeson's Fine if You're on Time". Morning report was always a highpoint for the small group of house staff who were privileged to attend. It was during this focused 30-minute period that one always experienced his total concentration on the problems at hand. A similar session took place early every Friday afternoon when patients on the Memorial Unit (where private patients were then located) were discussed. In contrast to the current era in which departmental heads often seem to be absent more than present, Dr. Beeson made being available in New Haven a high priority. As the result, he was rarely absent for morning report, which never seemed the same without him.

I recall an episode when he and I disagreed about a diagnosis. In those long ago days, to obtain appropriate literature one had to physically go to the Medical Library and obtain the bound volumes which contained the articles of interest. I had brought 6 volumes to morning report, after which he and I moved to his office for discussion of the diagnosis. Dr. Beeson was carrying some of these relatively heavy volumes when we encountered a member of the department. When asked why he was carrying old journals, Dr. Beeson responded by stating that his resident didn't think he was sufficiently informed and needed to do some reading.

He genuinely looked forward to the annual house staff softball game played between the interns and the assistant residents. Strikingly, this was the only day of the year on which he related informally to the house staff.

For this occasion, I purchased T-shirts with the logo "Fitkin Iron 'Terns", to acknowledge the rigors of their internship year, made more difficult by being an intern short. Gratifyingly, Dr. Beeson agreed to wear this T-Shirt. This group of former interns still refer to themselves as The Iron 'Terns. This group produced 13 full Professors.

And so, my Chief Residency year progressed, week by week, with Dr. Beeson providing a steadiness, surely one of his dominant characteristics, which benefitted all of us. I was sufficiently insightful to anticipate that my year of being Paul Beeson's Chief Resident would be the most gratifying and fulfilling year of my professional life. Despite the passage of over a half-century, my prediction has been correct; it was. During my subsequent academic career at The Johns Hopkins Hospital and the University of California School of Medicine (UCSF), I have interacted with many well established and famous professors of medicine, but none even distantly possessed the formidable presence or demonstrated the charisma of Paul Beeson.

A second disruption of the 1964-1965 hospital year occurred in the spring of 1965 when Dr. Beeson scheduled an unusual Friday afternoon departmental meeting in the Fitkin Amphitheater. At this meeting he announced, to a stunned department, that he was leaving Yale to join the faculty at Oxford University. As far as I know, only Dr. Beeson's secretary, Betsy Winters, I, and probably Bill Hollingsworth knew what he was about to say. It was truly a cataclysmic event.

Epilogue

In 1972, I went to Oxford on a mini-Sabbatical. Paul Beeson was then established as the Nuffield Professor of Medicine at Oxford. While I was there, many of his professional friends passed through, as though paying their respects. He had introduced his style of medicine to the medical service which he now headed. It was interesting to observe the response of the establishment to this new force.

He had retained his well-hidden sense of humor. We were en route to lunch at the "High Table" of Magdalen College when he said to me: "Don't expect to hear any interesting conversation." This despite High Table being populated exclusively by senior Oxford faculty.

In an extraordinary tribute to Dr. Beeson, the Iron 'Terns subsequently not only commissioned a portrait of Paul Beeson, but totally funded it. His superb portrait now appropriately hangs in the Fitkin Amphitheater. Given his professional and personal values, I am confident that this unequivocal demonstration of respect and affection by his last group of Yale interns was considered by him to have been one of his most meaningful honors.

Chapter 13

Memorial Service at Yale for Paul Beeson

Richard Rapport, Lawrence Freedman, Lewis Landsberg, Fred S. Kantor, Christine Hines, Peter Beeson

PROGRAM

Schubert: Impromptu No. 2	John N. Beeson Chief of Music Staff New York City Opera Assistant Conductor Metropolitan Opera
Welcome	Robert J. Alpern, MD Dean Ensign Professor of Medicine Yale University School of Medicine
Introduction of Speakers	John N. Forrest, Jr., MD Professor of Medicine, Yale University School of Medicine

"Paul B. Beeson: An Extraordinary Life in Perspective"
Richard Rapport, MD
Department of Neurological Surgery
Group Health Cooperative of Puget Sound

"Paul Beeson And His Early Years at Yale"
Lawrence R. Freedman, MD
Professor Emeritus
David Geffen School of Medicine at UCLA

"The Beeson Mystique: Perspectives From a Former Student and Current Dean"
Lewis Landsberg, MD
Professor of Medicine
Northwestern University Feinberg School of Medicine
Vice President for Medical Affairs
Northwestern University

"Paul B. Beeson's Legacy At Yale: Past, Present and Future"
Fred Kantor, MD
Paul B. Beeson Professor of Medicine
Yale University School of Medicine

"The Beesons' Redmond Years"
Christine Hines
Former Mayor, Redmond, Washington
The Redmond Historical Society

"A Perspective From the Family of Paul Beeson"
Peter G. Beeson, Concord, New Hampshire

Grieg: Springtime   John N. Beeson

Paul Beeson: An Extraordinary Life in Perspective
Richard Rapport

In one of those odd symmetries that make life so mysterious, I was 150 miles from Livingston, Montana, Dr. Beeson's birthplace, on the morning that Paul died. He was born in that little town in October 1908, on the second floor of a frame house built at 112th South Sixth Street. I went to find the place. It was a lovely plain little bungalow no doubt very white and pretty when first built by John Beeson in 1907. Some hippies had got a hold of it in the 70's and painted it that hideously tasteless two tones of purple that hippies were so unaccountably fond of. How Paul would have chuckled at that for after the Rockefeller Institute and the Brigham, after the Chairs at Emory, Yale, and Oxford, after the textbooks, the Kober Medal and the knighthood, Paul himself got hooked up with a bunch of unreconstructed hippies in 1980. I know that for sure. For all of those things I have just listed, I wanted to call his biography "The Last Great Man" but of course, he wouldn't allow that.

In these spreadsheet and technology driven days of our profession, it would be difficult for any single person to again accumulate the following and influence that Dr. Paul Beeson had. Paul accomplished about as much in medicine as it possible to achieve. Had he stayed in the lab and stuck with what he called Endogenous Pyrogen he might even have opened up Cytokine Biology earlier than it was and won a Nobel Prize. In a real sense he was the last great man but not for any of those things. Those things were the result of his greatness, not the cause.

Paul was a mesmerizing person without being charismatic in the usual sense, and his importance was out of proportion to the details of his accomplishments. It was by the example of his life that he embodied the virtues the physician moralist Edmund Pellegrino has used to define profession "a voluntary imposition of higher than ordinary standards" and this is not an easy thing to do because of the power of the aegon, our striving, our will, our ambition, that permits success is so often in competition with our more estimable selves.

Paul managed somehow to make all of those around him better, including me. In 1998 Lew Landsberg wrote to me about the Yale Department of Medicine when Paul was here and he said, "what was it we wondered, that contributed to the aura of greatness that surrounded this man?" It was some unnamed hold on the character of all those faculty and students he was charged with managing and educating. The last of Paul's interns at Yale all felt the same about him and recognized this special quality but couldn't name it. Of course, you were all 26 years old then.

After your lives of caring for sick people and students and faculties, I feel confident that all of you can name that quality, I think I can. It's the essence of love. Love is another of life's mysteries and if Paul was reluctant to use that word it was probably because of its poetic range. For here I mean his uncanny ability always to know the other, to put the patient first, to promote those around him rather than himself and to remember what

Ludwig Wittgenstein meant when he wrote, in what is perhaps the most perfect arrangements of words ever put onto paper, "whereof one cannot speak, thereof one must keep silent". And so, it was because of his character at the age of 73 Paul understood what those dozen Seattle hippies were talking about when they said, "maybe it wasn't such a great idea to build more nuclear weapons."

Paul was a secular person, an element that surprised me a first. He never saw the inside of a church during the thirty years that I knew him and he didn't dwell on the ineffable. William James teaches us that there are a variety of religious experiences and there certainly are a variety of people who believe that they are the chosen and can talk to God. We usually say of these people that they are hallucinating. But there are very few people who for whatever reason have so internalized the ideals of humanism in its most perfect form that they become the purest embodiment of empathy. In the end, I wrote that Paul was to the last half of the twentieth century what William Osler was to the first. Both were born on the frontier, went to medical school at McGill, spent time with the Pepper boys at Penn, chaired the dominant Departments of Medicine of their age at important east coast medical schools, wrote the principal textbooks of medicine of their time, occupied a named chair at Oxford, and both were knighted. Paul didn't cut off the distal phalanx of his sister's finger, but he didn't have a sister.

In the last chapter of his 2001 biography I finished with this: On the edge of the 21st Century the predictions of Paul Starr that Medicine will become progressively more industrialized seems probable, still there remains the example of Paul Beeson sitting beside a patient on an open ward surrounded by students listening to the clues, fears, and questions embedded in the story of a single sick person.

We daydream about how we are and how we wish to be, we construct a self from what we have been and what we imagine we might become. We look for examples, Paul Beeson was not only the finest person I have ever known, he was the best human being I can imagine.

Paul Beeson, the Early Years at Yale

Lawrence R. Freedman, MD Professor Emeritus
The David Geffen School of Medicine at UCLA

Two years ago Rina and I went to visit Paul and Barbara Beeson in their New Hampshire retirement community. We wanted to see them again and I wanted to discuss some ideas with Paul. But Paul was tired, I sadly accepted that the end of the Beeson era was approaching. I've thought a lot about Paul since he died. I thought about his arrival at Yale, in 1951, when I was half way through my intern year. He succeeded Francis Blake, an eminent and formal chairman and person.

It was a small department, only 12 full time members. He was an "outsider" from Emory, Georgia - a southerner at the Yankee Ivory Tower. We did not know that he was a hardy frontiersman - via Montana, Seattle and Alaska.

Suddenly, Grand Rounds, previously in mid-week, were at 8:00am on Saturday mornings, later to be adjusted to 11 am, but still on Saturday. Mumbled remarks that wives and children were upset, were met with a nod and a reserved smile. Grand Rounds were grand indeed because Paul was always there, and always so present. Paul introduced "morning report"- a congenial yet rigorous daily discussion of the previous day's admissions. The professor had a special way of engaging with house officers of any level; we came away knowing that he valued and considered our opinion. These interactions created a lasting bond between the house staff and the chairman and gave us all a magnetic sense of belonging.

Five years after Paul's arrival at Yale I was his chief resident. Paul established a particularly close and trusting relationship with his chief residents. He allowed me to get to know him as a person - how he thought, how he ticked. I remember being both touched and amazed when he remarked to me one day that he had been feeling uneasy and remiss that he had not, in his own estimation, paid enough attention to a particular fellow of his. He had not lived up to his own expectations of himself. He never cut himself any slack!

Paul Beeson's dedication to patient care and his total availability to discuss any personal problem of a resident or faculty member were a hallmark of his leadership. He was reserved, but never distant. Reserved – but in a very personal way – which made him such a trusted mentor.

Trust was a cornerstone of Paul's leadership. He exuded a sense of integrity and intellectual honesty and he expected the same from others. He did not suffer fools lightly and he did not care for excuses.

By 1956, Paul had established subspecialty divisions in the department: Hematology led by Stu Finch, Endocrinology with Phil Bondy, Dermatology with Aaron Lerner, Gil Glaser in Neurology, Howard Spiro in GI and Bill Hollingsworth in Rheumatology. We would meet in a small lunchroom on the 5th floor of the hospital. The meetings were fascinating. Medicine and politics frequently intermingled—and politics were everywhere. Paul was a Republican then, and I think, the only Republican in the department! We all looked forward to his quiet yet firmly stated political views. Paul was flexible in his thinking and open to evaluate matters on their merits; it was refreshing to realize that his views were not informed by loyalty to a party but that he was loyal to whatever his integrity and honesty required. For example, the breakthrough of Sputnik elicited from Paul a realization that we must no longer carry on medically as before.

He wanted to extend medical activity beyond our comfortable cocoon and participate in the wider world. When he was asked by the National Academy of Sciences to take over the Department of Medicine at the Atomic Bomb Casualty Commission in Hiroshima and Nagasaki; he brought it to a faculty meeting; we were all for it. Bill Hollingsworth and Dorothy were first to go to Hiroshima, Stu and Pat Finch were next, Rina and I followed, then Ken and Mary-Louise Johnson and finally Stu and Pat again. The department was extending its reach to Japan.

While many considered going to Japan a foolish departure from the Academic Royal Road, it was Paul Beeson's vision and personal backing that made the decision a life enriching choice both medically and personally.

A wide variety of issues were brought to the faculty meetings and under Paul's leadership it was the department which took the responsibility for the decisions.

In remarkable contrast stood the Dean's announcement of the establishment of a new curriculum just one day after the whole faculty almost unanimously rejected it.

Paul's outstanding ability to establish trust, to bring competitive groups together to work in productive friendship and harmony, gave birth, among other things, to the Interplanetary Society - affectionately called the Pus Club, a small group spearheaded by Paul, Walsh McDermott and Barry Wood. Work was openly discussed without fear of giving away a good idea prematurely. At our last meeting in Seattle in 1997 to honor Paul, the "membership list" had grown to nearly 100 persons representing an impressive gathering of contributors to the field of academic infectious disease.

What I had hoped to discuss with Paul when I visited him 2 years ago was whether there is a professional obligation for medical and scientific experts to publicly express their views concerning the health consequences of legislation influencing the environment; and, should the subject have a place in the medical school curriculum.

As it happens, just this month, the Physicians for Social Responsibility, an organization Paul had vigorously supported, acted on this very issue in a detailed publication. I think it would have pleased Paul to know that his quest for affirming the physician's social responsibility continues to gain momentum.

I want to close with what Bob Petersdorf, another of Paul's chief residents, and sadly no longer with us, said about Paul when he presented the Kober Medal to him in 1973: "Today I am going to tell you an adventure story. It's a story that has in it a bit of Marco Polo, Don Quixote, John Glenn and perhaps even Walter Mitty."

"The Beeson Mystique: Perspectives from A Former Student and Current Dean"
Lewis Landsberg

I am grateful for having the opportunity to speak on behalf of the many medical students and residents who had the good fortune to train under Paul Beeson at Yale.

The first time I saw Paul Beeson was in the fall of 1960 in the old Fitkin amphitheater of the Grace-New Haven hospital. In those days medical grand rounds were held at 11 am Saturday morning and medical students, even first year students, could attend. The memory of those grand rounds, five decades ago, is as clear and vivid to me as yesterday. Dr. Beeson always sat in the first row on the right hand side of the amphitheater. The other professors in the department, some of whom are here this afternoon, sat around him. In those days real patients were presented, frequently in person. The proceedings had an expectant solemnity. Dr. Beeson's presence dominated the room. Sometimes he said very little. But he had an aura of erudition, of elegance, of dignity, that we all felt was the very essence of physicianship. That image is as fresh today as it was fifty years ago.

So what is the basis Paul Beeson's enduring influence?

All those fortunate enough to train or work with him felt it. We treasured the copies of his Textbook of medicine that he signed for us, always including a personal comment. My wife always said that if there was a fire in the house she knew she had to get this signed book out first! We speculated endlessly on the indefinable essence of Paul Beeson but could never quite capture what it was. A classmate of mine called it the "Beeson mystique." When Dr. Beeson entered a room, everyone stood. In his presence we all felt greatness.

Humility was certainly an important component of his special character. In a profession historically characterized by arrogance, his humbleness stood as a sharp rebuke to the hubris of lesser men. And juxtaposed with this humility were an iron will, a strong discipline, and an insistence on excellence. We all felt this. He never shrank from disciplining a house officer who was derelict in his duty. We knew that he would never tolerate less than our best effort to understand the illnesses of our patients, and to ameliorate their suffering. Presenting our patients to Dr. Beeson always provoked anxiety. He looked right into your eyes, fully engaged in the presentation. But the anxiety that we felt was based on striving to do the very best, and fearing that our very best might not be good enough. We always wanted to live up to his expectations. We carefully watched the way he interacted with patients, and this left a lasting impression. He always sat when speaking with a patient on rounds. This avoided looking down on the patient, and conveyed a desire to listen, rather than an attitude of hurry or impatience.

The faculty at Yale felt the same way about him. His persona seemed to imbue the entire department – from the lowly clinical clerks to the world-renowned professors – with an organic unity, a unity based on his unique charisma. We all had the feeling that those of us who were lucky enough to have worked with Dr. Beeson were in some way different, as if some of his special character rubbed off on us and changed us.

In her book *The Healers' Tale*, Sharon Kaufman compiles a series of interviews with several influential physicians, Paul Beeson included. One of her chapters is entitled "Role Model on Two Continents," referring to Dr. Beeson's influence at Yale and at Oxford. But role model is not quite right. Role model implies that you want to be like someone. No one that I knew would ever presume to be like Dr. Beeson. We wanted to be worthy of him. And this is one key to his enduring influence: he inspired trainees and colleagues to be their best. His character demanded nothing less. He set an impossibly high standard. But reaching for it made us all better.

We all learned a lot from Paul Beeson. Here are some of the lessons that I took away; some of these lessons have been particularly helpful to me in my present role as a dean: I learned that it is a privilege to be a physician and that this privilege carries awesome responsibility. I realized that important lessons can be taught without words. I learned never to underestimate the influence you have on your trainees or those who report to you. I came to recognize the importance of humility in a physician.

I realized the importance of knowing a lot if you were going to help your patients, as I began to appreciate the marriage of the art and science of medicine in the master clinician. He taught me about the commitment to the patient and the importance of the relationship between patient and physician and the need to alleviate pain and suffering whatever the cause. Many of this is now, five decades later, referred to as "professionalism." All of his former trainees here today could generate a list of their own.

And we all appreciated the importance of his scientific work. His most important scientific contribution was the initial discovery of a biologically active molecule that he called endogenous pyrogen, a prototype for a whole class of mediators, now known as cytokines. He also did important work on pyelonephritis, leptospirosis, bacterial endocarditis and a landmark study with Bob Petersdorf on fever of unknown origin.

He was intrigued by the association of certain diseases, such as pulmonary alveolar proteinosis and nocardia infection, and he passed this curiosity on to his trainees and colleagues. He was instrumental in the development of subspecialties within internal medicine at Yale but always recognized the primacy of internal medicine itself as the parent and guardian of these offspring.

Paul Beeson's position in American medicine is a matter of historical record. The profound influence that he exerted at Yale was a microcosm of his importance in the profession at large. He was a founding father of academic internal medicine. He was president of every major academic medicine society at a young age. He was honored by every society with its most prestigious award: the Kober medal from the Association of American Physicians; the Phillips award from the American College of Physicians; the Williams award from the Association of Professors of Medicine. Obviously, his peers recognized the same qualities that so impressed his colleagues and trainees.

Does all of this capture the essence of Paul Beeson, the reasons for his enduring influence? I think not. He was larger than life but he never seemed to understand the awe in which he was held. He was kind, compassionate and loyal to his residents and faculty. Those of you who have read Jim Collins' book "Good to Great" will recognize Paul Beeson immediately. In this work, based on research into companies that markedly outperformed the competition for sustained periods of time, Collins emphasizes the importance of leadership, but leadership of a very special type. Analysis of these highly successful companies produced an unexpected picture of the CEO, whom he describes as the "level 5" leader. The cardinal feature of this leadership was in Collins' words, "a paradoxical blend of personal humility and professional will." Discipline and lack of egoism are important components. Self-effacing rather than self-aggrandizing leadership characterized these successful enterprises.

Yale benefited immensely from its "level 5" leader, Paul Beeson, and this benefit is still present today in the traditions of internal medicine that he helped to develop, and in the persons fortunate enough to have worked with him.

The whole community at Yale felt an enormous sense of loss when, at the peak of his prominence, he left to go to Oxford to become the Nuffield Professor at the Radcliff infirmary. For the faculty at Yale it was the end of a decade that many referred to as "Camelot." The department under Beeson attained a special status: an Athens situated between the Byzantium of Harvard to the east and the Rome of Columbia to the west. But his enduring influence lives on through those he trained and through the tradition of excellence that he engendered. Paul Beeson, we salute your memory.

Paul Beeson: Legacy at Yale, Past and Present
Fred Kantor

I would like to acknowledge the debt we owe to Elisha and Libby Atkins and their family who by endowing the Beeson Professorship ensured the timeless perpetuation of the Beeson legacy. What is this legacy? I believe it was his caring for the patient, the house staff, the fellows, and the social contract with an aging population. Francis Peabody wrote, "The secret of the care of the patient is in caring for the patient." This thought directed Paul Beeson at the patient's bedside. He pulled up a chair so that he was on eye level; this obviously made a big impression because two of us have mentioned it. The patient didn't have to look up at the physician towering over him.

He told us that no matter how crowded the day or hurried the program, by sitting next to the patient, he or she felt they had their unhurried physician's full attention. If a patient of his was in the hospital, even though they were doing well, he would still come in on Sunday when there was no need to do so, because he felt the patient waited anxiously upon his doctor's visit. He cared about families, and he knew and remembered the names of his house staffs' spouses. When a child was born to a house staff couple, a present like a warming dish appeared, from Paul and Barbara Beeson. For the Department Christmas party, Paul and Barbara personally gathered greenery from the Yale golf course to decorate and warm the somewhat stark Harkness lounge. The invitations to the party were hand written, and we all knew who wrote them because we knew his handwriting from notes in the chart.

Dr. Beeson cared deeply about the science of medicine and getting it right. In addition to his own considerable contributions, he reviewed and edited every paper form his department before submission to a journal. His joy was palpable at the "Pus Club", when his young people presented their work and themselves to perhaps prompt an offer for an academic job.

Then there was the social contract, what was that? It was caring for the people of the world by being anti-nuke when that seemed to be a young person's province. Developing and contributing to the somewhat new field of aging, when he perceived that the population was getting older and phy-sicians needed to know the special requirements of these patients. How is this rich legacy perpetuated? By his pupils who by perceiving how much he cared; they wanted to do better that they otherwise would do to not disappoint the professor. We're still doing it today in the department of medicine at Yale.

I'm not a student of the bible but I would like to close with a bit of poetic license in a quote from Ecclesiastes, Chapter 38. "Honor this physi-cian with the honor due unto him for of the most high cometh healing and he shall receive *honor of the king, Sir Paul Beeson.* The skill of the physician shall lift up his head: and in the sight of great men he shall be in admiration."

The Beeson's Redmond Years

Christine Hines

It was in 1975 that Dr. Beeson and his wife Barbara, came to live in the City of Redmond. One of the first things they did was to purchase the original homestead of one of Redmond's founders, The Perrigos. They restored the farmhouse and the barn and made sure all the trees stayed. Today that beautiful spot is home to the Eagle Rim Community and that farmhouse is the center for a clubhouse and yes, all the trees are still there. They became involved in the City of Redmond very quickly as there was a great deal of development going on, plus many environmental issues of concern to them. So they went to the City Council meetings, the County and State meetings and any other meet ings that affected the City.

At that time Redmond was a small town with one traffic light, but on its way to becoming a much larger city. And that is when I met Paul and Barbara. We were immediately attracted to the same issues and concerns. Since there were so many things going on in the community, including the development of the Redmond Golf Course, into a shopping center, the loss of valuable farmlands, apartments going to condominium usage and no places left for parks, trails or open space, we were a natural to team up. It was at this time that Paul mentioned I should run for the City Council. I must confess I had never thought to do that. But I did and with the backing of Paul and Barbara and others got on the Council. To me this is when

City of Redmond
WASHINGTON

PROCLAMATION

WHEREAS, Dr. Paul Bruce Beeson's prestigious medical career touched the lives of many patients and nurtured leaders practicing medicine throughout the world; and

WHEREAS, Paul Beeson was a man of world renown, yet his love for Redmond was unsurpassed; and

WHEREAS, Paul and Barbara were dedicated to environmental protection and historic preservation of Redmond for three decades; and

WHEREAS, Paul supported Barbara's activism in the city, and together, they made a dynamic duo looking after the future of Redmond; and

WHEREAS, Paul was often the reasoned and calming "humble man behind the woman"

WHEREAS , the city is indebted to Paul and Barbara for their vision and influence in defining and assuring Redmond's unique character for years to come; and

WHEREAS, the Beesons, through their unprecedented efforts, embodied the City of Redmond' s vision, "Together, we create a community of good neighbors ";

NOW, THEREFORE, I, ROSEMARIE IVES, Mayor of the City of Redmon d, on behalf of our community, do hereby proclaim November I 0, 2006, as

DR. PAUL B. BEESON MEMORIAL DAY
to celebrate his life and acknowledge his significant contribution to Red

Rosemarie M. Ives, Mayor

November 10, 2006

Redmond came of age. Paul and Barbara through their participation caused people to think and question what was happening in Redmond and what citizens could do about it.

A few years later I ran for Mayor and won. Then more and more people started paying attention. I was fortunate to have an excellent city staff and we went about setting goals and policies for park acquisitions and trail rights, all the while handling the myriad other challenges that go with running a city.

You know it has been said people come into your life for a reason and Paul and Barbara surely came into mine and for that I will always be eternally grateful. It was and is a precious relationship. Paul's knowledge and caring attitude is the gift left to the City of Redmond.

He even had time to help me, and my family, when one of my daughters was involved in a traffic accident. His caring came through again during my husband's illness. It is truly hard to put all this into words, but I am reminded of a quote from Dr. William C. Menninger, Founder of the Menninger Clinic and Foundation. He said, "Find a mission in life and take it seriously." Well that certainly exemplifies the life of Paul Beeson.

With his tireless efforts and generous contributions not only to medicine but also to the welfare of the citizens of Redmond, I say Peace to his memory, Peace to his achievements and accomplishments and I would like to close with my own personal quote to his memory: "What a Guy."

A Perspective from the Family of Paul Beeson

Peter Beeson

I have been asked to say some words from the Beeson family's perspective on behalf of my mother, my brother John, my sister Judy, my father's six grandchildren, Sylvia and Sabrina, Barry and Laura, and my Laura and my boys, Nick and Mike, and my father's great-granddaughter, Paula.

We want to thank everyone at Yale for the enormous effort and apparent affection that has gone into today's gathering. My father would appreciate, although probably with a great deal of self-consciousness, the thoughts and the memories that his professional colleagues and Chris have shared today.

My father spent time on a regular basis preparing himself and his affairs for death. John, Judy, and I for at least the last twenty years of my father's life would receive detailed, matter-of-fact, somewhat unsettling letters from my father in which he described the whereabouts of the bank accounts, life insurance policies, safety deposit boxes, bragging about how well TIAA-CREF was doing. He was a very orderly man and as a physician apparently quite unperturbed by the prospect of death. On the other hand he gave us very little help when the subject of a memorial service came up. On one occasion he did allow that if people wanted to have a small gathering at Yale, that would be nice. Now you never got much more than that out of my father but we in the family all know that what's happening today is what my farther hoped for and so, thank you very much for putting together this marvelous gathering of people who are so important and accomplished in their own right to remember by father's long professional career.

As you've heard today, my father is off the charts when it comes to professional accomplishment and recognition. When we were at Yale last for the unveiling of Richard Whitney's striking portrait and we listened to the speakers, one of my sons turned to Laura and asked, "Are we really related to this guy?"

As a parent, he would be the first to tell you that he was very much in the realm of the rest of us. Few of us can tackle the challenge of professional life and personal challenges and lay claim to have handled it with distinction and my father wouldn't either. He probably faced a particularly difficult job in that regard. This was captured in one of the hundreds of cards and emails that we received after my father's death. Richard Lee, a student in one of his last group of interns, described the competing demands on his time in the following way: "Paul was a very special and gifted man like his own father, committed to caring for the ignorant, ill and infirm and perhaps at time, less available to his family for whom he had great love and great confidence in their sturdiness and perseverance. In fact I suspect that you had no choice in the sharing, pupils and patients confiscated his attention and time."

Of course where Dr. Lee's comments are true, my father's family has obviously prospered and flourished never the less. In my own mind, this is because Dad very early in his career, very early in the Second World War, volunteered for service with the Harvard Red Cross Field Unit Hospital and Infectious Disease Hospital built in Salisbury, England and met my mother, who was then a beautiful 22-year-old nurse. My father would probably point to Soma Weiss or Gene Stead or other great medical figures to explain his own professional development and career. We in the family know that the real explanation for his succeeding is not his professional mentors but because he had the good sense to follow his heart during the war and court and marry my mother.

From that point forward, including their final five years together in a retirement community in New Hampshire, my mother was the cornerstone of his professional and personal life. In Atlanta, New Haven, Oxford, and finally Seattle, Mother took the lead in creating warm and memorable homes for us. She raised three very different and demanding children, she accepted and managed the enormous disruption that came with each of Daddy's key professional moves with grace and complete dedication to his career. These moves were of course, an essential part of my father's professional growth and extraordinary sweep of accomplishment.

A good number of us gathered in New Hampshire after my father's death. We had days to spend together; we thought back over the years with the help of photographs and our own memories and family weeklies. Family weeklies were letters that my father typed with carbon paper for decades in an effort to keep his geographically separated family in touch. There were endless random memories we had of my father, including Dad raising and lowering our flag outside the home in Seattle, intense debates about the Vietnam War, where he showed an amazing deference to the views of Rusk and McNamara and other decision makers of that time. Teaching his grandsons, Nick and Mike, the game of roulette at the small dining table at their house in Seattle, mucking out the Seattle paddock in loose rubber boots with Sylvia and Sabrina many mornings during the summers. Mucking out is a term of art for people who have horses. Convinced that we were going to loose the reservation??? We've heard Sputnik mentioned as a reason for my father reaching out to the International medical community, in our home Sputnik ended up resulting in a bomb shelter being built in the basement of our house in Woodbridge.

And then there is a memory of him reading to John and me, this marvelous book called "The Jumping Lions Of Borneo" while we waited for dinner during long summer vacations in Canada. And die hard loyalty to the fate of the Cleveland Indians and ultimately to the Seattle Mariners.

And finally, we three children, John, Judy, and I, remembered those moments between a father and his children that no one plans but create memories that endure forever. For John it was an instance when he was ten and Daddy provided him with quiet counseling on the wisdom of economy and the use of four-letter words. For Judy, it was my father's signature greeting of Jud-Pud and his warm, uninhibited affection when her small pony died. For me, it was the first part of a sabbatical year in England in the late fifties, when I had real difficulties adjusting to the rigorous expectations of the English Public School system and he spent many nights essentially home-schooling me until I caught up. These aren't remarkable but are they are special times for us to remember.

When Yale began to plan for this service, John Forrest asked for our suggestions for the speakers list. My wife Laura and I sat down with my mother and went through the various address books that she and Dad had assembled during their lives. It is amazing, how much my mother recalls of every person in those address books and how important their friends and colleagues had been as they moved through life together.

Before several of us in the family, got into the car to come South to New Haven this morning, we visited with my mother, as I am sure you can imagine, she was happily immersed in the New York Times reading about the election results and stories about the demise of Donald Rumsfeld and Nancy Pelosi's lunch with the President. She asked to be remembered to all of you, She asked me in particular to let you all know how important and treasured you have all been in the life she and my father shared. On behalf of the rest of the family, I thank you for this.

Early in his career Beeson was known for his scientific accomplishments: his discovery that hepatitis can be transmitted through blood transfusions and his identification of cytokines, proteins in white blood cells which included infection and cancer. Throughout his career he moved easily between laboratory and the wards, between the roles of scientist and doctor. And at Yale he oversaw the growth of Internal Medicine into one of the country's leading departments.

His main legacy, however, rests on his reputation as the most caring of physicians, teachers and mentors. As medicine becomes more industrialized and impersonal, wrote Richard Rapport MD, author of *Physician: The Life of Paul Beeson*, "there remains the example of Paul Beeson sitting beside a patient on an open ward, surrounded by students, listening to clues, fears and questions embedded in the story of a single sick person."

Born in 1908 in Livingston, Montana, Paul Beeson grew up in Alaska, where his father, John Beeson, was a general practitioner and surgeon for the Alaskan Railway. At the age of 19 Paul Beeson joined his older brothers Harold at McGill University Medical School. After an internship at the University of Pennsylvania, Dr. Beeson joined his brother and father in practice in Ohio. He soon left, however, to pursue research at the Rockefeller Institute and Hospital in New York.

In 1939 Dr. Beeson joined the Harvard University Medical Service and became chief resident to Some Weiss, MD, whose dedication to students and concern for patients included him deeply. During world War II, Dr. Beeson went to England as a volunteer at the Harvard Red Cross Field Hospital, where he met Barbara Neal, a young American nurse. They were married in 1942.

After the war Dr. Beeson went to Emory University, where he chaired the department of medicine. In 1952 he was recruited by Yale University and during his 13-year tenure as chair, the Department of Internal Medicine flourished.

In 1965, Dr. Beeson became the Nuffield Professor of Medicine at Oxford University. When he returned to the United States 10 years later, he and Barbara settled in Redmond, Washington, and he took an appointment at the University of Washington School of Medicine. He retired in 1981.

Dr. Beeson was a fellow of the American Academy of Arts and Sciences, a member of the National Academy of Sciences and a Master of the American College of Physicians, which gave him the John Phillips Memorial Award in 1976. He also received the Bristol Award from the Infectious Diseases Society of American and the Kober Medal from the Association of American Physicians. In 1973, Queen Elizabeth II named him an Honorary Knight Commander of the Most Excellent Order of the British Empire, in recognition of his service at Oxford.

Dr. Beeson was an editor or co-editor of Harrison's *Principles of Internal Medicine,* the *Cecil-Loeb Textbook of Medicine* and the *Oxford Companion to Medicine.* In 1981, the Paul B. Beeson Professorship in Internal Medicine was established at Yale. In 1996, the School of Medicine named its medical service in Dr. Beeson's honor.

Chapter 14

Two Articles by Paul Beeson

ROBERT G. PETERSDORF* AND PAUL B. BEESON

*From the Department of Internal Medicine, Yale University School of Medicine,
New Haven, Connecticut*

TABLE OF CONTENTS

INTRODUCTION

In 1868 Wunderlich, a German clinician, published in monograph form a convincing demonstration of the value of measuring the body temperature in various diseases. This work was soon translated into other languages (1), and the practice of making regular measurements of body temperature quickly became standard throughout the world. Thus the thermometer became the first instrument of precision to be used in medical practice. Long before Wunderlich, of course, physicians had known that illness was sometimes manifested by increased body warmth: in fact the word "Fever" came to be used to designate a certain form or forms of illness. Benjamin Rush maintained that there was "only one fever," but by the early part of the nineteenth century clinicians were able to distinguish between some of them, such as typhoid and typhus fevers, purely on clinical grounds. The introduction of clinical thermometry happened to come at the same time as the discoveries of Pasteur and the beginning of the Golden Age of Bacteriology; soon, therefore, it was no longer acceptable to say that a patient

* Present address: Dept. of Medicine, University of Washington and King County Hospital, Seattle.

was suffering from 'a fever': the challenge was to determine the cause of that fever. It was also recognized that although infectious processes were the commonest causes of fever, other kinds of disease could also affect temperature regulation, and that a great variety of causes required consideration in the differential diagnosis of febrile illness. This became one of the main fields in differential diagnosis, and many of the great clinicians of the first half of the twentieth century, such as Horder and Libman, owed their reputations in some part to successes in diagnosis of febrile disease.

Fever of unknown origin (F.U.O.) is a common clinical problem, encountered frequently in nearly all branches of practice. Fortunately the cause is oftenest an acute infection, which soon becomes evident and responds to treatment, or runs its course. In the present article we are not concerned with such short-term problems, but are restricting the discussion to cases of prolonged febrile illness of obscure cause. This is likely to be a source of perplexity and frustration to the physician, and for the patient the discomforts of illness are compounded by the anxiety of uncertainty. These unhappy victims understandably tend to seek additional medical opinions, and may wander from hospital to hospital, repeatedly enduring the same questions, the same examinations, the same laboratory tests. The fact to be accepted at the outset of a discussion of this problem is that there are diseases capable of provoking high fever for weeks or months, or even years, without progressing to a stage where the true nature of the malady reveals itself, and for which we have no accurate methods of diagnosis.

Much has been written and said about the diagnosis of prolonged febrile illness. We do not propose here to attempt a detailed review of previous discussions, other than to note that they show with remarkable clarity the great shifts which are constantly taking place in medical practice. For example, the well known article written by Hamman and Wainwright in 1936 (2), which reports on 90 cases of prolonged febrile illness studied at the Johns Hopkins Hospital, includes 11 instances of fever due to syphilis, and nearly all of the discussion is devoted to infectious diseases. That discussion does not mention by name the two present-day differential diagnostic favorites, periarteritis nodosa and systemic lupus erythematosus.

Previous writings on fever of unexplained origin have almost invariably depended upon the method of retrospective analysis for the collection of case material. That is to say, the cases were selected either by reliance on memory or by culling them from the hospital records according to diagnosis at the time of discharge. Obvious disadvantages are that cases assembled simply on the basis of recollection may present a distorted picture of the total problem; and that restricting the material to cases in which not even a tentative diagnosis had been achieved by the time of discharge from the hospital is certain to eliminate many in which there may have been long periods of uncertainty before a diagnosis could be made.

In an attempt to avoid some of the drawbacks just cited, and to obtain a present-day sampling of the problem of unexplained fever in adults, we undertook the present study in 1952. It was decided simply to note cases of prolonged unexplained fever satisfying certain criteria, at the time of their occurrence, with the intention of further study by follow-up methods at a later date. The criteria selected were: *Illness of more than three weeks' duration.* This tended to eliminate the acute self-limited infectious diseases.

In some reported series such cases have comprised as much as half of the case material. *Fever higher than 101°F on several occasions.* This eliminated the entity of 'habitual hyperthermia' (3). *Diagnosis uncertain after one week of study in hospital.* This time interval was selected as that which allows completion of the usual laboratory studies made initially in attempts to identify the cause of a febrile illness, examples being bacteriologic and serologic tests, radiologic examinations, skin tests, etc.

In 1957, when there were more than 126 cases on the list, the period of collection was terminated, and the follow-up investigation was begun. Our community is well suited to this type of study, because of its size and the stability of its population. Nevertheless some of the patients could not be traced. Furthermore, in reviewing the records it seemed reasonably certain that some of the febrile illnesses listed had represented combinations of such common entities as urinary tract infection and thrombophlebitis; accordingly these were eliminated. It was convenient, then, to base the analysis on just 100 cases, in all of which satisfactory follow-up information was available. We are aware of some bias in the final selections, and do not wish to imply that the statistical information to be presented has more than a very general significance; nevertheless the relative frequencies in the various categories are thought to give a rough picture of the probabilities in cases of fever of unexplained origin in the United States, at the mid-point of the twentieth century.

DIAGNOSTIC CATEGORIES OF THE 100 CASES

The diagnostic categories into which we finally placed the 100 cases are shown in Table I, arranged in order of frequency. It will be seen that in 93 of them a reasonably certain diagnosis was eventually possible.

The 7 cases in which not even a satisfactory tentative diagnosis could be made despite follow-up information represent 6 instances where the patients appear to have made complete recoveries. Many possibilities suggest themselves. Some of the patients may now only be in periods of remission during the long courses of diseases such as systemic lupus erythematosus. Some may have been suffering from indolent infections, e.g. tuberculosis, myocsis, toxoplasmosis, wherein host defense mechanisms finally gained the upper hand. Hypersensitivity reactions may have terminated. The disease called cranial arteritis tends to run a long course and then to subside; it would not be recognizable in the absence of involvement of a superficial artery or of sudden visual impairment. Whatever the nature of the diseases in these subjects, they comprise a sizeable portion of any series of cases of perplexing fever.

Among the 93 cases in which a reasonably certain diagnosis was eventually made we had not anticipated that more than one-third would prove to be examples of infectious disease. On the other hand we had predicted that the neoplastic and collagen groups would be larger. Five cases of periodic disease are undoubtedly an incorrect indication of the true frequency of this entity, since every one of these patients was referred to us because of our special interest in problems of unexplained febrile disease; however, it must be pointed out that patients with this disease are likely to consult many physicians and to be studied in several hospitals, because of the very long course of the disorder.

INFECTIONS

Tuberculosis

Despite many statements to the contrary, tuberculosis is still a common disease. It was the cause of fever in 11 of our patients, i.e. nearly one-third of cases due to infection. In general, these patients were younger than those with fever due to suppurative disease, and 5 of the 11 were Negroes, which stands in contrast to the racial distribution in the other categories, only 9 of the 89 being Negroes. Detailed information concerning the symptoms, signs and laboratory data of these patients is summarized in Table II.

In two patients (cases 1 and 2) the process was principally confined to the lung, although a transient pericardial rub occurred in one. Failure to establish the diagnosis earlier was attributable to the late appearance of an infiltrate in one case and to the initially negative tuberculin test in the other.

The remainder of the 11 patients had widespread tuberculosis and presented a variety of clinical pictures. For example, two (cases 3 and 4) presented with fever and hilar lymphadenopathy. Both developed pulmonary infiltrates while in the hospital. In both patients liver biopsy revealed granulomata suggestive of tuberculosis. It is likely, however, that the primary focus of infection was in the lungs, since mild pleurisy was the first symptom in one patient and acid-fast

TABLE I
Diagnostic Categories of the 100 Cases

Category	Number of Cases	
Infections		
Tuberculosis	11	
Liver and biliary tract infections	7	
Bacterial endocarditis	5	
Abdominal abscess	4	
Pyelonephritis	3	
Psittacosis	2	
Brucellosis	1	
Cirrhosis with E. coli bacteremia	1	
Gonococcal arthritis	1	
Malaria	1	
Total	—	36
Neoplastic diseases		
Disseminated carcinomatosis	7	
Localized tumor	2	
Lymphomas and leukemias	8	
No histologic diagnosis made	2	
	—	19
Collagen disease		
Rheumatic fever	6	
Systemic lupus erythematosus	5	
Unclassified	2	
	—	13
Pulmonary embolization		
Following myocardial infarction	1	
Endocardial fibroelastosis	1	
Thrombophlebitis migrans	1	
	—	3
Benign non-specific pericarditis		2
Sarcoidosis		2
Hypersensitivity states		
Granulomatous hepatitis	2	
Erythema multiforme	1	
Drug fever (dilantin)	1	
	—	4
Cranial arteritis		2
Periodic disease		5
Miscellaneous diseases		
Weber-Christian disease	1	
Thyroiditis	1	
Rupture of the spleen and pancreatitis	1	
Myelofibrosis	1	
		4
Factitious fever		3
No diagnosis made		7
Total		100

TABLE II

Clinical and Laboratory Data in 11 Patients with Tuberculosis

Case	Age	Race	Sex	Diagnosis	Symptoms	Signs	Fever Height	Fever Duration (mos.)	Anemia	WBC	Diff.	PPD	Other	Clues to Diagnosis	Method of Diagnosis	Outcome
1	26	N	F	Pulmonary tuberculosis, ?pericarditis	Fever, chills, anorexia, substernal pains	?Pericardial rub	102	2	+	Incr.	N	+		Developed pulmonary infiltrate	Gastric washing +	Improved
2	48	W	M	Pulmonary tuberculosis, silicosis	Arthralgia	Swelling fingers	104	2	+	N	N	0 to +		Conversion PPD; silicosis	Sputum +	Died
3	43	N	M	Pulmonary tuberculosis with dissemination	Chills, fever, sweats, pleurisy, cough	None	102	3	0	N	N	+		Hilar adenopathy, ?perihilar infiltrate, appearance nodular infiltrate	Liver biopsy, response to treatment	Improved
4	45	N	M	Pulmonary tuberculosis with dissemination	Malaise, fever	None	105	2	+	N	N	+		Hilar adenopathy, developed infiltrate	Liver biopsy, + sputum	Improved
5	57	W	M	Primary hepatic tuberculosis	Weight loss	Weakness, disorientation, hepatomegaly	104	1½	+	N	10% monos	0	Alk. p'tase 75 B.U.	Hepatomegaly	Liver and lymph node biopsy	Died
6	63	W	F	Primary hepatic tuberculosis	Fever	Rales	103	4	+	Incr.	N	+		?History tuberculosis	Laparotomy	Improved
7	30	W	F	Tuberculous meningitis with dissemination	Fever	Pregnant	104	1½	+	Incr.	Shift, left	0		Developed meningitis; miliary infiltrate	+ urine culture, response to treatment	Improved
8	56	N	M	Miliary tuberculosis	Weakness	Cachexia, fundal exudates	106	1½	+	N	25% monos	0		Fundal exudates	Autopsy	Died
9	46	W	M	Tuberculous pericarditis with dissemination	Fatigue, weight loss	Cachexia, generalized lymphadenopathy	103	2	0	N	N	+		Pericardial rub appeared	Liver and lymph node biopsy, sputum +, urine +	Improved
10	40	N	M	Tuberculous pericarditis	Fever	Heart enlarged, pericardial rub	103	3	+	N	N	+		Bloody pericardial fluid	Response to treatment	Improved
11	57	W	F	Tuberculosis of adrenals	Weakness	Hyperpigmented	103	2	+	N	6% eos	+	Na 129 K 6 NPN 49 ACTH test +	Calcified adrenals, history vertebral tuberculosis	Response to treatment	Improved

Incr. = Increase, N = Normal, + = Positive, 0 = Negative.

bacilli were isolated from the sputum in the second. Chapman and Whorton, in their review of 63 patients with miliary tuberculosis, stress that systemic symptoms usually overshadow evidence of localized disease and also point out the difficulty in arriving at the diagnosis which was made antemortem in only one-sixth of their patients (4).

The most likely route of dissemination from the lungs of these patients is to the hilar lymph nodes and thoracic duct and thence into the blood. A number of tubercle bacilli lodge in the liver, which is almost always involved in miliary tuberculosis. Even when the disease has appeared clinically to be confined to the lungs, tuberculous foci are found in the liver in 80 per cent of patients at autopsy (5).

At times hematogenous dissemination seems principally to involve the liver. Examples of this are cases 5 and 6, which may be representative of a form of the disease which has been called primary miliary tuberculosis of the liver (6). Patients with obvious pulmonary tuberculosis and metastatic tubercles in the liver or generalized miliary disease are excluded from this group. Symptoms consist of malaise, weakness, lassitude, abdominal distention and a notable absence of respiratory symptoms. Positive physical findings are usually confined to hepatosplenomegaly and ascites; anemia, leukopenia and hyperglobulinemia have been noted often. The concept of hepatic tuberculosis is, we think, a useful one and early recognition of this form of the disease may be lifesaving.

In two patients (cases 7 and 8), dissemination of acid-fast bacilli was first manifested by pericarditis. In one the diagnosis was most elusive and even pericardial biopsy was negative but an impressive response to anti-tuberculous therapy on two occasions, with lysis of fever and diminution in heart size, were accepted as strong evidence of tuberculosis. Several authors have commented upon the difficulty in making the diagnosis of tuberculous pericarditis; in 34 of the 95 patients described by Harvey and Whitehill the diagnosis could not be established with certainty (7). In our second patient pericarditis did not become obvious until late in the course, at a time when organisms could be recovered from liver and lymph node biopsies as well as from sputum and urine.

Two patients (cases 9 and 10) had classical miliary tuberculosis culminating in tuberculous meningitis. In one a "snow-storm" appeared in the lungs simultaneously with symptoms and signs of meningeal involvement; she responded well to therapy. The other had three spinal fluid examinations, all with normal findings, and an unsuccessful therapeutic trial with isoniazid and PAS. At necropsy he was found to have typical lesions of miliary tuberculosis, including early meningitis. An important but unappreciated clue in this patient was the presence of fundal exudates, most probably choroidal tubercles. It is of interest that both of these patients failed to react to PPD skin tests.

The last patient in this group had the classical stigmata of Addison's disease by physical examination and laboratory tests. Clues to the diagnosis were a history of tuberculosis of the vertebrae 9 years previously and calcification of the adrenals by x-ray, considered by Sanford and Favour the best sign differentiating tuberculous and nontuberculous adrenal insufficiency (8). Fever is unusual in Addison's disease, and its presence should suggest the possibility of active tuberculosis, particularly when associated with leukocytosis, elevation in sedimentation rate and a positive tuberculin test.

Delays in arriving at the diagnosis in our patients were related for the most part to the late involvement of organs likely to provoke characteristic manifestations, namely lung, pericardium and meninges. In 2 instances the waiting period necessary for the results of cultures was the cause of delay. In general, however, systemic dissemination seemed to be the most important factor in late diagnosis, since in several instances tuberculosis was not even seriously considered until several weeks after onset of fever.

Despite the fact that the tuberculin test was negative in 3 of our patients, it remains an important diagnostic procedure. The result was positive in 8 of 11 patients, 6 of whom had widely disseminated disease.

Because hematogenous spread was the rule in this group of patients, liver biopsy was very helpful in diagnosis; in fact, in 3 patients evidence of the disease was first obtained by means of this procedure. Acid-fast bacilli were seen in 2 of the specimens and were cultured from other tissues or body fluids in all three. In another patient tubercles were found in the liver at laparotomy.

When the condition of the patient will not

6   ROBERT G. PETERSDORF AND PAUL B. BEESON

allow liver biopsy to be done, or if this and other diagnostic maneuvers fail, a therapeutic trial with anti-tuberculous drugs is indicated. In one of our patients prompt response to isoniazid strongly implicated tuberculosis as the cause of the fever. In another (case 8), who ultimately expired, a more extended trial might have been lifesaving.

Acute Infections of the Biliary Tract and Liver

Another unexpected finding was the fact that the series included no less than 7 instances of suppurative infection of the liver and biliary tract. Two patients had large single liver abscesses of cryptogenic origin, and the other five had acute cholecystitis and cholangitis; two in the latter category had empyema of the gallbladder. The diagnosis was made at laparotomy in 4 of them, and at autopsy in 2. In the remaining case a gas-containing abscess of the liver was demonstrated radiographically; it apparently resolved during a prolonged course of antibiotic therapy. Six of these patients were males.

Clinically detectable icterus was noted in only 2 patients. Pain and tenderness in the right upper abdomen were not notable in any of them. The fevers in these patients tended to be exceptionally high; temperature elevations exceeded 103°F in 7 of the cases, and 6 of them had more than one shaking chill. All but 1 had an elevation in leukocyte count, and in 3 it was more than 20,000 per cu.mm. Needle biopsy of the liver was done in 4 of the 7 cases, and the evidence obtained was not very helpful, showing at most some evidence of cholangitis.

One factor contributing to the difficulties in diagnosis in this group is found in their ages. All were more than 50 years old, and 4 were more than 70. It is common clinical knowledge that manifestations of acute intra-abdominal disease may be comparatively mild in elderly patients, who often experience little pain, and exhibit no tenderness or muscle splinting. One of our patients, a man of 78, complained only of chills and feverishness. He was examined many times during a period of 3 weeks, since the tentative clinical diagnosis was probable neoplasm, nevertheless no abdominal mass or tenderness was detected. At laparotomy, however, he was found to have empyema of the gallbladder and a subhepatic abscess containing 70 ml. of pus. The frequent absence of tenderness or muscle splinting in elderly patients with biliary tract infection has been mentioned by Fisher and White (9).

Review of the histories of these patients has made us conclude that one must always give serious consideration to the advisability of exploratory laparotomy in a person with prolonged unexplained fever, especially when the subject is a male past 50 pears of age. Failure to discover a curable disease such as empyema of the gallbladder is inexcusable.

Bacterial Endocarditis

Bacterial endocaritis was the eventual diagnosis in 5 cases in the series. In one patient, a man of 58 years, the delay in diagnosis was attributable to a confident clinical impression that he had another disease, and to the fact that he did not have a heart murmur early in the course of his illness. This man was admitted because of a brief episode of aphasia, which, in retrospect, should have received more consideration, but at the time was looked upon merely as a coincidental minor cerebral vascular accident. Our major focus of attention in the early stage of his hospital course was a small pulmonary infiltrate, thought to be due to tuberculosis. However, during a three-week period of observation, although fever continued, the pulmonary shadow became less conspicuous, a murmur of aortic insufficiency became audible, and there was a widening of the pulse pressure. Blood cultures were finally obtained and revealed the presence of *Streptococcus viridans*. He made a good clinical response to penicillin therapy. The occurrence of bacterial endocarditis on the aortic valve in males past the age of 50, with development of a murmur during the course of the illness is a not too rare sequence of events (10).

In the other patients bacterial endocarditis was one of the diseases considered from the beginning of the period of clinical observation. Delay in establishing the diagnosis was attributable in two cases to negative blood cultures, that is to say, these patients had the abacteremic form of the disease. One of them died and the diagnosis was verified at autopsy. The other was a 26-year-old man with tetralogy of Fallot. After many blood cultures had failed to give growth he was given a 3-week course of penicillin and streptomycin, with no subsidence of his fever; however, when therapy was discontinued his temperature quickly returned to normal and he has remained well for several years. It was concluded that he probably had bacterial endocarditis, cured during the chemotherapy, but the beneficial effect of antibiotic treatment was obscured by the development of a drug fever. In the remaining 2 cases delay in making the diagnosis was the result of courses of antibotic therapy given to the patients before admission to the hospital; consequently the first few blood cultures taken after admission to the hospital yielded no growth, and not until the antibiotic effect had worn off was bacteremia demonstrable.

Thus the diagnosis of bacterial endocarditis was truly 'missed' in only 1 of these cases, the first described. In the other 4 that diagnosis was under serious consideration from the beginning, but there was delay because of negative blood cultures. It should be pointed out, on the other hand, that bacterial endocarditis nearly always comes up for consideration in any case of prolonged unexplained fever. In fact, several of the other cases in this series were 'given the benefit of a trial' of chemotherapy for that disease. This seems impossible to avoid: the physician can never be certain that he is *not* dealing with an abacteremic case-of bacterial endocarditis, and often feels compelled to try the effect of antibiotic therapy, fearful that he may be overlooking a possible curative treatment of an otherwise fatal disease.

Abdominal Abscesses

Four patients were eventually discovered to have deep-seated abscesses within the abdominal cavity. In two Negro females, the abscesses were in the pelvis. One, aged 32, entered the hospital for an elective surgical procedure, and was found to have a fever for which there was no obvious cause. She was transferred to the Medical Service, for investigation of the fever, and subjected to the usual battery of diagnostic tests, including chest x-ray, bacteriologic and serologic examinations, L.E. tests, etc. After three weeks of this a mass was discovered in her lower abdomen, and exploratory laparotomy was carried out. This revealed a large tubo-ovarian abscess, removal of which resulted in prompt cessation of the fever. Even after the nature of this illness was recognized the patient denied having had abdominal pain or menstrual abnormality; nevertheless, we feel that the correct diagnosis should have been made much earlier than it was. The case illustrated one of the weaknesses inherent in the increasing specialization of modern medical practice. The diagnostic study was in the hands of people whose thinking was more likely to turn

in the direction of collagen diseases than such every-day entities as pelvic inflammatory disease.

The second patient, aged 57, had suffered fever and night sweats for 6 months, and had lost a considerable amount of weight. When admitted to the hospital her hemoglobin was 5.8 Gm. per 100 ml., and leukocyte count 22,000 per cu. mm. Her temperature rose as high as 103°F. Carcinoma of the gastrointestinal tract was strongly suspected, but radiographic studies, including barium enema were interpreted as showing normal patterns. Liver biopsy, agglutination tests, L.E. tests, etc., were not helpful. After one month she complained, for the first time, of abdominal pain. It was decided to carry out a laparotomy; this revealed the presence of a pelvic abscess, almost certainly originating from appendicitis many months previously. She made an excellent recovery.

The other two intra-abdominal abscesses occurred in males, and the causative bacteria belonged to the Salmonella group. One patient was a 70-year-old Negro, who had been ill for 2 weeks, with fever and chills, but who denied all other symptoms. In the past he had suffered some indigestion, and his physician had made a diagnosis of peptic ulcer. Examination revealed no abdominal tenderness, and no mass was detected; however, radiologic study of the upper gastrointestinal tract did show a large gastric ulcer, possibly malignant. Because of his high fever, many blood cultures were made, and eventually some of these yielded *S. choleraesuis*. Treatment with chloramphenicol caused some improvement, but there was a relapse at the end of the course of chemotherapy. It was then decided to go ahead with laparotomy, and this disclosed that the patient had suffered a perforation of a large benign gastric ulcer, with the formation of a large abscess in the lesser peritoneal sac. Partial gastrectomy was done, the abscess was drained, and chloramphenicol therapy was resumed. He made an excellent recovery.

The last patient in this group was 57 years of age, and gave a history of intermittent chills and fever for the preceding 10 months. Studies in another hospital had revealed hepatosplenomegaly, and liver biopsy had been interpreted as showing hemochromatosis, but the cause of the chills and fever had not been determined. In our hospital many blood cultures were negative, but eventually *S. montevideo* was recovered from cul-

8   ROBERT G. PETERSDORF AND PAUL B. BEESON

ture of material aspirated from the bone marrow. Later the same organism was identified occasionally in blood cultures. Chloramphenicol therapy did not affect his fever. Laparotomy was carried out; the gallbladder appeared abnormal and was removed. Chloramphenicol treatment was continued, and his fever abated. He made a partial clinical recovery, but died one year later as a result of hemorrhage from esophageal varices. At autopsy he was found to have the remnant of a large abscess in the left subphrenic area. Presumably this focus of infection had been sterilized during the long course of chemotherapy.

An interesting clinical feature of the case just described is that there was an inversion of the usual temperature rhythm. For many weeks his highest daily elevation occurred in the early hours of the morning, whereas the lowest was in the afternoon. In our experience this is a surprisingly rare phenomenon. It has been said to characterize the fever of tuberculosis, but must be exceptional, and merely a consequence of the frequency of tuberculosis as a cause of long- continued fever.

Pyelonephritis

Coliform bacterial infection of the kidney was the disease of 3 patients in this series. They were females, aged 40, 60 and 71 years. None had symptoms of cystitis, and pyuria was absent, or scanty and intermittent. Urine cultures were negative in one, intermittently positive in the second, and consistently positive in the third.

The diagnostic clue in the oldest patient was detection of a tumor in the region of the left kidney after a two-month febrile illness. Intravenous pyelogram had been done elsewhere at the beginning of this illness, and interpreted as normal. However, retrograde pyelogram done after the finding of the 'tumor' showed a deformity of the renal pelvic outline, with a large opacity in the region of that kidney. The tentative preoperative diagnosis was hypernephroma. She was found, however, to have a chronically infected kidney and a large peri-nephric abscess, from which *E. coli* was recovered in pure culture. It is of interest to note that the mass, which consisted of kidney and its surrounding purulent mass, was thought to move freely with repiration, a characteristic not rare in perinephric abscesses (11). Extension of the suppuration to the perinephric space is, of course, uncommon in *E. coli*

infection, and most likely to occur when there is complete ureteral obstruction. Calculi were not found in this patient, and the pyelographic findings were not consistent with complete ureteral obstruction.

The second patient was a 60-year-old woman with hypertension who gave a history of several episodes of pyelitis of pregnancy. Urine cultures revealed the presence of *E. coli*, but no pyuria was demonstrated, and she was thought at first merely to have asymptomatic bacteriuria. Antimicrobial therapy did not affect her fever. Many diagnostic tests were performed, searching for signs of a variety of kinds of illness. Intravenous pyelogram showed renal opacification on the right; therefore, it was decided to explore the region surgically. The right kidney was found to be a small, severely scarred organ, with some evidence of active bacterial infection. Nephrectomy was done, and her fever subsided, although urine cultures continued to yield *E. coli*.

The third patient, a woman of 40, had hypertensive heart disease and mild congestive heart failure. Intravenous pyelograms were interpreted as normal, and urine cultures never revealed large numbers of bacteria, although *E. coli* in quantities of borderline significance, i.e. 1000 to 5000 per ml., was present several times. Many blood cultures were made, but these gave no growth. Nevertheless because of unexplained fever and a heart murmur it was thought possible that she had bacterial endocarditis in an abacteremic phase. Accordingly she was given a course of penicillin and streptomycin. This had no effect on the fever. In view of the questionably significant urine cultures it was then decided to try the effect of a prolonged course of streptomycin and tetracycline. At the end of ten days of that therapy her fever subsided and the urine cultures became negative. The diagnosis of pyelonephritis was assumed to be the probable one, though not definitely established. Although the only example in the present series, this is not the only instance in which we have observed pyelonephritis to simulate bacterial endocarditis. This disease can simulate many other syndromes as recently discussed by Schreiner (12).

Miscellaneous Bacterial Infections

Brucellosis with hepatitis. Brucellosis is generally regarded as one of the 'classic' causes of pyrexia of unknown origin, hence the possibility of this infection is nearly always brought up for consideration. Only one instance qualified for inclusion in this series of cases, and there the delay in diagnosis was due to the fact that the principal manifestations were those of liver disease. The patient worked in a meat packing house, and had been ill for 7 weeks before admission with fever, and weakness. A few days before admission to the hospital he noted that his urine was dark and that his eyes appeared yellow. On examination, in addition to the icterus there was noted considerable enlargement of the liver and spleen. Liver function tests indicated active parenchymatous disease. Liver biopsy was interpreted as showing a subacute hepatic necrosis and a granulomatous hepatitis, consistent with brucellosis (13). Agglutination reaction was strongly positive, and he improved rapidly following treatment with tetracycline and streptomycin. Reviewing this case it appears that failure to give sufficient thought to the patient's work, as well as preoccupation with other causes of hepatitis, were responsible for delayed recognition of an unusual form of brucellosis.

Gonococcal arthritis. A 49-year-old Negro man had been ill for 3 weeks before admission, with fever and a swollen knee. He denied symptoms of gonococcal urethritis and no evidence of that could be detected. During 4 weeks in the hospital other joints became swollen and painful, and his temperature rose as high as 104°F. Three years previously he had recovered from miliary tuberculosis. Diagnoses under consideration included recurrence of tuberculosis, as well as rheumatic fever and rheumatoid arthritis. At length fluid was aspirated from the knee, which, on examination by Gram stain, showed Gram-negative cocci; culture of the fluid, however, gave no growth. Complement fixation test for gonococcal infection was postive. The patient's signs and symptoms cleared gradually under treatment with penicillin and chloramphenicol, and he progressed to complete recovery. It seems reasonable to assume that this was a case of gonococcal arthritis.

Hepatic cirrhosis with E. coli bacteremia. Occasionally patients with Laennec's cirrhosis suffer acute febrile episodes associated with *E. coli* bacteremia (14, 15). One of our cases belongs in this category. He was 50 years of age, had been addicted to alcohol for many years, and had been told 12 years previously that he had cirrhosis. For

2 weeks prior to admission, and for 1 week afterward he had a febrile illness, with elevations as high as 104°F. Physical examination revealed hepatosplenomegaly and other signs of chronic liver disease, and liver function tests supported this. While in the hospital one blood culture was positive for *E. coli.* His febrile illness subsided without antibiotic therapy and he was permitted to return to his home. However, he suffered a relapse 1 week later, with elevations to 105°F. He was re-admitted, and blood cultures this time showed no growth; however, in view of the clinical picture and the previous demonstration of bacteremia, chloramphenicol treatment was instituted. The patient made rapid improvement. He died 14 months later in another hospital, following an intestinal resection for mesenteric thrombosis. Autopsy revealed only the presence of cirrhosis, and there was no clue to the original focus of the *E. coli* infection.

Episodes of coliform bacteremia in patients with severe liver disease have been recognized for a long time, but the paucity of literature about them suggests that they occur rarely. A recent report from Paris, however, tends to refute this and suggests that this is the most frequent kind of septicemia in cirrhotics. These authors report observation of 15 examples of this complication among 450 patients with cirrhosis (16). The curious thing about the episodes is that they often occur 'out of the blue,' without any indication of the existence of a primary focus of infection. The suggestion has been made that they occur as a result of the shunting of portal blood into the peripheral circulation because of portal hypertension. This is not wholly satisfying, because it has not yet been conclusively demonstrated that living bacteria frequently gain access to the portal circulation of man. The pathogenesis of these episodes is deserving of further study.

Psittacosis

Before giving further details of these two cases of psittacosis it seems worth while to emphasize the fact that infections by viruses rarely produce prolonged febrile illness. While it is true that lymphogranuloma venereum, trachoma and infectious hepatitis (if that is a viral infection) may be cited as viral infections in which there is chronic progression of the lesion, none of these is characterized by fever. For the most part, then, the clinician faced with a problem of long-term

10   ROBERT G. PETERSDORF AND PAUL B. BEESON

unexplained febrile illness, can dismiss viral infections from primary consideration.

The only instances of infection by viruses which appear in this group of cases are 2 cases of psittacosis. They barely qualify for inclusion on the basis of illness of 3 weeks or slightly longer, with the diagnosis still uncertain at the end of one week's study in the hospital. In both cases it was clear that there was a pathologic lesion of the lung, but differentiation from primary atypical pneumonia, tuberculosis, mycosis, 'allergic pneumonitis' and other entities could not be made promptly.

The two cases of psittacosis occurred in females, aged 32 and 46. A history of contact with parakeets was later obtained in both patients. Their illnesses were characterized by fever and systemic manifestations with comparatively little cough and no expectoration. In each one of them a pulmonary infiltrate was demonstrated by x-ray during the third week of illness, and in one there were physical signs of consolidation. One patient developed a few macular lesions on the trunk somewhat resembling rose spots of typhoid fever. This has been noted before, and may indeed cause confusion with typhoid (17), in view of the fact that psittacosis may be manifested by fever, headache, abdominal distension, leukopenia and splenomegaly. The many diagnostic possibilities which may be suggested by cases of psittacosis have been discussed more recently by Seibert et al. (18). In both of our cases the diagnosis was established by rising titer of complement fixing antibodies for psittacosis virus. One of our cases made a good recovery after four weeks without specific therapy. The other improved during a course of penicillin treatment.

Malaria

A typical case of malaria qualified for admission to this series of cases, simply because the possibility was not considered at first. The patient was a 34-year-old man who, 7 months previous to onset of symptoms, had been engaged in entomological investigations in Panama. While there he had taken suppressive doses of chloroquin, but had had no antimalarial therapy since his return to Connecticut. His illness began with myalgia, headache and malaise, and fever to 101°F. A tentative diagnosis of infectious mononucleosis was made. After two weeks of febrile illness at home without improvement he was ad-

mitted to the hospital for study. Blood cultures, agglutination tests, radiological examinations, etc. revealed nothing of significance. Meanwhile his temperature rose as high as 105°. At length the significance of recent exposure to malaria was appreciated, and smears of the peripheral blood revealed *Plasmodium vivax*. He was cured by appropriate antimalarial therapy.

NEOPLASTIC DISEASES

Nineteen of the cases in this series had fever as a symptom of neoplastic disease. Eight of these were in the lymphoma-leukemia category; 11 were carcinoma or sarcoma.

Fever is a well known manifestation of neoplastic disease, and was given considerable attention in the writings of clinicians 50 years ago. Briggs reviewed 238 malignancies, and found fever, unrelated to other causes, to be present in 38 per cent (19). In the majority of his cases there were only occasional rises in temperature; only 7 of them had sustained fever. On the basis of these and other figures it would appear that roughly 3 per cent of patients with visceral carcinoma have fever as the presenting complaint.

Disseminated Carcinoma

In 7 patients there was wide dissemination of carcinoma, from primary foci in the pancreas, stomach, esophagus, carotid body, eye and bone. The organs most frequently affected by metastatic lesions were the liver and bones four times each, lungs three times and adrenals and abdominal lymph nodes in two cases each. Pyrexia could not be correlated with the locus of metastatic disease, and the pattern of dissemination in these febrile patients did not seem to differ from that which is usually observed (20).

Of note is the relative youth of these patients, 5 of whom were between 20 and 50 years of age. In general, the illnesses followed acute courses. In 6 patients symptoms had been present for less than 3 months, and consisted of fever, weakness, weight loss and pain, usually referable to a site of neoplastic infiltration.

Carcinoma of the pancreas. The two patients with this disease had remarkably similar illnesses. Both were middle-aged men; their symptoms were vague, and they maintained high fevers for many weeks. The correct diagnosis was eventually achieved by biopsy of an inguinal lymph node in one patient, and by laparotomy in the other. Both of these men had leukemoid blood pictures; in one the leukocyte count remained in the vicinity of 60,000. The other's leukocyte count was about 30,000 and there was an eosinophilia of 25–30 per cent. Leukemoid reactions have been noted in a variety of malignant tumors (21). Isaacson and Rapaport called attention to eosinophilia in malignant disease, and described this phenomenon in 0.5 per cent of all malignancies at one hospital (22). Eosinophilia can be particularly confusing in patients with pyrexia of unknown etiology; for example, most of the attending physicians favored the diagnosis of periarteritis nodosa in our patient until the true nature of his disease was recognized.

The frequency of fever in all cases of carcinoma of the pancreas does not appear to be unusually high. In Bell's series fever was the presenting symptom in 6 of 466 cases (23). Cliffton points out that 50 per cent of patients with neoplastic infiltration in the ampulla of Vater have intermittent fever, but cites an incidence of only 2% in lesions elsewhere in the pancreas (24).

Carcinoma of the stomach. A 67-year-old woman complained of fever, with vague aches and pains, and was first thought to be suffering from psoriatic arthritis. Two months later x-rays of her skeleton revealed evidence of widespread metastatic malignancy, and the level of blood alkaline phosphatase was found to be 64 Bodansky units. Lymph node biopsy revealed an adenocarcinoma, which was later found to have originated in the stomach. This patient, then, had fever attributable to carcinoma of the stomach for 3 months. Gastric malignancy was thought by the older clinicians to be the prototype of a fever-producing tumor (19). This view was recently supported by Berlin and Porter (25), who reported 39 episodes of fever among 81 admissions for gastric malignancy, but in all but 6 of those the temperature elevations did not exceed 101°F. Hartmann analyzed the records of 271 patients with carcinoma of the stomach and found 8.8 per cent to have fever due to intercurrent infections and 7.7 per cent to have rhythmical "malaria-like" elevations in temperature occurring at intervals of 3–5 days. One of his patients became afebrile following gastrectomy (26).

Carcinoma of the esophagus. One of the worst

diagnostic errors in this series occurred in the case of a 34-year-old Puerto Rican male who gave a history of vague epigastric pain for 5 months, and mild dysphagia for 2 months, with one minor episode of hematemesis. He had some fever, and one of the main possibilities under consideration was schistosomiasis. Radiographic examination of the upper gastrointestinal tract and colon were reported as normal. Esophagoscopy was planned, but not completed because of a hyperactive gag reflex. His fever subsided spontaneously and he was discharged, only to be re-admitted 3 weeks later because of chills and fever. At this time he underwent an extensive "F.U.O. work-up" including liver and lymph node biopsy, bone marrow examination and numerous culutres and x-rays. A tentative diagnosis of Hodgkin's disease was made, on the basis of low-grade eosinophilia, lymphocytic infiltration in the liver, and a rather classical Pel-Ebstein fever. When admitted for the third time, nausea, vomiting and dysphagia were the presenting complaints. Radiographic examination revealed a constricting lesion in the mid-esophagus, and the presence of carcinoma was established by biopsy. X-ray examination demonstrated metastases in the ribs and lungs and a broncho-esophageal fistula. Possibly the pyrexia was related to the communication between the bronchus and esophagus, and the several spontaneous defervescences may have followed intermittent drainage of infected material from the bronchial tree into the esophagus.

The lesson to be re-learned here is that dysphagia is by far the most common symptom of carcinoma of the esophagus and that failure to consider this possibility is the single most important cause for a delay in the diagnosis (27, 28).

Uncommon neoplasms. One patient had malignant melanoma. He had been febrile for 8 weeks and under study in the hospital for 2 weeks when the possible connection between the present illness and an ocular prosthesis inserted 8 years previously was brought up for consideration. The diagnosis was made by biopsy of the liver. Here we were chagrined at our failure to remember the old axiom about "the patient with a glass eye and a big liver." The interval between the removal of ocular melanoma and the appearance of metastases, usually in the liver, may be extremely long, a fact illustrated here as well as by a number already in the medical literature (29).

One of the most unusual cases in this series involved a *fibrosarcoma of bone* in a young woman, who complained of fever and diffuse aches and pains. The initial impression was acute rheumatic fever, but discovery of a lesion in her rib 3 months after the onset of illness led to a biopsy which showed fibrosarcoma of bone. This tumor was first described by Steiner in 1944, and consists of numerous lesions widely-distributed in the reticuloendothelial and hematopoietic tissues of the marrow (30). It is thought to be of multicentric origin, and has some resemblance to multiple myeloma. The initial impression of acute rheumatic fever is reminiscent of the occasional diagnosis of that disease in young patients with acute leukemia, as emphasized by Aisner and Hoxie (31).

Another unusual tumor was a *carcinoma of the carotid body*, with metastases. Many fruitless diagnostic procedures, including liver biopsy, were done in this patient, before a small mass in the neck, previously believed to be due to 'nonspecific lymphadenitis,' was excised and found to be a primary tumor of the carotid body.

Localized Tumors

In two patients localized neoplastic processes were the cause of fever. One of these was a 53-year-old woman who had daily elevations to 102°F for 18 months. She had been examined in several hospitals, had undergone innumerable radiographic studies, including intravenous pyelograms, cultures, and biopsies of bone marrow and liver, and had been subjected to therapeutic trials with a variety of drugs. There was clinical evidence of thyrotoxicosis, but propylthiouracil failed to affect the fever. A course of antituberculous therapy was likewise unsuccessful. Finally, repetition of the intravenous pyelogram revealed a slight irregularity of the calyceal pattern on the right. Retrograde pyelogram then demonstrated a mass at the upper pole of that kidney. Nephrectomy confirmed the impression of hypernephroma. The fever disappeared promptly following removal of the kidney and she was well 3 years later.

Fever as a sign of renal carcinoma is, of course, well known. Usually, however, the diagnosis of a fever-producing hypernephroma is not difficult since other signs are present. For example, in 273 patients with renal carcinomas reported by Berger and Sinkoff (32), 44 had fever but only 7 had pyrexia as the sole manifestation. It has been pointed out, however, that the diagnosis of renal carcinoma may be extraordinarily difficult particularly since some tumors produce little or no defect in the pelvis or calyces on pyelography. Lateral expansion of the tumor may result in only slight displacement of the kidney or increase in its size (33). This was the case with our patient, since she had at least 3 "negative" intravenous pyelograms during her long course. A clue which went unappreciated was a slightly high alkaline phosphatase. This enzyme has been found in increased quantities in several patients with hypernephroma and the level has returned to normal following nephrectomy (34). It is said that persistence of fever following removal of a hypernephroma is strong evidence of the existence of metastasis (35).

The second patient in this group had an anaplastic carcinoma of the lung, which was difficult to visualize radiographically. At a second bronchoscopic examination histologic evidence was obtained. Pneumonectomy resulted in lysis of fever, but involvement of hilar nodes implied a poor prognosis. The resected specimen contained an area of infection distal to the tumor mass, and it is likely that infection rather than tumor was responsible for the fever. In a series of 100 patients analyzed by Bloomer and Lindskog, fever was never the presenting symptom (36).

Lymphomas and Leukemias

Lymphosarcoma and reticulum cell sarcoma. Four patients with these diseases all had widespread involvement of abdominal and retroperitoneal nodes, and the disease was far-advanced when the diagnosis was finally made by biopsy. Lymphomas constitute the most common tumor of the retroperitoneal space; this area is notorious for its clinical silence and is an ideal site for the multiplication of cancer cells (37). The disease is usually widespread before displacement of the kidneys, stomach or colon becomes apparent radiographically. Deviation in the course of the ureter, as demonstrated by intravenous pyelogram, may be the earliest clue; this was true of two of our patients.

Hodgkin's disease. Two patients had courses

fairly typical of Hodgkin's disease. In one of them arthralgia delayed the diagnosis, while "collagen" diseases were being considered. Biopsy of a cervical node provided the correct answer. She is receiving intermittent therapy with triethylene melamine—the only survivor in this group. The other patient had had chills and fever for several months; chest x-ray revealed a slight widening of the mediastinum and the diagnosis was established by supraclavicular node biopsy. Both patients had Pel-Ebstein fever, which is said to be a disappearing phenomenon in Hodgkin's disease. A likely explanation for the reduction in the incidence of Pel-Ebstein fever is that present-day methods of treatment with steroid hormones, radiation therapy or radiomimetic agents may affect the temperature course in such a way that the classical periodicity does not become evident. In one of our patients administration of salicylates had little effect on the course of the temperature fluctuations, an experience which has been noted by others (38).

Monocytic leukemia. Two patients with monocytic leukemia gave great difficulty in diagnosis, and, in fact, the nature of their disease was determined only by autopsy. The first was a 41-year-old woman who had complained of fever, back pain, weakness and nervousness for 6 weeks prior to admission. The only noteworthy physical findings were thyroid enlargement and a few palpable nodes in the neck and axilla. There was severe anemia, the hematocrit ranging between 20 and 29 per cent. The white blood cell count was normal with a slight shift to the left and 8 per cent monocytes. Bone marrow was not diagnostic of any hematologic disorder. The appearance of a small infiltrate in the left upper lobe prompted a vigorous search for tubercle bacilli. Her condition deteriorated rapidly over the next 6 weeks; terminally, nucleated red cells appeared in the blood and the alkaline phosphatase rose to 23.8 Bodansky units. Autopsy revealed monocytic leukemia involving the bone marrow, liver, spleen, kidney, adrenals and pituitary; there was evidence of extramedullary hematopoiesis and a small residual focus of nontuberculous pneumonia.

The second patient suffered the abrupt onset of paraplegia. Laminectomy showed infarction of the spinal cord at T6–T8. During the next several months there was a high spiking fever,

initially attributed to pyelonephritis or infection in a decubitus ulcer. However, the persistence and height of the fever despite treatment of these processes, led to consideration of other causes for fever. Biopsy of bone marrow, liver, skin and muscle and exploratory laparotomy, together with numerous bacteriologic, serologic, and radiographic examinations gave unhelpful results. Just before death a hemorrhagic rash appeared on the legs. This was thought to be due to an allergy to a drug. In addition there was noted terminally a palpable spleen and some enlargement of the liver. At autopsy, findings typical of monocytic leukemia were discovered in many organs.

Of all the leukemias, the monocytic type is notoriously difficult to recognize. We were interested to note that this was the only form of leukemia in the present series. The course in these patients tends to be subacute, lasting several months. Such manifestations as oral lesions, and presence of blast cells in the peripheral blood are often absent. Most cases described in the literature are characterized by a vague onset, weakness and symptoms of anemia. Fever may be a prominent symptom and 1 of the 8 cases described by Sinn and Dick was for some weeks a problem in diagnosis of unexplained fever (39). The clues to the diagnosis usually lie in some hematologic abnormality—either anemia, leukopenia or thrombocytopenia—which may antedate by months and even years the appearance of the full-blown picture of leukemia. Bone marrow examinations show a normal or aplastic picture, and immature cells in the marrow may not be found (40).

The diagnosis in the second patient was confused by the presence of several acute infections, which were held responsible for the fever. The significance of fever in acute leukemia has recently been studied by a group at the National Institutes of Health (41). Of 92 febrile episodes in their patients with acute leukemia, 59 were clearly related to infection. On the basis of these studies, the authors recommend that fever in patients with leukemia be considered due to infection until proved otherwise.

COLLAGEN DISEASES

Rheumatic Fever

Six of the 100 cases are now regarded as having suffered from acute rheumatic fever. This

14   ROBERT G. PETERSDORF AND PAUL B. BEESON

diagnosis was always among those given prominent consideration, but in the absence of the
full-blown picture satisfying Jones' criteria (42)
the diagnosis cannot be made with certainty,
and one must depend on the long-term course
of the illness for a reasonably certain answer. It
is inevitable, therefore, that some cases of rheumatic fever would appear in a series compiled
in the manner of this one. The principal problems in our cases were to distinguish between
acute rheumatic fever and such diseases as rheumatoid arthritis, systemic lupus erythematosus,
bacterial endocarditis and tuberculosis.

The ages of these six patients were 15, 29, 36,
42, 59 and 70 years. Active rheumatic fever is
not rare in middle-aged or elderly persons (43,
44), and may be encountered more commonly
in the future, because of the availability of effective prophylaxis and therapy for streptococcal infections in young persons. Two of our patients had histories of previous rheumatic fever.
In 3 the present illness had begun with soreness
of the throat. Three had arthritis or arthralgia
involving several joints. Repeated electrocardiographic examinations revealed "acute changes"
in 3 of them. Heart murmurs were described in
4, but only one was a diastolic murmur. One of
the 2 without any murmur had a transient pericardial friction rub. The oldest patient in the
series had moderately severe congestive heart
failure with cardiac enlargement during her illness. Leukocyte counts were normal in 3, elevated in 3, with one of the latter group having
a count of 60,000 per cu. mm. on one occasion.
The antistreptolysin titer was elevated in 4,
normal in 2 patients. Fever and symptoms responded well to acetylsalicylic acid therapy in
4, and to ACTH in one case. Only one patient,
the youngest, had a skin lesion, but in that instance the development of typical erythema
marginatum was of considerable help in point-
ing to the correct diagnosis.

Rheumatic fever stands out in the present
series of cases as the entity in which the findings
on physical examination, and the course of the
illness, were of paramount importance in diagnosis.

Systemic Lupus Erythematosus

During the 5-year period of this study it is
estimated that between 20 and 25 new cases of
systemic lupus erythematosus were recognized

among our hospital patients. Thanks principally
to the ready availability of the L.E. test, rapid
diagnosis was possible in most of those. There
were, however, 5 cases in which early diagnosis
by the L.E. test could not be made, and since
all had fever as a prominent manifestation they
are included in this series of cases of prolonged
febrile disease of obscure etiology. As was true
of our cases of rheumatic fever, it can be said
here that the diagnosis of lupus erythematosus
was under serious consideration from the beginning in all of the cases, but immediate differentiation from such other diseases as hematogenous
dissemination of tuberculosis, acute rheumatic
fever, rheumatoid arthritis, acute glomerulo-
nephritis, bacterial endocarditis, etc. could not
be made with certainty. In 2 of these 5 cases the
L.E. phenomenon eventually became demonstrable and they can be considered unequivocal
cases. In the remaining 3, however, a positive
test was never obtained; furthermore even after
their deaths (2 by bacterial pneumonia, 1 by
renal failure) typical morphologic evidence of
this disease was not found. This may be due in
part to the fact that all had received intensive
steroid therapy, which may have made the histologic evidences of the disease less conspicuous.
All 3 of these cases were characterized by typical
skin lesions and other manifestations, such as
arthritis, pleural effusions, active renal disease,
etc. We feel justified in this diagnosis despite
the absence of substantial proof. The data of
Harvey and his associates are of interest on this
point (45). They report negative L.E. tests in
19 of 96 cases with unequivocal systemic lupus
erythematosus. Thirty-eight of their cases were
examined at autopsy. Of those, 16 had severe
complicating infection, but among the 22 without complicating infection were 5 cases in which
little evidence of structural change could be
found. One of their pathologists is quoted as
remarking that the findings were "as if they
had died a 'chemical death,' leaving behind no
structural clues as to its nature."

Unclassified Collagen Disease

Two male adults, each about 25 years of age
at the onset of his illness, have had rather similar chronic illness, characterized at times by
high fever. The duration of illness in one patient
is 13 years, in the other it is 3 years. These two
diseases seem to belong in the general category

of collagen disease, since there are resemblances to systemic lupus erythematosus, rheumatoid arthritis and rheumatic fever. They are presented in a separate category, however, because it is thought they may represent a special syndrome.

In both men the illness began suddenly, with high fever and sore throat. The fever continued for weeks, and reached levels of 105 and 106°F. Cultures of throat and blood revealed nothing of significance. The hematologic response was distinctive, in that each had leukocytosis in the range of 20,000 to 35,000. Their illnesses have waxed and waned, but neither patient has been completely free of fever and other manifestations at any time since the onset. They have been subjected to the most searching study: roentgenograms, bacteriologic and serologic tests, skin tests, biopsies, etc. Antistreptolysin titer, sheep cell agglutination test (Rose), and L.E. test have been consistently negative in both patients.

Some months after the onset of illness both patients began to have rheumatic manifestations, with arthralgia, muscle pain and stiffness, and occasional true arthritis with joint swelling, and some atrophy of the adjacent muscle groups. For the most part the joints involved have been large ones. The rheumatic manifestations have come to be the patients' chief complaints and their appearance at the present time is more like rheumatoid arthritis than any other disease. Neither patient has shown evidence of renal, pulmonary or pleural involvement. Neither received much benefit from treatment with acetylsalicylic acid, but both showed great symptomatic improvement by steroid administration. However, this seemed to be merely a damping of the intensity of the process, since both patients continue to have low-grade fever, and suffer some discomfort because of muscle and joint pain.

PULMONARY EMBOLIZATION

Fever is a well known manifestation of pulmonary infarction, though its duration ordinarily is a matter of only a few days (46). In 3 of our cases, however, recurrent infarction of the lungs eventually was identified as the cause of long-continued fever. The disease predisposing to pulmonary embolization differed in each case. One was that of a 68-year-old woman who

had been kept in bed for two weeks because of coronary insufficiency. A nightly temperature elevation to 102–103°F began, and persisted for the next 4 weeks. Examination in the hospital revealed basal pulmonary congestion and a small pleural effusion. Tests for tuberculosis, bacterial pneumonia and collagen-vascular disease gave negative results. During the fourth week in the hospital thromboembolic disease was suggested by the appearance of tenderness in the right thigh, and a transient pleural friction rub. Administration of heparin was begun, and within 4 days her fever subsided, and all other symptoms ceased. The use of anticoagulants has been advocated as a therapeutic trial in suspected cases of pulmonary infarction (47); we have observed several patients with overt pulmonary infarcts who became afebrile coincident with employment of anticoagulant treatment.

The second patient was a 41-year-old woman who had gradually developed signs of heart failure over a period of several years. The etiology of her heart disease was undetermined, although fluctuating antistreptolysin-O titers suggested the possibility of rheumatic myocarditis. However, she failed to improve after treatment with salicylates or adrenal cortical hormones. Terminally she developed signs of thrombophlebitis and pleuritic pain. Autopsy revealed dilatation and hypertrophy of the heart with foci of myocardial sclerosis. There were mural thrombi in the right ventricle, and multiple old and recent clots in the pulmonary vessels with areas of infarction distal to them. The course and findings are compatible with those of the disease called endocardial fibroelastosis of the adult type (48).

The pathogenesis of the fever in this patient is of interest. It is conceivable that fever was secondary to disease of the myocardium, but this seems unlikely in view of the fact that pathological changes in the myocardium were limited to fibrosis and no significant foci of inflammation were seen. Heart failure can in itself cause low-grade temperature elevations (49, 50). We believe, however, that the most likely cause for fever was recurrent infarctions of the lung. The multiplicity of lesions of different age is in keeping with the view that repeated emboli are a prerequisite for prolonged fever, and that a single embolus is probably associated with but a brief elevation in temperature.

The third patient, a 38-year-old man, had

an acute febrile illness lasting just 5 weeks and associated terminally with jaundice, cough, pleuritic pain and petechiae and ecchymoses. The laboratory data were consistent with a severe hemolytic anemia and thrombocytopenia. Terminally he had nitrogen retention and massive edema. Thromboembolic disease was obviously present and he was treated by anticoagulants and bilateral femoral vein ligation, but expired. Autopsy revealed numerous pulmonary emboli and infarcts. In addition there were thromboses of the inferior and superior vena cavae, and the renal and mesenteric veins. This case resembles the entity which has been termed visceral thrombophlebitis migrans (51), although hemolytic anemia has not been mentioned as part of this syndrome. Possibly hemolysis was responsible in part for this patient's fever.

HYPERSENSITIVITY STATES

Erythema multiforme. A 56-year-old white man complained of chills and fever for 2 weeks, and was found on examination to have tender muscles and papular lesions over his legs. Biopsies of the liver and skin showed mild acute inflammatory changes about small arteries, and he was first thought to have periarteritis nodosa. However, his symptoms and signs subsided spontaneously during 2 weeks in the hospital, and on follow-up examination 4 years later he appeared to be entirely well. While it is possible that he had periarteritis nodosa, the course of illness was not the usual one of that disease, and it seems more reasonable in retrospect to list him as an example of erythema multiforme. The etiology of that disorder is obscure but it is generally thought to be a "manifestation of hypersensitivity" since it frequently occurs following ingestion of drugs, particularly phenolphthalein derivatives, bromides, sulfonamides and salicylates, and tends to recur in some patients.

Drug fever. It is important to keep in mind the fact that fever is one of the most frequent systemic manifestations of hypersensitivity and that the drugs used to combat infection may themselves give rise to sensitization and pyrexia. A great many of them have been shown to be capable of causing fever, but penicillin, sulfonamide, propylthiouracil, iodides, and barbiturates are among the most common offenders (52). Apparently, however, almost any drug can do

this occasionally, and there may be no other signs or symptoms of hypersensitivity. When fever is caused by one of the agents known to be a frequent offender, such as penicillin or a barbiturate, the diagnosis may not be difficult, but when fever is caused by a drug which has been given "routinely", for sedation or analgesia, the diagnosis may be more elusive. Such was the case in one of our patients who entered the hospital because of an acute pulmonary infection but continued to have fever for four weeks after resolution of the pulmonary infiltrate. At that time consideration was given to the fact that she was receiving phenylhydantoin (Dilantin) because of ill-defined seizures which had occurred some months previously. The therapy was discontinued, and her fever subsided promptly. Toxic potentialities of this drug, notably rash, leukopenia and hyperplasia of the gums, are well recognized; fever, however, is relatively rare although it has been reported as part of a generalized reaction characterized by jaundice and exfoliative dermatitis (53).

Granulomatous hepatitis. Liver biopsy may be the best practical means of identifying diseases characterized by the formation of granulomas, and occasionally it is possible to make an etiologic diagnosis by this means. In certain metazoan infestations recognizable fragments of larvae may be demonstrable, and now and then in such infections as histoplasmosis, tuberculosis or actinomycosis the parasite may be identifiable. More often the finding of granulomatous disease in the liver is a valuable adjunct to etiologic diagnosis, as was the case in patients with sarcoidosis and brucellosis in the present series. In 2 additional cases granulomas were found in liver tissue obtained by needle aspiration, but there was no other sound basis on which to establish an exact diagnosis. They are therefore listed simply as granulomatous hepatitis.

The first was a 32-year-old man who had been treated with a sulfonamide compound for acute pyelonephritis 3 weeks previously. One week before admission he complained of chilly sensations, fever and malaise. On entry to the hospital he was found to have fever of 104°F, and enlargement of liver and spleen. His temperature fluctuated between 101°F and 103°F for the next 3 weeks in the hospital, then subsided gradually without specific treatment. Extensive investigations were carried out but the only positive findings were in the demonstration of granulomas in the liver and bone marrow. This man then made a complete recovery, and was in good health at the time of follow-up 2 year later.

The second patient, a woman aged 71, who was known to be sensitive to penicillin, had been given a sulfonamide and tetracycline for an ear ache four weeks before admission. Shortly thereafter she began to have a remittent fever, and suffered some myalgia and chilly sensations. On admission to the hospital her temperature was found to vary between 101 and 103°F. There were no remarkable physical findings. Laboratory tests showed mild anemia and leukocyte count of 19,000, with 4 to 7% eosinophils. Numerous cultures for bacteria, fungi and acid-fast bacilli were negative, as were skin tests, agglutinations, extensive radiologic studies and bone marrow examinations. Liver function studies showed 34% bromsulfalein retention, and alkaline phosphatase was elevated to 29 Bodansky units. Liver biopsy revealed diffuse granulomatosis. Her fever subsided after 2 weeks in the hospital, and liver functions returned to normal. Two years later she was reported to be in good health.

In view of the failure to find evidence of specific diseases known to cause granulomatosis, and of the subsequent clinical recoveries of these 2 patients it seems reasonable to postulate that these illnesses were the result of hypersensitivity reactions. The second patient had other evidences to support the diagnosis of an allergic reaction—eosinophilia and a history of penicillin sensitivity. Both of our patients had been given sulfonamides, drugs notorious for producing a multiplicity of lesions, including granulomas. In 22 patients who were thought to have "sulfonamide" lesions at autopsy, granulomas were found in the liver in 8; 2 of these patients had also been febrile (54). It is of interest also that granulomas can be produced in dogs by the administration of sodium sulfadiazine, although the lesions are usually limited to the kidneys and myocardium (55).

NON-SPECIFIC PERICARDITIS

In retrospect, and on the basis of adequate follow-up observation, this diagnosis appears probable in the cases of 2 elderly men, aged 68

and 71. In both of them fever was the predominant clinical manifestation, ranging between 101 and 104°F. One patient had recurrent attacks of pain in the left lateral chest in association with daily remittent fever for 18 weeks. A transient pericardial rub was occasionally audible, and the electrocardiogram showed changes compatible with pericarditis. Initially the diagnosis of acute "benign" pericarditis was favored but this was questioned later because of the long duration of illness. Diagnostic tests for other causes of pericarditis were all negative. His symptoms were eventually controlled by a long course of steroid therapy, and did not recur when this was terminated. Two and one-half years later he was asymptomatic and appeared well.

The second patient's febrile illness lasted 9 weeks, and the clinical problem was similar, except that chest X-ray revealed bilateral pleural effusion in addition to the pericardial effusion. These roentgenographic signs cleared without specific therapy during a period of 3 weeks.

Because of the ages of these 2 patients the so-called post-myocardial-infarction syndrome (56) had to be given consideration. However, there was no evidence of recent myocardial infarction in either case, and the duration of their febrile periods is longer than has been described.

Non-specific or idiopathic pericarditis is at best a diagnosis which must be made by exclusion. Evidence tending to implicate the Coxsackie viruses or infectious mononucleosis is occasionally obtained, but in most instances no specific etiology can be established. Fever may be a prominent feature of this syndrome. In Levy's series, 20 of 27 patients had fever, ranging between 100.4 and 105°F and lasting as long as two months; indeed, prolonged fever of obscure origin was the chief problem in one of his cases (57). It is noteworthy that pericardial rub may be absent in a significant number of cases, and that pulmonary infiltrations or pleural effusions are not uncommon (58).

SARCOIDOSIS

Fever is usually believed to be so rare an accompaniment of sarcoidosis, that its presence should suggest a search for some complicating disease (59, 60). Nevertheless 2 of the patients in our series had fever as a prominent manifestation.

The relation between erythema nodosum and

sarcoidosis is of special interest here since erythema nodosum is characterized by fever. This entity has been thought to be a manifestation of a number of infections, particularly those caused by the tubercle bacillus and the hemolytic streptococcus. Lofgren, however, has presented evidence that erythema nodosum in the presence of hilar lymphadenopathy, fever and arthralgia represents the first, or "lymph node", stage of sarcoidosis (61).

One of our cases seems to provide a typical example of the hilar-lymph-node syndrome. She complained of fever and night sweats for 3 weeks, and was found to have enlargement of the liver and spleen. While in the hospital the characteristics of erythema nodosum made their appearance, and chest x-ray revealed enlarged hilar glands bilaterally. The tuberculin test was weakly-positive in 1:100 dilution, and the serum globulin was 4.7 Gm per cent. Biopsy of axillary and supraclavicular nodes and of the liver revealed granulomata and no acid-fast bacilli. Fever subsided without specific therapy, although it is of interest that aspirin aggravated her malaise and myalgia. The patient still had hilar adenopathy 3 months later although she was entirely well. As judged by Lofgren's observations the prognosis is good, since only 8 per cent of patients progressed to the stage of chronic pulmonary disease (62).

The second of our patients, a 62-year-old white man had fever as high as 103°F and shaking chills for 4 weeks. One week before admission he developed severe conjunctivitis and tender spots under the fingernails. Physical examination revealed an acutely ill man with splinter hemorrhages of the nail beds and petechiae. He had a severe conjunctivitis but the iris was spared. There was no heart murmur or enlargement of liver and spleen. The initial diagnosis was bacterial endocarditis, but 20 negative blood cultures, failure to develop a heart murmur and unsuccessful trials with numerous antibiotics argued against this diagnosis. The diagnosis of sarcoidosis was suggested by a left hilar mass, weakly positive tuberculin test, peculiar papular rash and hyperglobulinemia. Liver biopsy was normal but a lymph node removed from the hilar area of the left lung revealed granulomata of sarcoidosis. His fever gradually subsided over a period of 3 months, and chest x-rays 6 months later showed a reticular infiltrate compatible with the diagnosis of sar-

coidosis. Five years later the infiltrate had not changed. Despite the confusing picture at the onset of the illness, it seems probable that this patient had sarcoidosis, although we cannot exclude the possibility that this syndrome developed in response to a specific infectious disease, e.g. hemolytic streptococcal infection. Regarding the splinter hemorrhages it is interesting to note that a careful study indicates they are in no sense pathognomonic of endocarditis (63).

CRANIAL ARTERITIS

Two elderly women, ages 67 and 73, had febrile illnesses which were eventually regarded as being due to giant cell (cranial) arteritis. In one the diagnosis was substantiated by biopsy of the temporal artery. Her illness had begun 12 weeks previously, with fever, malaise and chills, which seemed to follow an injection of typhoid vaccine. She had been admitted to another hospital and had received antibiotic treatment without effect. The principal laboratory finding was moderate leukocytosis with 8 to 12 per cent eosinophils. She complained of severe headache at times. After some days in our hospital she had a recurrence of the severe headache, and that symptom led to a careful palpation of the temporal arteries; one of them was found to be thickened, though it was not tender. Biopsy revealed the typical histologic picture. Steroid therapy was begun and brought about prompt subsidence of fever and relief of headache. When the treatment was terminated after two months, there was no recurrence of symptoms, and follow-up inquiry 2 years later revealed that the patient felt quite well.

The second patient was admitted to the hospital twice during a 4-month period, because of fever in the range of 101–102°F. Her symptoms had begun following a tooth extraction. In addition to the fever she complained of mild joint pains. Because of that the tentative clinical diagnosis for a time was rheumatoid arthritis. She also had some headache, as well as vague pains in the mastoid and parotid regions. Her leukocyte count was 9,000–11,000, with 2–4% eosinophils. Three months after the onset of fever she experienced sudden impairment of vision; visual field studies revealed bilateral right inferior quadrantic defects. This raised the possibility of cranial arteritis, although palpable abnormality of the temporal and occipital vessels could not be found, so a biopsy was not done. Her fever and other symptoms gradually subsided at the end of 6 months, and did not recur. The diagnosis in this case is based on clinical findings, course of illness, age of the patient, and especially on the sudden occurrence of visual defect in the distribution of the cerebral optic radiations.

This disease deserves special consideration in elderly patients with unexplained fever. Severe headache is an uncommon complaint in persons of this age period, and, when combined with fever, is probably a sign of serious disease. In view of the present evidence that prompt treatment with adrenal steroid hormones may reduce the incidence of visual impairment (64) early recognition becomes particularly desirable.

PERIODIC DISEASE

In 1947 and 1951 Reimann pointed out the possible interrelationship of a group of periodic disorders, characterized by such manifestations as fever, abdominalgia, arthralgia, neutropenia, purpura and edema (65, 66). He suggested that they be grouped under the term Periodic Disease, and described them thus: "of unknown origin, often begin in infancy, recur uniformly at predictable times for decades without affecting the general health and resist treatment." The regularity of the recurrences was stressed, and emphasis was placed on the point that the cycles were frequently 7 days in length, or in multiples of seven, as 14, 21, 28 and 56 days. He mentioned that "seven always has had a special significance and looms large in folklore," and, in discussing possible etiology, remarked that "some cosmic association may be suspected."

It seems to us that Reimann performed a valuable service in directing the attention of American clinicians to this kind of periodically recurring disorder, and that his designation for it is satisfactory for the present. However, there seems to have been a peculiar reluctance to accept the concept, and this group of disorders receives little or no mention in our textbooks of medicine. A possible reason for this skepticism may be the emphasis placed on associations with the figure seven and cosmic influence. Actually, some of the cases quoted by Reimann had illnesses recurring at irregular intervals and the cycles were from 2 days to 6 months or even longer.

The cases in our series seem to resemble closely some of those described by Reimann. Our

5 patients were all males, ages 33, 33, 42, 53 and 54 years. Their episodes of febrile illness had been occurring for 10, 25, 23, 7 and 25 years. Two of them stated that parents or siblings were subject to similar episodes. The intervals between attacks were 7–9 days in one, 3–4 weeks in another, and 2 or 3 times a year in the other three. All were in good general health between episodes and able to hold responsible positions; however, all found it necessary to go to bed during attacks. The duration of the episodes varied from 1–2 days to several weeks. The chief complaints were sudden onset of malaise and fever, with temperatures reaching 101° to 105°F. Joint pains and skin manifestations were denied, but 3 of them stated that abdominal pain was sometimes present. Three had moderate leukocytosis during their attacks and splenomegaly was noted in 3. Otherwise, extensive studies in our hospital, as well as in other clinics, had not yielded findings of significance.

One of our patients is of special interest because he manifested some abnormalities which may have provided a clue to the pathogenesis of his disorder. The patient was a physician, aged 33, who had had bouts of fever since the age of 8. During investigation of his illness at another hospital it was noted that he gave a history of salt-craving and hyperpigmentation, and this had led to studies of his adrenal cortical function. These revealed a fall in eosinophils but no rise in 17-ketosteroids following an infusion of ACTH. He was also found to have increased excretion of pregnanetriol in the urine. The possible existence of a mild form of adrenogenital syndrome had therefore been suggested. During the course of his study in our hospital, Dr. Philip Bondy was consulted regarding the disordered adrenal function. Dr. Bondy then suggested that the entire clinical picture could conceivably be due to an abnormal metabolism of steroid hormones, citing the finding of Kappas et al. (67) that etiocholanolone is capable of inducing fever and malaise in man. Subsequent tests of our patient did in fact reveal the presence of abnormal quantities of unconjugated etiocholanolone in the blood during febrile periods, whereas this steroid was absent when he was free of symptoms. Dr. Bondy and his associates carried out similar observations on one of the other 4 patients with periodic disease, and he too showed this abnormality of steroid metabolism (68). Much more work will be needed to assess the significance of these findings, particularly on the question of whether unconjugated etiocholanolone may be found in the blood during other kinds of febrile disease.

Another entity, which closely resembles periodic disease, and, doubtless has been confused with it, has recently been characterized by Heller et al (69), who have suggested the name Familial Mediterranean Fever. They describe 74 cases personally observed in Israel, together with 179 cases culled from previous reports in the medical literature, some of which had been labelled periodic disease. Familial Mediterranean Fever has so far been recognized almost exclusively among Jews and Armenians, and there is a tendency for more than one case to occur in a family. Symptoms usually begin before the age of 10 years, and consist of bouts of fever with pain in abdomen, chest or joints, and, in some cases, erysipelas-like lesions on the extremities. Some patients show evidence of renal dysfunction, probably because of amyloidosis.

It is possible that one or more of the cases we have labelled periodic disease is actually an example of Familial Mediterranean Fever. Our records do not contain adequate information regarding ethnic background to assist in classifying them in retrospect. At any rate, the lead about possible role of etiocholanolone in periodic diseases and the genetic aspects of Familial Mediterranean Fever tend to implicate metabolic disorders in the etiology of both kinds of febrile disease.

Recently Priest and Nixon (70) have reviewed reports on these periodic illnesses, and suggested that a new name be applied to them: familial recurring polyserositis. It is obvious that the confusion will not be resolved until we have clearer concepts regarding pathogenesis.

MISCELLANEOUS DISEASES

Weber-Christian disease. The patient was a 66-year-old physician who had fever for 3 weeks before entry. At the onset of his illness he had had fairly typical erythema nodosum. When seen in our hospital he showed edema of the legs and feet, and enlargement of the spleen. As the edema receded, subcutaneous nodules were found to be present on the extensor surfaces of the legs. Biopsy of one of these revealed panniculitis and arteritis compatible with the histologic picture of Weber-Christian disease. There was considerable improvement in the fever and cutaneous lesions when ACTH was given. In contrast to other cases in this series in which there were atypical symptoms of relatively common diseases, this patient suffered from a relatively straightforward, but rare entity. Fever, tender nodules on the extremities, erythema nodosum and anemia have all been found in other cases of Weber-Christian disease (71). Our failure to consider that possibility accounted for the delay in diagnosis.

Thyroiditis. A 53-year-old woman noted afternoon temperature elevation to 103°F 8 weeks before admission. Two weeks after onset of fever she began to have pain in the jaw and neck. Several teeth were extracted, but without improvement, and the patient was admitted to the hospital for further study. Physical examination revealed slight enlargement of the thyroid, which was barely tender. The temperature ranged between 100 and 102.4 in the hospital. The diagnosis was established by the laboratory findings typical of thyroiditis—I^{131} uptake of 7.5 per cent, butyl extractable iodine of 7.8 mcg. per cent and serum precipitable iodine of 11.0 mcg. per cent. Tests for other causes for fever were unproductive. There was a salutory response to prednisone therapy.

Fever is commonly present in the syndrome of subacute thyroiditis, and its duration may be long. In a series of cases from the Presbyterian Hospital, New York (72), fever was present for 3–8 weeks. Thirty-three of 38 patients reported by Crile had fever, which was present for weeks and even months (73). Usually, of course, swelling and tenderness of the thyroid gland makes the diagnosis simple but the peculiar radiation of the pain to the back of the neck, jaw and throat has in some instances led to the incorrect diagnosis of meningitis, impacted wisdom teeth and tonsillitis. It is of interest that several of Crile's patients underwent dental extractions, as did our patient.

The most definitive method of making the diagnosis of thyroiditis is, of course, biopsy. Studies of thyroid function, which characteristically demonstrate depression of I^{131} uptake and usually elevation of blood iodine levels, and demonstration of antibodies against thyroglobulin, may be helpful.

Rupture of the spleen and pancreatitis. A 35-year-old man had a brief episode of fever, chills and malaise 3 months before admission. Two months later he developed fever, rigors, malaise and upper abdominal pain. On admission to the hospital physical examination showed only the signs of a small left pleural effusion. He was anemic and the leukocyte count was 16,900. Blood sugar, serum amylase and electrolytes, liver function tests, sputum studies for tubercle bacilli, bronchoscopy and bronchography were normal.

Although the source of his difficulty was first thought to be in the thorax, a retroperitoneal mass was later demonstrated by radiologic studies. Exploratory laparotomy disclosed the presence of a ruptured spleen with intracapsular hematomata and necrotizing pancreatitis involving the tail of the pancreas. Removal of the spleen and parts of the pancreas resulted in complete recovery.

It is interesting to speculate upon the course of events in this case. Rupture of the spleen may have occurred spontaneously at the time of fever and malaise 3 months before. Although spontaneous rupture usually involves diseased spleens notably in patients with leukemia, malaria or infectious mononucleosis, it may also be seen in previously healthy organs following minor trauma. The usual symptoms of splenic rupture are left upper quadrant pain and collapse, but fever may be the dominant sign (74). Perhaps our patient had infectious mononucleosis at the onset of his illness.

Pancreatitis has not, to our knowledge, been reported following rupture of the spleen, but certainly occurs after splenectomy, particularly when there is difficulty in dissecting the spleen from the tail of the pancreas.

Pancreatitis may have antedated splenic hemorrhage here, presumably due to erosion of a vessel by liberation of pancreatic enzymes. Such a course of events has been reported (75). It seems worth while to emphasize that pleural effusion is frequently a clue to disease below the diaphragm as well as above it, and is a common finding in acute pancreatitis (76). Consideration of this association might have led to earlier correct diagnosis in our patient.

Myelofibrosis. A 62-year-old man had fever, chills, drenching sweats and myalgia for 9 months. Treatment with various antimicrobial drugs had been without effect. On examination he was found to have ulcerations and petechiae of the oral mucosa and enlargement of the liver and spleen. Pertinent laboratory data were hemoglobin of 8.1 Gm. per cent, leukocyte count of 16,100, with a shift to the left, and 13 nucleated red blood cells per 100 leukocytes on the peripheral smear. Reticulocyte count was 4.2 per cent and platelet count 60,000. Liver biopsy showed extramedullary hematopoiesis. Two bone marrow aspirations were unsuccessful but a bone marrow biopsy revealed fibrosis. Extensive search for evidence of other febrile diseases, especially tuberculosis, gave negative results. The temperature, which had reached 105°F. nightly, fell to normal following administration of aspirin, and remained within the normal range while he received 10 mg. prednisone per day.

Fever must be a rare occurrence in myelofibrosis and is not mentioned as a sign in 2 recent reviews (77, 78). Its presence in a patient with myelofibrosis should strongly suggest the diagnosis of tuberculosis in addition to the hematologic disorder. One review which compares myelofibrosis with and without tuberculosis states categorically that pyrexia is the single most important sign which distinguishes myelofibrosis with tuberculosis from idiopathic fibrosis of the marrow (79).

There are a number of reasons for thinking that our patient did not have tuberculosis in addition to myelofibrosis. The course was too protracted; the clinical status of patients with tuberculosis and myelofibrosis has generally deteriorated rapidly. The tuberculin test was negative, and culture of the bone marrow did not yield acid-fast bacilli. His fever did not subside when streptomycin was given, and no granulomata were found when the spleen was removed 6 months after admission. He expired a year later at another hospital.

FACTITIOUS FEVER

Determination of the body temperature is so firmly incorporated in all clinical practice that the reliability of results is seldom questioned. Yet it is possible for patients to feign illness by falsifying their temperatures. Such was the case in 3 of the patients in this series, who masqueraded as diagnostic problems for long periods of time. Their case records, along with those of

11 others, have been reported in detail elsewhere (80).

The first patient, a 23-year-old woman, complained of fever and abdominal pain for several weeks following uterine curettage for spontaneous incomplete abortion. She was treated with penicillin, streptomycin, chloramphenicol, erythromycin and sulfonamides, but continued to be "febrile." Finally exploratory laparotomy was undertaken, but no abnormality could be found. Following operation the fever disappeared, and the patient later boasted to her room-mate that she had been deliberately shaking the thermometer in the wrong direction. As is true of most patients with factitious fever she had other evidences of abnormal behavior. The difficulty in recognizing the problem here lay in the fact that there was a plausible cause for illness.

The second patient was an 18-year-old student nurse who was seen in consultation at another hospital, because of intermittent fever of several weeks' duration. Inspection of the temperature chart revealed a discrepancy between the temperature fluctuations and the graphic record of her pulse; furthermore her general appearance was surprisingly good when considered in relation to a prolonged febrile illness. When confronted with the possibility that she might be falsifying the temperature readings, her "fever" terminated abruptly. The motives for this behavior and the exact means by which it was accomplished were not established. This patient provides an example of several common findings in factitious fever. She was a student nurse; in our experience nurses and others familiar with hospital routine are likely to be successful in this form of deception. She did not have tachycardia despite abrupt spikes in temperature. Other clues of this nature are failure of the temperature to follow the normal diurnal gradient, rapid defervescence unaccompanied by diaphoresis, and fever of 106°F or higher, a rare phenomenon in adults (81).

The most spectacular case of factitious fever was presented by a 38-year-old man, weighing 325 pounds, who complained of "black-out" spells. The history was bizarre and characterized by episodes of unconsciousness during one of which he was "pronounced dead." In addition, he had peripheral vascular disease which had required lumbar sympathectomy and a left mid-thigh amputation. Despite this there was no evidence of vascular disease elsewhere, and

except for the amputation and sharply demarcated left hemi-anesthesia the findings on physical examination were normal. Numerous laboratory studies failed to reveal significant abnormality. In the hospital he had several sharp rises in temperature. Malingering was suspected when the temperature dropped from 106.6°F to 99.6°F in less than 4 hours without concomitant sweating or change in heart rate. Thereafter, with a nurse in constant attendance during temperature determinations his fever disappeared. He left the hospital against medical advice, but subsequent letters from other hospitals confirmed the diagnosis of factitious fever. Aside from the dissociation between pulse and temperature, this patient's fever was only one aspect of a factitious symptom complex.

Factitious fever must be differentiated from habitual hyperthermia—sometimes called psychogenic or hysterical fever (3). This disorder is most likely to occur in young women with overt neurotic traits in whom body temperature elevations to the neighborhood of 100°F occur frequently, even daily, for months or years. Habitual hyperthermia is probably a manifestation of vasomotor instability, much like labile hypertension or dermographia.

The diagnosis of fraudulent fever is not difficult if the possibility is considered. Attendance of a nurse at the time the temperature is recorded may solve the riddle. In some instances simultaneous oral and rectal temperatures will disclose a disparity. Finally, a thorough search of the patient's belongings for a cache of pre-set thermometers or a supply of vaccines, toxins, and syringes and needles may provide the answer. The prolonged courses of these "fevers" with intensive diagnostic study in many institutions, however, is proof that many of the patients avoid apprehension for long periods of time.

PATIENTS IN WHOM NO DEFINITIVE DIAGNOSIS
COULD BE ESTABLISHED

Despite vigorous efforts, no diagnosis was established in 7 patients. Six of these, in all of whom the duration of illness was less than 2 months, made apparently complete recoveries. None developed significant anemia, weight loss or cachexia. In short, these illnesses resembled acute self-limited infections rather than prolonged, chronic disease.

The first patient, a 52-year-old woman, was

thought at first to have multiple myeloma and an infection. Confusing features in her case were moderate hyperglobulinemia and an elevation in the titer of cold agglutinins. Usually cold agglutinins are elevated only in primary atyical pneumonia but high titers have also been noted in mumps, hemolytic anemia, various liver diseases and some peripheral vascular disorders. In retrospect, the course of this illness is most compatible with a low-grade infection which subsided spontaneously.

The second patient presented a confusing problem characterized primarily by fever. Unexplained were leukocytosis, a slight rise in the titer of brucella agglutinins and the finding of "mild colitis" by x-ray. Fever receded following a course of tetracycline and streptomycin and 2 years later the patient felt well. Although the therapeutic response favors the diagnosis of brucellosis, the rise in agglutinin titer was not in the significant range. Furthermore, one might have expected spontaneous defervescence in less than 7 weeks in brucellosis. Salmonella enteritis has to be considered because of the radiologic findings and therapeutic response. However, leukocytosis is unusual in salmonellosis in the absence of metastatic abscesses. Another possibility is amebiasis, which can cause prolonged fever of obscure origin (82).

An even more convincing case can be made for amebiasis in the next patient whose illness was preceded by diarrhea and who had a persistent low-grade eosinophilia. More intensive examination of the feces for parasites might have led to the diagnosis. Therapeutic trial with antiamebic drugs is less popular now than formerly, but doubtless is justifiable in instances such as these.

Disseminated lupus erythematosus was the tentative diagnoisis at the time of admission of the 4th patient. The laboratory findings and subsequent course did not substantiate this and instead seemed to point more toward the category of "atypical infectious mononucleosis." The clinical findings were compatible, but the characteristic hematologic abnormalities and rise in heterophile agglutinin titer were lacking. Seronegative "infectious mononucleosis" has been described in a number of reports, and, in general, is said to be milder, associated with less pyrexia, a higher incidence of cutaneous eruptions and fewer abnormal lymphocytes, than the classical heterophile-positive form of the dis-

ease (83). Toxoplasmosis is also capable of producing this clinical picture in adults (84). Tests for this disease were not carried out in our patient.

The illness of the fifth patient was characterized by seven weeks of fever and recurrent bouts of abdominal pain. In retrospect, this may have been an infection by one of the Coxsackie viruses. While Bornholm disease, or epidemic pleurodynia is perhaps the prototype of infection with this virus, atypical forms presenting mainly with abdominal pain and fever have been described.

In the sixth patient in this group we probably have an example of two well known diseases occurring in sequence and causing relatively prolonged fever. The patient was first seen because of cough and chest pain and showed electrocardiographic evidence of an acute myocardial infarction. He subsequently developed hematuria, proteinuria, and excreted red blood cell casts. The clinical manifestations improved upon administration of steroid hormones. For a time he was thought to be suffering from periarteritis nodosa, but that diagnosis could not be substantiated by histologic methods, and he made an apparently complete recovery. We now feel that the best explanation for this course of events is that the patient had a myocardial infarction associated with considerable pericarditis, and that this was followed by infarction of the kidneys giving rise to transient hematuria and azotemia.

The last patient may have had thrombotic thrombocytopenic purpura. This syndrome (85, 86) consists of the triad of bizarre central nervous system manifestations, hemolytic anemia, and thrombocytopenia with hemorrhagic manifestations. Our patient had been under treatment for tuberculosis for several years when these symptoms made their appearance. In an effort to control his bleeding tendency splenectomy was performed but he succumbed shortly afterward, and permission for autopsy could not be obtained.

DIAGNOSIS IN FEVER OF UNKNOWN ORIGIN

The means by which the diagnosis was finally achieved in 93 patients is summarized in Table III. In several instances two procedures carried out at about the same time provided helpful information; for that reason the total in the table is 106. As mentioned in the previous sec-

24   ROBERT G. PETERSDORF AND PAUL B. BEESON

TABLE III

Method of Diagnosis in 93 Cases of Fever of Obscure Etiology

Diagnosis	Number of cases	Biopsy	Laparotomy	Bacteriology	Serology	Other	X-ray	Clinical course	Response to Treatment	Autopsy
Infections										
Tuberculosis	11	4	1	4					4	1
Pyogenic	15		8	4			2		1	3
Bacterial endocarditis	5			3				1		1
Other	5	1		1	4	1				
Neoplastic diseases										
Disseminated carcinoma	7	6	1				1			
Localized carcinoma	2		2				1			
Lymphoma	8	5	1							2
No histologic diagnosis	2						1			
Collagen										
Rheumatic fever	6							6	2	
Lupus erythematosus	5				2			3		
Unclassified	2							2		
Cranial arteritis	2	1						1		
Factitious fever	3							3		
Periodic disease	5							5		
Pulmonary emboli	3							1	1	2
Non-specific pericarditis	2							2		
Sarcoidosis	2	1	1							
Hypersensitivity	4	3							1	
Miscellaneous	4	2	1			1		1		
Total	93	23	15	12	6	2	5	25	9	9

tion, no diagnosis could be made in 7 cases, and they will not be considered further here.

The cause of fever was not apparent until autopsy in 9 instances—this included 2 cases of monocytic leukemia, 1 miliary tuberculosis, 1 liver abscess, 1 subphrenic abscess, 1 ascending cholangitis, 1 abacteremic bacterial endocarditis and 2 with multiple pulmonary emboli. The fact that some of these were potentially curable diseases will be discussed in the section on Prognosis.

Histologic examination of tissue and exploratory surgery stand out as diagnostic procedures of special value in this kind of clinical problem, since in 23 instances the diagnosis was made by needle or excisional biopsy, and in 16 cases laparotomy or thoracotomy provided the needed information. When the atypical nature of most of the cases in this series is taken into consideration, the high yield of positive information by examination of tissue seems impressive. As might be predicted most of the disorders identified by

biopsy were neoplastic disease or tuberculosis. Other diagnoses made by biopsy were cranial arteritis, sarcoid, granulomatous hepatitis, Weber-Christian disease and myelofibrosis.

It seems worth while to give detailed consideration here to biopsy as a diagnostic technique in this type of clinical problem. As is summarized in Table IV, one or more biopsies were performed in 58 of our patients, and in 23 of them this was the means of diagnosis. However in only 15 was the first attempt productive. Furthermore, there were 8 cases in which one or more excisional or needle biopsies were negative, yet a diagnosis could be made from tissue obtained at laparotomy. Exploratory laparotomy failed to provide the diagnosis in 2 patients, who were later found to have monocytic leukemia and systemic lupus erythematosus.

Of 95 biopsy specimens examined, 65, from 35 patients, were not helpful. Many of the uninformative biopsies were from patients with

TABLE IV
Value of Biopsy in Different Disease Categories

	Neoplastic diseases				Infections				Collagen diseases			Miscellaneous diseases								No diag. made	Total
	Disseminated carcinoma	Localized carcinoma	Lymphomas and leukemias	Presumed	Tuberculosis	Pyogenic	Bacterial endocarditis	Other	Rheumatic fever	Lupus erythematosus	Unclassified	Cranial arteritis	Factitious fever	Periodic disease	Pulmonary emboli	Non-specific pericarditis	Sarcoidosis	Hypersensitivity	Other		
Number of cases	7	2	8	2	11	15	5	5	6	5	2	2	3	5	3	2	2	4	4	7	100
Cases in which biopsy used	7	2	7	1	7	7	1	2	0	4	2	1	0	2	2	2	2	3	2	4	58
Biopsy diagnostic	6	0	5	0	4	0	0	1	0	0	0	1	0	0	0	0	1	3	2	0	23
Biopsy not diagnostic	1	2	2	1	3	7	1	1	0	4	2	0	0	2	2	2	1	0	0	4	35
Initial biopsy not diagnostic; subsequent biopsies diagnostic	3	0	2	0	0	0	0	0	0	0	0	0	0	0	0	0	0	1	2	0	8
Biopsy not diagnostic; laparotomy diagnostic	1	2	0	0	1	3	0	0	0	0	0	0	0	0	0	0	1	0	0	0	8

bacterial infections. In the case of liver tissue these showed only ascending cholangitis or nonspecific inflammatory changes. Other diseases in which biopsy was not helpful included the collagen groups, nonspecific pericarditis, and periodic disease. Almost one half of our biopsies were from the liver. This procedure is employed comparatively frequently in our hospital, not only when primary liver disease is believed present, but also because we regard liver tissue as likely to reveal the presence of generalized processes such as tuberculosis, sarcoid or lymphoma. Disease was detected by this method in patients without hepatomegaly and with normal liver function tests.

Biopsy of skin or muscle was helpful twice, but in both instances the patients had palpable and visible lesions. With regard to lymph node biopsy, our experience is in line with the general impression that any palpable node in the neck or axilla may provide diagnostic information, especially when tuberculosis or neoplastic disease are under consideration. We usually resist the temptation to carry out biopsy of palpable inguinal nodes, because they are so likely to show only 'nonspecific inflammatory change.' Bone marrow aspiration was of little help in this series of cases, but trephine biopsy did provide the diagnosis in 2 of the 4 cases in which it

was done; in both of those x-ray had already disclosed the presence of some kind of bone disease. Renal biopsy was carried out twice and did not yield the correct answer in either instance.

Bacteriologic studies provided the diagnosis in 12 cases in the series. In 4 of them *M. tuberculosis* was demonstrated, and in 7 others the causative organism was eventually demonstrated in blood culture. Lastly, Gram-stain of synovial fluid revealed Neisseria in 1 case. Serologic tests were helpful in the diagnosis of brucellosis, psittacosis and gonorrhea.

Although x-rays were credited with being responsible for arriving at the correct diagnosis in only 5 cases, they provided valuable hints in a number of others. In patients with unexplained fever, radiographic study of the chest and intravenous pyelography should be among the first procedures to be done. Studies of the gastrointestinal and biliary tract are then indicated, and later a bone survey must receive consideration. Although none of these procedures stands out as being of particular value in the present series of cases it must be kept in mind that radiologic diagnostic tests were successful in hundreds of instances during the time period of this study. The cases under consideration qualify for inclusion only because conventional diagnostic tests were not helpful.

The diagnosis of a number of diseases, particularly acute rheumatic fever, which may present in bizarre fashion in adults, and other collagen diseases, can only be made on clinical grounds, sometimes only after prolonged observation. The same applies to the diagnosis of recurrent pulmonary emboli, nonspecific pericarditis, and periodic disease. Recognition of factitious fever requires only that the clinician keep this possibility in mind.

Therapeutic trials are warranted under certain conditions, and may occasionally be of great value. In our group these included the use of isonicotinic acid hydrazine in tuberculosis, aspirin in rheumatic fever, heparin in thromboembolic disease and the withdrawal of drugs suspected of causing drug fever. Occasionally prompt response to bacterial infections such as brucellosis, tularemia or even pyelonephritis due to Gram-negative pathogens may be the principal means of diagnosis; usually, however, it is only confirmatory.

PROGNOSIS IN FEVER OF UNKNOWN ORIGIN

Of the 100 patients in the series, 32 succumbed to the disease responsible for fever. This included 17 of 19 patients with tumors, 5 with infections, 5 with collagen disease, 2 with pulmonary emboli, and 1 each with Weber-Christian disease, myelofibrosis, and suspected thrombotic thrombocytopenic purpura. Twenty of our patients, including 6 in whom no diagnosis could be established, recovered without specific therapy. In 10 there has been progress of disease or failure to improve; half of these are the patients with periodic disease, the remainder had collagen disease, Hodgkin's disease and sarcoid. Attention should be focused on the largest group, comprising 38 patients, who were eventually helped by specific medical and surgical therapy. Twenty-nine of these had infections, and 20, including 8 with tuberculosis, recovered following the use of proper chemotherapeutic agents. Nine patients required surgery in addition to antimicrobial therapy; all had abscesses in the abdominal cavity, pelvis, kidneys, gallbladder or liver. Aspirin and adrenocorticoids were of value in the collagen diseases, and steroids also induced remissions in cranial arteritis and nonspecific pericarditis. Therapy with anti-

coagulants resulted in disappearance of fever in one patient. The efficacy of specific therapy in these patients convinces us that the clinician should feel obliged to make unremitting effort to establish an etiologic dagnosis in a patient with prolonged unexplained fever.

Of special, indeed tragic, significance is the fact that 7 of the 9 patients in whom the correct diagnosis was made only at autopsy had diseases for which there is effective treatment.

CONCLUDING REMARKS

The Changing Spectrum of F.U.O.

It seems worth while to compare briefly this analysis with some others in the medical literature. Since 1930 several groups of patients with fever of unknown origin have been described, notably those of Alt and Baker (87), Kintner and Rowntree (88), Hamman and Wainwright (2), Keefer (89), Bottiger (90) and Geraci et al. (91). Comparison of reports such as these is difficult because the criteria employed for selection of patients have differed considerably. For example, more than half of Alt and Baker's 101 patients were febrile for less than three weeks, which would disqualify them from our study. In 90 of Bottiger's 158 cases the diagnosis had been made, or the symptoms had subsided within 10 days. It is reasonable to assume that the majority of his patients had self-limited viral infections. Inclusion of patients with prolonged low-grade fever, between 99° and 101°F, in some series skews the distribution toward habitual hyperthermia and nearly 50 per cent of those in Kintner and Rowntree's series fitted into this diagnostic category. The present report is the only one which was planned in advance as a prospective study. The others depended to some extent on review of charts in which the diagnosis at the time of discharge from hospital was unexplained fever.

Despite these obvious limitations certain trends, summarized in Table V, are apparent. There has been a lessening of pyogenic infection, particularly the varieties caused by Gram-positive cocci. On the other hand, infections with Gram-negative enteric pathogens appear to be increasing, perhaps as a consequence of antibiotic therapy (92). The continued importance of tuberculosis as a cause of prolonged pyrexia is noteworthy and bears out the contention that the prevalence of this disease has not changed greatly, despite lowering of the morbidity and mortality (93). The relatively low incidence of tuberculosis in the series of Geraci *et al.* may be due to the fact that their material was limited to cases of tuberculous peritonitis discovered at laparotomy, while all other studies included tuberculosis of lung, lymph nodes and liver. Cases of fever due to neoplastic disease constitute a relatively constant part of all series. The same can be said for the collagen diseases, in spite of the present great interest in them.

Some Tentative Conclusions

A point deserving emphasis is that most patients with F.U.O. are not suffering from unusual diseases; instead they exhibit atypical manifestations of common illnesses— tuberculosis, sepsis, cancer, blood dyscrasias, pulmonary emboli, rheumatic fever, etc. Furthermore, in the present series of cases delay in diagnosis occasionally resulted because we did not make proper use of available information. Examples of this were our failure to think of brucellosis in an abattoir worker, or of malaria in a man who had visited Panama, or to give sufficient weight to the complaint of dysphagia in a young man who had esophageal carcinoma.

The most important lesson we have learned from this study is that, in many instances, attempts to obtain tissue for diagnosis were instituted too late. Many of our patients remained ill for long periods of time, undergoing numerous radiographic examinations and therapeutic trials, while lymph node or liver biopsy was not even under consideration. Procrastination in obtaining tissue for diagnosis is particularly blameworthy when there are palpably enlarged organs and masses. Sutton's Law* needs to be kept in mind by the diagnostician.

A possible exception to the principle of Sutton's Law is found in the procedure of needle

---

* We are indebted to Dr. William Dock for the term Sutton's Law. It recommends proceeding immediately to the diagnostic test most likely to provide a diagnosis, and deplores the tendency to carry out a battery of "routine" examinations in conventional sequence. The derivation of the term is as follows: When Willie Sutton, a hold-up man, was being interviewed by newsmen he was asked why he always robbed banks. Sutton, with some surprise, replied, "Why, that's where the money is."

TABLE V

Diagnostic Categories in Various Case Series

Authors	Hamman, Wainwright	Keefer	Bottiger	Geraci *et al*	Petersdorf, Beeson
Year	1936	1939	1953	1959	1960
Number of cases	54	75	34	70	100
Percentage of:					
Infections	59	65	46	24	36
Tuberculosis	17	11	17	7	11
Pyogenic	20	49	20	13	22
Other	22	5	9	4	3
Neoplastic diseases	23	20	30	30	19
Carcinoma	15	13	24	16	11
Lymphoma	7	7	6	14	8
Collagen disorders	0	11	12	8	15
Miscellaneous	0	4	12	24	23
No diagnosis made	19	0*	0*	14	7

* Not included in analysis

biopsy of the liver. Liver tissue is likely to reflect the presence of many systemic diseases, and biopsy was of great value to us in the diagnosis of neoplasms, tuberculosis, sarcoidosis and granulomatous hepatitis, even when the liver was not enlarged and function tests were normal.

When facilities for liver biopsy are not available, laparotomy and open biopsy should be given serious consideration. Geraci *et al.* (91) described 70 patients with F.U.O., only 30 of whom had signs or symptoms referable to the abdomen, who were subjected to laparotomy. In 80 per cent of these abdominal exploration provided the diagnosis. While needle biopsy of the liver might have sufficed in many of their cases, several instances of localized abscess, retroperitoneal tumor and tuberculous peritonitis would have been missed. The importance of laparotomy to establish the diagnosis of tuberculous peritonitis has been emphasized by Bennett (94).

We believe that laparotomy should be performed in most jaundiced patients with long-continued high fever of uncertain origin. All of our patients in that category had intra-abdominal or liver abscesses, or obstructive disease of the biliary tract; nevertheless liver biopsy showed only mild cholangitis. Under these circumstances exploratory laparotomy not only led to correct diagnosis, but sometimes also to a curative procedure. The problem is particularly

28   ROBERT G. PETERSDORF AND PAUL B. BEESON

difficult in patients with cirrhosis. Tisdale has recently reviewed 150 cases of Laennec's cirrhosis and found that more than half of these exhibited fever at some time (95). In about 70 per cent of instances the elevation in temperature could be attributed to the cirrhotic process, but among the remainder were several who required surgical treatment.

At the present time it is difficult to refrain from treating the patient with F.U.O. with various antibiotics in the hope that he may have bacterial endocarditis, brucellosis, pyelonephritis, cryptic sepsis, tuberculosis, and the like. At least 90 per cent of our patients had received one or more courses of antimicrobials. This sometimes led to confusion by transient suppression of signs and symptoms, or the appearance of drug fever. We do not mean to imply that therapeutic trials do not have a place in the management of such cases; on the contrary, judicious use of aspirin in rheumatic fever, specific chemotherapeutics such as chloroquine, emetine, penicillin, isoniazid and arsenic, and occasionally even cortisone, heparin or nitrogen mustards may be of value in diagnosis and treatment. However, we believe that in most cases therapeutic trials should be postponed until rational methods of diagnosis have been tried.

No patient with prolonged pyrexia should be subjected to a "routine" battery of laboratory tests, x-rays and biopsies. Each must be evaluated individually. We believe, however, that the quest should be a vigorous one, since in many instances the patient can be helped. In our group of cases nearly two-thirds of the patients recovered or improved, or could be helped to "live with" their disease, because positive diagnosis had provided more accurate knowledge of the future course.

REFERENCES

1. WUNDERLICH, C. A.: On the temperature in diseases. London, New Sydenham Society, 1871.
2. HAMMAN, L. AND WAINWRIGHT, C. W.: Diagnosis of obscure fever. Bull. Johns Hopkins Hosp. **58**: 109 and 307, 1936.
3. REIMANN, H. A.: Habitual hyperthermia. J. Amer. Med. Assn. **99**: 1860, 1932.
4. CHAPMAN, C. B. AND WHORTON, C. M.: Acute generalized miliary tuberculosis in adults. New Eng. J. Med. **235**: 239, 1946.
5. SAPHIR, O.: Changes in the liver and in the pancreas in chronic pulmonary tuberculosis. Arch. Path. **7**: 1026, 1929.
6. TERRY, R. B. AND GUNNAR, R. M.: Primary miliary tuberculosis of the liver. J. Amer. Med. Assn. **164**: 150, 1957.
7. HARVEY, A. M. AND WHITEHILL, M. R.: Tuberculous pericarditis. Medicine **16**: 45, 1937.
8. SANFORD, J. P. AND FAVOUR, C. B.: The interrelationships between Addison's disease and active tuberculosis; a review of 125 cases of Addison's disease. Ann. Int. Med. **45**: 56, 1956.
9. FISHER, H. C. AND WHITE, H. M., JR.: Biliary tract disease in the aged. Arch. Surg. **63**: 536, 1951.
10. MACGREGOR, G. A.: Murmurless bacterial endocarditis. Brit. Med. J. **1**: 1011, 1956.
11. SIMEONE, F. A.: Perinephric abscess. Arch. Surg. **45**: 424, 1942.
12. SCHREINER, G. E.: The clinical and histologic spectrum of pyelonephritis. Arch. Int. Med. **102**: 32, 1958.
13. SPINK, W. W., HOFFBAUER, F. W., WALKER, W. W. AND GREEN, R. A.: Histopathology of the liver in human brucellosis. J. Lab. and Clin. Med. **34**: 40, 1949.
14. WHIPPLE, R. L. AND HARRIS, J. F.: B. coli septicemia in Laennec's cirrhosis of the liver. Ann. Int. Med. **33**: 462, 1950.
15. MARTIN, W. J., SPITTEL, J. A., MORLOCK, C. G. AND BAGGENSTOSS, A. H.: Severe liver disease complicated by bacteremia due to Gramnegative bacilli. Arch. Int. Med. **98**: 8, 1956.
16. CAROLI, J. AND PLATTEBORSE, R.: Septicémie porto-cave. Cirrhoses du foie et septicémie a colibacille. Sem. hôp. Paris **34**: 472, 1958.
17. HORDER, T. AND GOW, A. E.: Psittacosis; record of 9 cases with special reference to morbid anatomy in 2 of them. Lancet **1**: 442, 1930.
18. SEIBERT, R. H., JORDAN, W. S. JR. AND DINGLE, J. H.: Clinical variations in the diagnosis of psittacosis. New Eng. J. Med. **254**: 925, 1956.
19. BRIGGS, L. H.: The occurrence of fever in malignant disease. Am. J. Med. Sci. **166**: 846, 1923.
20. ABRAMS, H. L., SPIRO, R. AND GOLDSTEIN, N.: Metastases in carcinoma. Analysis of 1000 autopsied cases. Cancer **3**: 74, 1950.
21. WINTROBE, M. M.: Clinical Hematology. 4th Edition, Lea and Febiger, Philadelphia, 1956, pp. 248–250.
22. ISAACSON, N. H. AND RAPAPORT, P.: Eosinophilia in malignant tumors: its significance. Ann. Int. Med. **25**: 893, 1946.
23. BELL, E. T.: Carcinoma of the pancreas. I. A clinical and pathologic study of 609 necropsied cases. Am. J. Path. **33**: 499, 1957.
24. CLIFFTON, E. E.: Carcinoma of the pancreas. Am. J. Med. **21**: 760, 1956.

25. BERLIN, D. A. AND PORTER, W. B.: Fever: a common symptom of carcinoma of the stomach. Virginia Med. Monthly **77**: 59, 1950.

26. HARTMANN, H.: Intermittierende, Malaria ähnliche Fieberparoxysmen bei Magenkarzinomen. Deutsche Klin. Wchnschr. **75**: 1153, 1955.

27. SHEDD, D. P., CROWLEY, L. G. AND LINDSKOG, G. E.: A 10 year study of carcinoma of the esophagus. Surg., Gynec. and Obs. **101**: 55, 1955.

28. MERENDINO, D. A. AND MARK, V. H.: Analysis of 100 cases of squamous-cell carcinoma of esophagus; with special reference to delay periods and delay factors in diagnosis and therapy, contrasting state and city and county institutions. Cancer **5**: 52, 1952.

29. WILLIS, R. A.: In Pathology of Tumors, 2nd Ed. C. V. Mosby Co., St. Louis, Mo., pp. 911–913.

30. STEINER, P. E.: Multiple diffuse fibrosarcoma of bone. Am. J. Path. **20**: 877, 1944.

31. AISNER, M. AND HOXIE, T. B.: Bone and joint pain in leukemia, simulating acute rheumatic fever and subacute bacterial endocarditis. New Eng. J. Med. **238**: 733, 1948.

32. BERGER, L. AND SINKOFF, M. W.: Systemic manifestations of hypernephroma: a review of 273 cases. Am. J. Med. **22**: 781, 1957.

33. GREENBURG, D.: Obscure fever caused by carcinoma of the kidney; a possible explanation for difficulties in diagnosis. Arch. Int. Med. **90**: 395, 1952.

34. PLIMPTON, C. A. AND GELLHORN, A.: Hypercalcemia in malignant disease without evidence of bone destruction. Amer. J. Med. **21**: 750, 1956.

35. HEMPSTEAD, R. H. AND PRIESTLY, J. T.: Fever as a predominant symptom of hypernephroma: report of two cases. Proc. Staff Meet. Mayo Clin. **27**: 67, 1952.

36. BLOOMER, W. E. AND LINDSKOG, G. E.: Bronchogenic carcinoma. A report comparing three consecutive series of 100 cases each. Cancer **4**: 1171, 1951.

37. MELICOW, M. M.: Primary tumors of the retroperitoneum. J. Internat. Coll. Surgeons, **19**: 401, 1953.

38. BOTTIGER, L. E.: Fever of unknown origin. II. A discussion around four typical cases. Acta med. scand. **154**: 215, 1956.

39. SINN, C. M. AND DICK, F. W.: Monocytic leukemia. Amer. J. Med. **20**: 588, 1956.

40. MEACHAM, G. C. AND WEISBERGER, A. S.: Early atypical manifestations of leukemia. Ann. Int. Med. **41**: 789, 1954.

41. SILVER, R. T., UTZ, J. P., FREI, E. III AND McCULLOUGH, N. B.: Fever, infection and host resistance in acute leukemia. Amer. J. Med. **24**: 25, 1958.

42. JONES, T. D.: The diagnosis of rheumatic fever. J. Amer. Med. Assn. **126**: 481, 1944.

43. FERRIS, E. B. JR. AND MYERS, W. K.: Initial attacks of rheumatic fever in patients over 60 years of age. Arch. Int. Med. **55**: 809, 1935.

44. GRIFONE, J. W. AND KITCHELL, J. R.: Active rheumatic heart disease in patients over sixty. J. Amer. Med. Assn. **154**: 1341, 1954.

45. HARVEY, A. McG., SHULMAN, L. E., TUMULTY, P. A., CONLEY, C. L. AND SCHOENRICH, E. H.: Systemic lupus erythematosus: review of the literature and clinical analysis of 138 cases. Med. **33**: 291, 1954.

46. SAGALL, L. E., BORNSTEIN, J. AND WOLFF, L.: Clinical syndrome in patients with pulmonary embolism. Arch. Int. Med. **76**: 234, 1945.

47. CHAPMAN, J. S.: Pulmonary infarction. So. Med. J. **45**: 597, 1952.

48. THOMAS, W. A., RANDALL, R. V., BLAND, E. F. AND CASTLEMAN, B.: Endocardial fibroblastosis: a factor in heart disease of obscure etiology. New Eng. J. Med. **251**: 327, 1954.

49. COHN, A. E. AND STEELE, N. J.: Unexplained fever in heart failure. J. Clin. Invest. **13**: 853, 1934.

50. PETERSDORF, R. G. AND MERCHANT, R. K.: A study of antibiotic prophylaxis in patients with acute heart failure. New Eng. J. Med. **260**: 565, 1959.

51. GERBER, I. E. AND MENDLOWITZ, M.: Visceral thrombophlebitis migrans. Ann. Int. Med. **30**: 560, 1949.

52. ALEXANDER, H. L.: In Reactions with Drug Therapy. Philadelphia, W. B. Saunders Co., 1955, pp. 49–65.

53. CLARKSON, B. H., GOLDBERG, B. L. AND SEGAL, J. P.: Dilantin sensitivity. Report of a case of hepatitis with jaundice, pyrexia and exfoliative dermatitis. New Eng. J. Med. **242**: 897, 1950.

54. MORE, R. H., McMILLAN, G. C. AND DUFF, L. G.: The pathology of sulfonamide allergy in man. Am. J. Path. **22**: 703, 1946.

55. MAISEL, B., McSWAIN, B. AND GLEM, F.: Effects of administration of sodium sulfadiazine in dogs. Arch. Surg. **46**: 326, 1943.

56. DRESSLER, W.: A post-myocardial-infarction syndrome. J. Amer. Med. Assn. **160**: 1379, 1956.

57. LEVY, R. L. AND PATTERSON, M. C.: Acute serofibrinous pericarditis of undetermined cause. A study of 27 cases. Am. J. Med. **8**: 34, 1950.

58. GELFAND, M. L. AND GOODKIN, L.: Acute benign nonspecific pericarditis without a pericardial friction rub. Ann. Int. Med. **45**: 490, 1956.

30   ROBERT G. PETERSDORF AND PAUL B. BEESON

59. LONGCOPE, W. T. AND FREIMAN, D. G.: A study of sarcoidosis. Medicine **31:** 1, 1952.
60. COWDELL, H.: Sarcoidosis: with special reference to diagnosis and prognosis. Quart. J. Med. **23:** 29, 1954.
61. LOFGREN S.: Primary pulmonary sarcoidosis. I. Early signs and symptoms. Acta med. Scand. **145:** 424, 1953.
62. LOFGREN, S.: Primary pulmonary sarcoidosis. II. Clinical course and prognosis. Acta med. Scand. **145:** 465, 1953.
63. PLATTS, M. M. AND GREAVES, M. S.: Splinter hemorrhages. Brit. Med. J. **2:** 143, 1958.
64. BIRKENHEAD, N. C., WAGENER, H. P. AND SHICK, R. M.: Treatment of temporal arteritis with adrenal corticosteroids: results in 55 cases in which lesion proved at biopsy. J. Amer. Med. Assn. **163:** 821, 1957.
65. REIMANN, H. A.: Regularly periodic fever of eleven years' duration. Acta. med. Scand. **196:** 666, 1947.
66. REIMANN, H. A.: Periodic disease. Medicine **30:** 219, 1951.
67. KAPPAS, A., HELLMAN, L., FUKUSHIMA, D. AND GALLAGHER, T. F.: The pyrogenic effect of etiocholanolone. J. Clin. Endocrinol. **17:** 451, 1957.
68. BONDY, P. K., COHN, G. L., HERRMANN, W. AND CRISPELL, K. R.: The possible relationship of etiocholanolone to periodic fever. Yale J. Biol. and Med. **30:** 395, 1958.
69. HELLER, H., SOHAR, E. AND SHERF, L.: Familial Mediterranean fever. Arch. Int. Med. **102:** 50, 1958.
70. PRIEST, R. J. AND NIXON, R. K.: Familial recurring polyserositis: a disease entity. Ann. Int. Med. **51:** 1253, 1959.
71. HALLAHAN, J. D. AND KLEIN, T.: Relapsing febrile nodular nonsuppurative panniculitis (Weber-Christian disease). Ann. Int. Med. **34:** 1179, 1951.
72. WERNER, S. C.: Thyroiditis in "The Thyroid." New York, Paul B. Hoeber, 1955.
73. CRILE, G., JR. AND RUMSEY, E. W.: Subacute thyroiditis. J. Amer. Med. Assn. **142:** 458, 1950.
74. MAYER, L.: Die Wunden der Milz. Leipzig, F. C. W. Vogel, Verlag, 1878.
75. LaBREE, R. H., FULLER, J. AND BOMAN, P. G.: Spontaneous rupture of the spleen after acute pancreatitis. J. Amer. Med. Assn. **172:** 816, 1960.
76. RICHMAN, A.: Acute pancreatitis. Amer. J. Med. **21:** 246, 1956.
77. LEONARD, B. J., ISRAELS, M. C. G. AND WILKIN-

SON, J. F.: Myelosclerosis. Quart J. Med. **26:** 131, 1957.
78. KORST, D. R., CLATANOFF, D. V. AND SCHILLING, R. F.: On myelofibrosis. Arch. Int. Med. **97:** 169, 1956.
79. CRAIL, H. W., ALT, H. L. AND NADLER, W. H.: Myelofibrosis associated with tuberculosis. Blood **3:** 1426, 1948.
80. PETERSDORF, R. G. AND BENNETT, I. L., JR.: Factitious fever. Ann. Int. Med. **46:** 1039, 1957.
81. DuBOIS, E. F.: Why are fever temperatures ove 106 F. rare? Am. J. Med. Sci. **217:** 361, 1949.
82. STROBER, M.: Fever of undetermined origin: presumptive cause, amebic colitis. U. S. Armed Forces Med. J. **7:** 1055, 1956.
83. SHUBERT, S., COLLEE, J. G. AND SMITH, B. J.: Infectious mononucleosis—a syndrome or a disease? Brit. Med. J. **1:** 671, 1954.
84. BEVERLY, J. K. A. AND BEATTY, C. P.: Glandular toxoplasmosis. Survey of 30 cases. Lancet **2:** 379, 1958.
85. BARONDESS, J. A.: Thrombotic thrombocytopenic purpura. Amer. J. Med. **13:** 294, 1952.
86. ADELSON, E., HEITZMAN, E. J. AND FENNESSY, J. F.: Thrombohemolytic thrombocytopenic purpura. Arch. Int. Med. **94:** 42, 1954.
87. ALT, H. L. AND BARKER, H.: Fever of unknown origin. J. Amer. Med. Assn. **94:** 1457, 1930.
88. KINTNER, A. R. AND ROWNTREE, L. G.: Long-continued, low-grade, idiopathic fever. Analysis of 100 cases. J. Amer. Med. Assn. **102:** 889, 1934.
89. KEEFER, C. S.: The diagnosis of the causes of obscure fever. Texas State J. Med. **35:** 203, 1939.
90. BOTTIGER, L. E.: Fever of unknown origin. With some remarks on the normal temperature in man. Acta med. Scand. **147:** 133, 1953.
91. GERACI, J. E., WEED, L. E. AND NICHOLS, D. R.: Fever of obscure origin—the value of abdominal exploration in diagnosis. Report of 70 cases. J. Amer. Med. Assn. **169:** 1306, 1959.
92. FINLAND, M., JONES, W. F., JR. AND BARNES, M. W.: Changes in the occurrence of serious bacterial infections since the introduction of antibacterial agents. Tr. Assn. Amer. Phys. **72:** 305, 1959.
93. Editorial: Prevalence of tuberculosis in large cities. J. Amer. Med. Assn. **157:** 512, 1955.
94. BENNETT, I. L., JR.: A consideration of fever of undetermined origin. J. Med. Assn. Georgia **45:** 389, 1956.
95. TISDALE, W. A.: Personal communication.

Too many specialists, too few generalists
Paul B. Beeson, M. D.

Dr. Beeson (AΩA, Emory, 1946) is professor of medicine emeritus at the University of Washington School of Medicine. Previously, after heading the Department of Medicine at Emory University and Yale University, respectively, he was Nuffield Professor of Clinical Medicine at Oxford University. For many years, he was coeditor, with the late Walsh Mc Dermott, of the Cecil-Loeb Textbook of Medicine.

Everybody seems unhappy about America's health care system. Doctors complain about "the hassle factor": loss of their traditional autonomy, excessive paperwork, malpractice litigation, et cetera. Patients say that doctors can see them only by appointment in their offices, and then appear to be hurried, cold, interested mainly in use of expensive technologic procedures. Government officials and economists are alarmed by ever-increasing expenditures for health services. Sociologists point out that tens of millions of Americans have neither insurance nor defined access to health care, although we have the world's highest per capita cost for health service $2,000, compared with $1,500 in Canada and $800 in Britain. Public health authorities note that although we possess an abundance of the newest technological aids for diagnosis and therapy, we rank below most developed nations, as judged by such indices as infant and maternal mortality.

An indication of the public's attitude is found in a recent opinion poll, conducted simultaneously in three English-speaking nations: Canada, Great Britain, and United States, by the Harvard School of Public Health and Louis Harris and Associates. Here are excerpts from the report:

> Americans express the greatest degree of dissatisfaction with their health care system. Most Americans (89 percent) see the need for fundamental change in the direction and structure of the U.S. health system. In the view of citizens of both Canada and Great Britain, the least desirable system would be the American system. Over 90 percent of the Canadian people underscore their high level of satisfaction with their current system by expressing a preference to remain with it (1).

How did we get into this predicament? In this essay I offer my perception, based on half a century in the profession (which included a decade in Britain's national health service). My thesis is that most of our difficulties stem from two related happenings: our national determination, at the close of World War II, to invest unprecedented sums of money in medical research, and the change in style of medical practice that resulted. Thus, a laudable aim –indeed its success—led to unforeseen side effects, responsible for what is now thought of as a crisis in health care.

American medicine prior to World War II

Medical students of my era (early 1930s) were introduced to clinical medicine in charity hospitals maintained by cities or counties. Most of our teachers served on a voluntary basis, earning their incomes in private practice elsewhere. (Teaching medical students and caring for people unable to pay were accepted obligations of the profession.) In addition to the voluntary practitioners, most schools had a few salaried clinical teachers; these were broadly competent in such branches as medicine or surgery, and were looked on by the students as role models.

After graduation, most of us obtained rotating internships, to prepare for careers in family practice. Mine was a two-year appointment, first a series of two-month assignments in fields such as pediatrics, obstetrics, radiology, and neurology; then six months in medicine and six months in surgery. (I then spent two years in family practice in a small Ohio town, before deciding to obtain further training in internal medicine. That led me, quite unexpectedly, into a career in academic medicine.)

In the prewar years, American family doctors saw patients either in their homes or in private offices. Hospitals were mainly reserved for surgery, obstetrics, and grave medical illnesses. For home visits the doctor's bag could carry nearly all that was available for diagnosis and therapy: clinical thermometer, stethoscope, sphygmomanometer, otoscope, ophthalmoscope, bandages, antiseptic solutions, vials of pills for treatment of symptoms, and a prescription pad. A doctor's office might possess an X-ray machine or fluoroscope, a microscope, and equipment for blood counts and urinalyses.

Research and development during World War II

Between 1939 and 1945 the warring nations mounted large scientific programs, which produced better military machines, radar, jet propulsion, and the atomic bomb. Medical research and development also yielded some advances, including large-scale production of penicillin, effective vaccine for yellow fever, better antimalarial drugs, and blood banks.

These achievements were seen by the public as evidence of what a large research effort can bring about; consequently, at the end of the fighting we launched a great national campaign to purchase better health. ·

The postwar surge in medical research

Support for medical research came from many sources: private donors, foundations such as the American Heart Association and March of Dimes, but, most importantly, the federal government, through the National Institutes of Health (NIH). Here is the way Arthur Kornberg described the contribution of the NIH:

NIH grew at a modest rate, occupying six small buildings in Bethesda when I arrived there in 1942. Then came the explosive expansion in the post-World War II decades which changed the face of medical science—13,000 people working in fifty buildings on a 300-acre site in Bethesda, along with 52,000 scientists at 1600 institutions around the world, supported by an annual budget of near $7 billion. (2)

After about 1948, those of us who were employed by medical schools found ourselves being beseeched to accept financial help! Grants, traineeships, and money for new research laboratories were easy to obtain. We had only to indicate a need and that need was satisfied: to employ and train more people, or to build and equip research laboratories.

Turbulence created by advances in medical science: Changes in our medical schools

During the past four decades most of our medical schools have been incorporated into large conglomerates containing other health profession schools, research buildings, and university teaching hospitals. Most voluntary clinical teachers have disappeared, replaced by hordes of salaried teacher/ researchers. Medical school budgets have increased greatly, especially to pay the salaries of the large clinical faculties, salaries on a par with incomes earned in private practice. The medical schools in turn depend on faculty members to devise innovations that will attract special kinds of patients, for such needs as cancer therapy, organ transplant, or joint replacement. This kind of practice generates large hospital charges and high professional fees, which help the schools to remain solvent. Obviously though, the trainees in such institutions are exposed to a skewed spectrum of human illness.

Senior faculty members, the people who formerly were the good clinicians and role models, have retreated from the bedside in order to fulfill executive responsibilities, worrying about collection of professional incomes, bed occupancy, and money to support outpatient services.

Thus, within a short time our medical schools have changed from comparatively compact branches of universities into components of large medical centers, institutions that emphasize two things: research and tertiary clinical care.

Interestingly, our full-time clinical faculties keep on growing in size, although the number of medical school entrants has declined slightly in recent years. The actual numbers of salaried clinical faculty members, and also the numbers of active practitioners in the whole nation, as reported to the Association of American Medical Colleges (AAMC) and the American Medical Association (AMA), cannot be ascertained exactly, but a conservative estimate would indicate that about 8 percent of all active clinicians in the United States are salaried. employees of medical schools. Because of the requirement to engage in research, together with the associated national activities, clinical teachers are likely to feel some insecurity about competence in broad areas of clinical medicine; consequently, they have a tendency to steer discussions in teaching sessions toward their special areas of expertise. This practice can result in far too much detail about limited fields. Academic life used to carry with it a splendid opportunity for continued medical education resulting from the collegial relationship of fellow faculty members. Nowadays, it is saddening to note how few faculty members even attend the weekly teaching conferences in their own departments.

Today's entrants to the medical profession

The 1989 AAMC Graduation Questionnaire indicated that the average medical school graduate has a debt of $42,000. This potential indebtedness selects medical school applicants from affluent families and also influences newly qualified graduates to choose fields of practice that yield large incomes, in order to pay off loans. The same AAMC study showed that only about one-fifth of senior students were contemplating the primary care specialties: family practice 11.7 percent, general internal medicine 6.0 percent, and general pediatrics 4.8 percent. Among the remainder, 5.8 percent intended to become anesthesiologists, 3.4 percent ophthalmologists, 5.3 percent radiologists, and 5.1 percent orthopedists.

In the 1930s, about 80 percent of American practitioners were family doctors. (3) Today, the Physician Data Services division of the AMA reports that only 11.7 percent of practicing physicians designate themselves as general or family practitioners. (4) While some of the latter may be reporting family practice as a specialty, it seems fair to note that American medicine has experienced a specialist boom, somewhat like the postwar baby boom. This increase contrasts with Canada and Great Britain, where governmental mechanisms control practice choices: about 60 percent of British doctors are in family practice, and just over 50 percent of Canadians belong in that category.

Internships, residencies, traineeships, and practice localities

Among the changes following the war was a shift in kinds of internships offered by most teaching hospitals, from rotating to straight services. And, inasmuch as board certification has become the immediate goal after the M.D. degree, three-year packages of internship and residency training have become more or less the rule. This postgraduate experience may be followed by one or more years in subspecialist training. Thus, our graduates make career choices early and then sequester themselves within limited areas of clinical medicine, where the role models are full-time faculty members who confine their work and thought to special fields. In these circumstances it is not surprising that most young doctors decide to become specialists.

There are of course other attractions to specialty practice. The average income is higher than that of generalists. Specialists practice in proximity to one another, usually in suburban areas, where hospitals are equipped for the procedures they carry out. Suburban locations offer advantages in living conditions, schools, et cetera. As a consequence, the nation now has voids of professional service, both in inner cities and in rural areas.

Drawbacks of a health care system staffed mainly by specialists

While not denying that there is greater need for specialist practice now than before, I maintain that the pendulum has swung much too far, resulting in maldistribution of doctors and excessive cost of medical services. I am sure that most people would like to have a continuing relationship with one practitioner who knows them and the family setting and who can deal with most problems or, when indicated, arrange for appropriate referral. Today, however, people too often try to decide for themselves which specialist to consult and may then be passed on to a different doctor—a wasteful and expensive business.

Specialists have been trained to use complex technology, and undoubtedly do so more than necessary. When appointed to the staff of a hospital, they urge its administrator to install costly equipment. This works against regional sharing of expensive facilities. Also, the fragmentation of medical services and facilities handicaps efforts of third-party payers to negotiate efficient arrangements for medical care.

Distasteful as the notion is, we have to recognize that specialists may decide (perhaps subliminally) to use procedures, whether elective surgery or techniques like echocardiography or endoscopy, · because their incomes will be augmented. As early as 1911, George Bernard Shaw said this in the preface to The Doctor's Dilemma:

> That any sane nation, having observed that you could provide for the supply of bread by giving bakers a pecuniary interest in baking for you, should go on to give surgeons a pecuniary interest in cutting off your leg, is enough to make one despair of political humanity (5).

Indubitably, the primary care fields of practice yield lower incomes than the specialty fields. The last year for which I was able to obtain figures on net incomes of certain groups of practitioners is 1986 (6). These were: family practitioners and pediatricians, $80,000; general internal medicine, $93,000; all internal medicine (half in subspecialties), $106,000; all practicing doctors, $119,000.

The case for primary care

It is generally accepted that family practitioners can deal with about 90 percent of medical episodes. They do so promptly and inexpensively. In Canada and Britain, where national policies and regulations have assured that the majority of doctors are family practitioners, health bills are substantially lower, every person has a designated doctor, and, generally speaking, the people are better satisfied.

As already mentioned, I engaged in family practice for two years. Later, during a decade as a hospital-based physician in Britain, I had an opportunity to observe the quality of work of general practitioners there. It seemed to me that patients were referred to consultants for the right reasons, and at the right times. I was impressed, too, by the information in their letters of referral, telling about the patient as a person, and including relevant past medical history.

Measures designed to encourage primary care practice

1. Family Practice: In the 1960s a scarcity of primary care doctors began to be recognized. In 1969 the American Board of Family Practice was established. This board stipulated a three -year residency training program, and conducted an examination for certification as specialist in family practice. There are now some 36,000 diplomates of this board, among the more than 500,000 doctors in active practice in the United States. The residency training programs are mainly in hospitals affiliated with medical schools, though not usually the main university teaching hospitals. The programs include rotations in several fields and emphasize care of ambulatory patients. About 90 percent of our medical schools have now established departments of family practice.

In 1978 the Institute of Medicine issued a report entitled "A Manpower Policy for Primary Health Care," which dealt with many aspects of family practice. A noteworthy, and frequently quoted passage in that report listed these components of good primary care: accessibility, comprehensiveness, coordination, continuity, and accountability (7).

In 1988 the Council on Long Range Planning and Development of the American Medical Association issued an important statement about · the need for, and the many opportunities of, family practitioners. It noted a growing demand for family practitioners by group practices and health maintenance organizations, and also emphasized the desirability of more competitive incomes (6).

2. General Internal Medicine and General Pediatrics: The nation's pool

of general internists and pediatricians represents another important source of primary medical care. Maintaining and expanding that pool is hampered because so many board certified internists and pediatricians, about 60 percent, go on to qualification as subspecialists. In defense of that tendency, it is claimed that specialists serve as family practitioners for many of their patients—the so-called "hidden system" of primary care (8). In my view, this approach is not the best way to attack the problem.

In about 1970, when the fashion was to break up departments of medicine and pediatrics into subspecialty divisions, a countermeasure was launched in some medical schools, by establishing divisions of general internal medicine and general pediatrics. This trend has gained in popularity. Recently, the AMA Council on Long Range Planning and Development made the following statement about general internal medicine, a statement that also applies, with allowance for the age group, to general pediatrics:

General internal medicine is a discipline composed of specialists trained broadly and extensively to meet the health care needs of most adults. An internist combines knowledge of the basic medical sciences with the humanistic aspects of medicine and the intricacies of complex and serious illness. As a personal, primary care physician, the internist works with patients toward health maintenance; when illness strikes, the internist establishes the diagnosis and institutes prompt treatment. An internist has been educated to manage complex illnesses and multiple severe illnesses in the same patient. The training of internists is designed to ensure competence in the organ system specialties such as cardiology, gastroenterology, and rheumatology, and in integrative disciplines such as allergy, geriatric medicine, and oncology and to prepare the general internist to provide continuous, coordinated care for adults. An internist 's practice, therefore, can include a range of services from preventive medicine to comprehensive patient care to consultative services (9).

Two private foundations have made important contributions here. In the early 1970s the Robert Wood Johnson Foundation began to make grants to finance programs intended to serve as demonstration projects in the broad area of health care, for example, inner cities, perinatal care, community health services. Also, the foundation awarded more than 500 two-year scholarships to trainees, about 54 percent in departments of medicine and 20 percent in departments of pediatrics. Johnson scholars carried out investigations of methods of prevention and treatment, in and out of hospitals.

Ten years ago, the Henry J. Kaiser Family Foundation launched a program of scholarships in general internal medicine, offering five years of support for young internists who wished careers as generalists within departments of internal medicine. Many of these awards have gone to former holders of Johnson scholarships. These Kaiser scholars have not only been prized as clinical teachers, but also have shown themselves capable of conducting worthwhile research: clinical epidemiology, cost benefit analysis, clinical problem solving, clinical trials, computers in medicine, industrial medicine, evaluation of units for intensive care or for geriatric assessment, and ethical issues. They have also engaged in clinical studies in areas that cross subspecialty lines, such as fever, syncope, dementia, and pain.

The Society of General Internal Medicine has existed for a decade and it has become a vigorous academic organization, now numbering about 2000. It sponsors the *Journal of General Internal Medicine*.

Conclusion—some personal biases

My focus here has been narrow, with emphasis on what I believe to be an obstacle to efficient and equitable medical care for all people: an excessive proportion of specialist practitioners. Of course, the medical profession is not solely responsible for all our problems; nonetheless we do contribute importantly, by our choices of field of practice, our incomes, and our tendency to use costly tests and procedures. Other factors, for which we are not responsible, include lack of insurance for 15 percent of the population, lifestyles including substance abuse, public expectation of care without delay and in handsome surroundings. There is also the morass of malpractice litigation and resulting high cost of malpractice insurance.

I do not believe we can adopt in whole the health care system of some other country, even though that system appears to work better, and to be fairer to all people. To accomplish something like that, in our pluralistic system, containing thousands of private hospitals and diagnostic laboratories, along with our varying schemes of professional practice, would generate great resistance and dislocations. Sounder strategy, it seems to me, is to attempt correction of important faults in the framework of existing conditions.

We can make primary care medicine more attractive to young doctors by the policies of our medical schools. Departments of family practice deserve fullest support. Departments of medicine and pediatrics can ensure that their generalist members have high visibility.

We can begin to correct the over supply of specialist practitioners by working for changes in pay scales, for example, the sometimes exorbitant fees for procedures, both medical and surgical, and the inadequate reward for cognitive, communicative, and preventive services. We need to emphasize studies of cost effectiveness and quality assurance.

References

1. Blendon, RJ, and Taylor, H: Views on health care: Public opinion in three nations. Health Affairs 8:149-57 , Spring 1989.
2. Kornberg, A: For the Love of Enzymes: The Odyssey of a Biochemist. Cambridge, Massachusetts, Harvard University Press, 1989, p. 130.
3. Donabedian , A, Axelrod, SJ, Wyszewianski, L, et al.: Medical Care Chartbook , Ann Arbor , Michigan, Health Administration Press, 1986, p. 176.
4. Robeck, G, Randolph, L, and Seidman, B: Physician Characteristics and Distribution. Chicago, American Medical Association, 1990, p. 90.
5. Shaw, GB: Preface on doctors. In: The Doctor's Dilemma, p. 9. New York, Penguin Books, 1982.
6. Council on Long Range Planning and Development of the American Medical Association: The future of family practice: Implications of the changing environment of medicine. JAMA 260:1272 -79, 1988.
7. Institute of Medicine, Division of Health Manpower and Resources Development: Report of a Study: A Manpower Policy for Primary Health Care. Washington, DC, National Academy of Sciences, May 1978.

8. Aiken, LH, Lewis, CE, Craig, J, et al.: The contribution of specialists to the delivery of primary care: A new perspective. N Engl J Med 300 :1363-70, 1979.

9. Council on Long Range Planning and Development of the American Medical Association: The future of general internal medicine. JAMA 262 :2119-24, 1989.

Reprinted from The Pharos of Alpha Omega Alpha Spring, 1991, Vol. 54, No. 2,Pages 2-6.

Chapter 15

Curriculum Vitae and Bibliography of Paul Beeson

CURRICULUM VITAE
Paul Bruce Beeson

Birthplace and date: Livingston, Montana; October 18, 1908

Education: 1925-1928, University of Washington M.D., C.M., 1933, McGill University Hon. D.Sc., 1968, Emory University D.M., 1969, Oxford University
Hon. D.Sc., 1971, McGill University Hon. D.Sc., 1975, Yale University
Hon. D.Sc., 1975, Albany Medical College Hon. D.Sc., 1979, Medical College of Ohio

Experience:
1933-1935 – Intern, Hospital of the University of Pennsylvania
1935-1937 - General Practice, Wooster, Ohio
1937-1939 - Resident, Rockefeller Institute Hospital 1939-1940 - Resident in Medicine, Peter Bent Brigham Hospital
1940-1942 - Chief Physician, American Red Cross - Harvard Field Hospital Unit, Salisbury, England
1942-1944 - Assistant Professor of Medicine, Emory University
1944-1946 - Associate Professor of Medicine, Emory University
1946-1952 - Professor and Chairman, Department of Medicine, Emory University
1952-1965 - Professor and Chairman, Department of Medicine, Yale University
1965-1974 - Nuffield Professor of Clinical Medicine, Oxford University
1974-1981 - Distinguished Physician, Veterans Administration
1974-1981 - Professor of Medicine, University of Washington (now Emeritus)

Honors and Awards

1962 - Member, American Academy Arts & Sciences

1963 - Co-Editor, Cecil Textbook of Medicine (to 1979)

1963 - Fiftieth Anniversary Gold Medal, Peter Bent Brigham Hospital

1966 - Fellow, Royal College of Physicians

1967 - President, Association of American Physicians

1968 - Alumnus Summa Laude Dignatus, University of Washington

1968 - Member, National Academy of Sciences

1970 - Master, American College of Physicians

1972 - Bristol Award, Infectious Diseases Society of America

1973 - Kober Medal, Association of American Physicians

1973 - Honorary Knight Commander of the British Empire

1975 - Honorary Fellow, Royal Society of Medicine

1975 - Honorary Fellow, Magdalen College, Oxford

1976 - Phillips Award, American College of Physicians

1977 - Flexner Award, Association of American Medical Colleges

1980 - Honorary Member, Reticuloendothelial Society

1981 - Paul B. Beeson Professorship created, Yale University

1981 - Honorary Fellow, Green College, Oxford

1981 - Gold-Headed Cane Award, University of California, San Francisco

1982 - Founders Award, Southern Society for Clinical Research

1984 - Willard Thompson Award, American Geriatrics Society

1984 - Honorary Member, Canadian Society of Internal Medicine

1986 - Co-Editor, Oxford Companion to Medicine

1990 - Distinguished Teacher Award, American College of Physicians

Publications

1. Hoagland, C.L., Beeson, P.B., Goebel, W.F., The capsular polysaccharide of the type XIV pneumococcus and its relationship to the specific substances of human blood. Science, 88(2281): 261-3. Sep 16, 1938.

2. Beeson, P.B., and Hoagland, C.L. Use of calcium chloride in relief of chills following serum administration. Proc. Soc. Exp. Biol. (N.Y.), .3.8. 160, 1938.

3. Hoagland, C.L., Beeson, P.B., and Goebel, W.F. The capsular

polysaccharide of the Type XIV pneumococcus and its relationship to the specific substances of human blood. Science .8 &:261, 1938.

4. MacLeod, C.M., Hoagland, C.L., and Beeson, P.B. The use of the skin test with the type specific polysaccharides in the control of serum dosage in pneumococcal pneumonia. J. Clin. Invest. 1. I:739.

5. Goebel, W.F., Beeson , P.B., and Hoagland, C.L., Chemicoimmunological studies on the soluble specific substance of pneumococcus, IV. The capsular polysaccharide of Type XIV pneumococcus and its relationship to the blood group A specific substance. J. Biol. Chem. 1.2_2:455, 1939.

6. Beeson, P.B., and Goebel, W.F. The immunological relationship of the capsular polysaccharide of Type XIV pneumococcus to the blood Group A specific substance. J. Exp.

7. Beeson, P.B., and Hoagland, C.L. The use of calcium chloride in the treatment of chills. N.Y. St. J. Med. :803, 1940.

8. Beeson, P.B., and Janeway, C.A. The antipyretic action of sulfapyridine. Am. J. Med. Sci. 2.00:632, 1940.

9. Beeson, P.B., and Goebel, W.F. Immunological crossreactions of Type B Friedlander bacillus in Type 2 antipneumococcal horse and rabbit serum. J. Immunol. .3.8.:231, 1940.

10. Janeway, C.A., and Beeson, P.B. The treatment of pneumococcal pneumonia; with special reference to the use of sulfathiazole, intramuscular serum, the Francis test and histaminase. New Engl. J. Med. 2.44.:592, 1941.

11. Beeson, P.B. Factors influencing the prevalence of trichinosis in man. Proc. Roy. Soc. Med. M: 585, 1941.

12. Beeson, P.B. Trichinosis. Clinical manifestations and diagnosis. Lancet 2:67, 1941.

13. Levine, S.A., and Beeson, P.B. The Wolff-Parkinson-White syndrome,with paroxysms of ventricular tachycardia. Am. Heart J. 22.:401, 1941.

14. Beeson, P.B., and Scott, T.F. McN. An epidemic myalgia distinct from Bornholm disease, which chiefly affected the muscles of the neck. Ann. Rheum. Dis. 2.:1, 1941.

15. Beeson, P.B., and Scott, T.F. McN. Clinical, epidemiological and experimental observations on an acute myalgia of the neck and

shoulders; its possible relation to certain cases of generalized fibrositis. Proc. Roy. Soc. Med .3.5:733, 1942 .

16. Scott, T.F. McN., Beeson, P.B., and Hawley, W.L. Paratyphoid B infection. The ineffectiveness of sulphaguanadine. Lancet 1:487, 1943.

17. Beeson, P. B. Jaundice occurring one to four months after transfusion of blood or plasma. Re biopsies, cultures, smears, auto-inoculations and report of seven cases. J.A.M.A. 12.1:1332, 1943.

18. Beeson, P.B., and Westerman, E. Cerebrospinal fever. Analysis of 3,575 case reports, with special reference to sulphonamide therapy. Brit. Med. J. 1:497, 1943.

19. Beeson, P.B. Fever. Clinics 2.: 1361, 1944.

20. Beeson, P.B., and Miller, E.S. Relationship of Lymphogranuloma venereum infection to the incidence of hyperglobulinemia. Am. J. Med. Sc. 2111: 643, 1944.

21. Beeson, P.B. Chesney, G., and McFarlan, A.M. Hepatitis following injection of mumps convalescent plasma. I. Use of plasma I., Use of plasma in the mumps epidemic. Lancet 1: 814, 1944.

22. Beeson, P.B., and Miller, E.S. Epidemiological study of lymphogranulama venereum, employing the complement-fixation test. Am. J. Publ. Health 3.1: 1076, 1944.

23. Beeson, P.B. Brannon, E.S., and Warren, J.V. observations on the sites of removal of bacteria from the blood in patients with bacterial endocarditis. J. Exp. Med. 81: 9, 1945.

24. Beeson, P.B. and Heyman, A. Studies on chancroid, II. Efficiency of the cultural method of diagnosis. Am. J. Syph. 2.9: 633, 1945

25. Beeson, P.B., A study of the fever resulting from intravenous injection of pyrogens. Proceedings. 2: 79, 1945.

26. Heyman, A., Beeson, P.B., The significance of immunologic tests in lymphogranuloma venereum and chancroid. Proceedings, 2:88, 1945.

27. Heyman, A., Beeson, P.B., and Sheldon, W.H. Diagnosis of chancroid. The relative efficiency of biopsies, cultures, smears, auto-inoculations and skin tests., J.A.M.A. 12.9: 935, 1945.

28. Beeson, P.B., and Miller, E.S. Murine typhus fever. Medicine (Baltimore) 2.5.:1, 1946.

29. Heyman , A., and Beeson, P.B. Studies on chancroid. II I. Ducreykin reactions in Negro hospital patients. J. Vener. Dis. Inform. 21: 104,

1946.

30. Beeson, P.B. Studies on chancroid. IV. The Dubrey bacillus: growth requirements and inhibition by antibiotic agents. Proc. Soc. Exp. Biol. (NY): 81, 1946.

31. Beeson, P.B. Development of tolerance to typhoid bacterial pyrogen and its abolition by reticulo-endothelial blockage. Proc. Soc. Exp. Biol (NY): 248, 1946.

32. Beeson, P.B., Wall, M.J., and Heyman, A. Isolation of virus of lymphogranuloma venereum from blood and spinal fluid of a human being. Proc. Soc. Exp. Biol. (NY) 62: 306, 1946.

33. Heyman, A., Wall, M.J., and Beeson, P.B. The effect of sulfonamide therapy on the persistence of the virus of lymphogranuloma venereum in buboes. Am. J. Syph. 31. 1:81, 1947.

34. Heyman, A., Wall, J., Beeson, P.B., The effect of sulfonamide therapy on the persistence of the virus of lymphogranuloma venereum in buboes. Proceedings. 3(1 Vol): 31, 1947.

35. Michael, M., Jr., Beeson, P.B., Bacteriological and clinical studies on streptomycin therapy with observations on the pathogenesis of urinary tract infections. Proceedings 3(1 Vol): 25, 1947.

36. Beeson, P.B. Effect of reticulo-endothelial blockade on immunity to the Shwartzman phenomenon. Proc. Soc. Exp. Biol. (NY) 6.4:146, 1947.

37. Wall, M.J. Heyman, A., and Beeson, P.B. Studies on the complement fixation reaction in lymphogranuloma venereum. Am. J. Syph. 3.1:289, 1947.

38. Beeson, P.B. Tolerance to bacterial pyrogens. I. Factors influencing its development. J. Exp. Med. 8. 6:39, 1947.

39. Beeson, P.B. Tolerance to bacterial pyrogens. I. Factors influencing its development. J. Exp. Med. 8. 6:29, 1947.

40. Cargill, W.H., and Beeson, P.B. The value of spinal fluid examination as a diagnostic procedure in Weill's disease. An. Int. Med. 21:396, 1947.

41. Beeson, P.B., Temperature-elevating effect of a substance obtained from polymorphonuclear leucocytes. Journal of Clinical Investigation. 27(4): 524, July 1948.

42. Heyman, A., and Beeson, P.B. Influence of various disease states upon

the febrile response to intravenous injection of typhoid bacterial pyrogen; with particular reference to malaria and cirrhosis of the liver. J. Lab. Clin. Med. 3A: 1400, 1949.

43. Michael, M., Jr., Cole, R., Beeson, P.B., Olson, B., Sarcoidosis: preliminary observations from an analysis of 350 cases. Transactions of the Annual Meeting. 46: 208-12, 1950.

44. Michael, M. Jr., Cole, R.M., Beeson, P.B., and Olson, B.J. Sarcoidosis. Preliminary report of a study of 350 cases with special reference to epidemiology. Am. Rev. Turberc. 62:403, 1950.

45. Bennett, L.L. Jr., and Beeson, P.B. The properties and biologic effects of bacterial pyrogens. Medicine 2.9: 365, 1950.

46. Beeson, P.B., and Hankey, D.D. "Benign aseptic meningitis" as a manifestation of leptospiral infection. Trans. Assoc. Am. Phys. 6.3: 130, 1950.

47. Beeson, P.B. Fever of obscure origin. Veterans Adm. Med. Bull., pg. 10, 1951.

48. Beeson, P.B. Hankey, D.D., and Cooper, C.F. Leptospiral iridocyclitis. Evidence of human infection with leptospira Pomona in the United States. JAMA. 1.45: 229, 1951.

49. Beeson, P.B., and Hankey, D.D. Leptospiral meningitis. Arch. Int. Med. 8.9: 575, 1952.

50. Beeson, P.B. Cryptococcic meningitis of nearly sixteen years' duration. Arch. Int. Med. 8.9: 797, 1952.

51. Beeson, P.B. Leptospiral infections of man (editorial). Am. J. Med. 1.5: 591, 1953.

52. Bennett, L.L. Jr., and Beeson, P.B. Studies on the pathogenesis of fever. I. The effect of injection of extracts and suspensions of uninfected rabbit tissues up on the body temperature of normal rabbits. J. Exp. Med. 9.8: 477, 1953.

53. Bennett, I.L. Jr., and Beeson, P.B. Studies on the pathogenesis of fever II. Characterization of fever-producing substances from polymorphonuclear leukocytes and from the fluid of sterile exudates. J. Exp. Med. 9.8: 493, 1953.

54. Bennett, I.L. Jr., and Beeson, P.B. The effect of cortisone upon reactions of rabbits to bacterial endotoxins with particular reference to acquired resistance. Bull. Johns Hopkins Hosp. 9.3: 290, 1953.

55. Bennett, I.L. Jr., and Beeson, P.B. Bacteremia: a consideration of some experimental and clinical aspects. Yale J. Biol. Med. 2.6: 241, 1954.

56. Beeson, P.B. Subacute bacterial endocarditis: optimal duration of treatment (editorial). Am. J. Med. 19:1, 1955.

57. Hollingsworth, J.W., and Beeson, P.B. Experimental bacteremia in normal and irradiated rats. Yale J. Biol. Med. 28: 56, 1955.

58. Beeson, P.B. Factors in the pathogenesis of pyeolonephritis. Yale J. Biol. Med. 28: 81, 1955.

59. Hollingsworth, J.W., Finch, S. C., and Beeson, P.B. The role of transfused leukocytes in experimental bacteremia of irradiated rats. J. Lab. Clin. Med. 4.8: 227, 1956.

60. Guze, L.B., and Beeson, P.B. Observations on the reliability and safety of bladder catheterization for bacteriologic study of the urine. New Engl. J. Med. 255: 474, 1956.

61. Guze, L.B., and Beeson, P.B. Experimental pyelonephritis. I. Effect of ureteral ligation on the course of bacterial infection in the kidney of the rat. J. Exp. Med. liM: 803, 1956.

62. Guze, L.B., and Beeson, P.B. The effect of cortisone on experimental hydronephrosis following ureteral ligation. J. Urol. (Baltimore) Z.8: 377, 1957.

63. Beeson, P.B., Rocha, H., and Guze, L.B. Experimental pyelonephritis: influence of localized susceptibility to hematogenous infection. Trans. Assoc. Am. Phys. 10: 120, 1957.

64. Beeson, P.B. The case against the catheter (editorial). Am. J. Med. 24:1, 1958.

65. Guze, L.B., and Beeson, P.B. Experimental pyelonephritis. II. Effect of partial ureteral obstruction on the course of bacterial infection in the kidney of the rat and the rabbit. Yale J. Biol. Med. Iii: 315, 1958.

66. Rocha, H., Guze, L.B., Freedman, L.R., and Beeson, P.B. Experimental pyelonephritis. III. The influence of localized injury in different parts of the kidney on susceptibility to bacillary infection. Yale J. Biol. Med. Iii: 341, 1958.

67. Freedman, L.R. and Beeson, P.B. Experimental pyelonephritis IV. Observations on infections resulting from direct inoculation of bacteria in different zones of the kidney. Yale J. Biol. Med. Iii: 406, 1958.

68. Beeson, P.B., and Rowley, D. The anticomplementary effect of kidney tissue: Its association with ammonia production. J. Exp. Med. 11.0: 685, 1959.

69. Rocha, H., Guze, L.B., and Beeson, P.B. Experimental pyelonephritis. V. Susceptibility of rats to hematogenous pyelonephritis following chemical injury of the kidneys. Yale J. Biol. Med. 32: 120, 1959.

70. Freedman, L.R., Kaminskas, E., and Beeson, P.B. Experimental pyelonephritis. VII. Evidence on the mechanisms by which obstruction of urine flow enhances susceptibility to pyelonephritis. Yale J. Biol. Med. 3-3: 65, 1960.

71. Beeson, P.B. Clinical medicine and the future. Yale J. Biol. Med. 3-3: 235, 1960.

72. Freedman, L.R., and Beeson, P.B. Experimental pyelonephritis. VIII. Effect of acidifying agents on susceptibility to infection. Yale J. Biol. Med. 3-3: 318, 1961.

73. Petersdorf. R. G., and Beeson, P.B. Fever of unexplained origin. Report of 100 cases. Medicine: 1, 1961.

74. Beeson, P.B., and McDermott, W. (editors) The Cecil-Loeb Textbook of Medicine, 11the Edition, Philadelphia, W.B. Saunders Co., 1963.

75. Beeson, P.B., Nocardiosis as a complication of pulmonary alveolar proteinosis (editorial). Ann. Int. Med. Fill: 1964.

76. Beeson, P.B. Bondy, P.K., Donnelly, R.C., and Smith, J.E. Panel discussion: moral issues in clinical research. Yale J. Biol. Med. 3Ji: 455, 1964.

77. Beeson, P.B. The Academic Doctor. Presidential Address, Transactions of the Association of American Physicians, 1xxx, 1967.

78. Beeson, P.B., and McDermott, W. (editors) The Cecil-Loeb Textbook of Medicine, 12the Edition, Philadelphia, W.B. Saunders Co., 1967.

79. Beeson, P.B. Special Book Review of "Sickness and Society" by Duff and Hollingshead. Yale J. Biol. Med . .41:226, 1968.

80. Beeson, P.B. Eugene A. Stead, Jr.: A biographical note. Ann. Int. Med. 6.9: 986, 1968.

81. Basten, A., Boyer, M.H., and Beeson, P.B. Mechanism of eosinophil response of rats to Trichinella spiralis. J. Exp. Med. 1.3.1: 1271, 1970.

82. Basten, A., and Beeson, P.B. Mechanism of eosinophilia II. Role of the lymphocyte. J. Exp. Med. 13.1: 1288, 1970.

83. Boyer, M.H., Basten, A., and Beeson, P.B. Mechanism of eosinophilia. III. Suppression of eosinophilia by agents known to modify immune responses. Blood. 3. Fi(No-4): 458, 1970.

84. Beeson, P.B., and McDermott, W. (editors), The Cecil-Loeb Textbook of Medicine, 13th Edition, Philadelphia, W.B. Saunders Co., 1971.

85. Morgan, J.E., and Beeson, P.B. Experimental observations on the eonsinopenia inducted by acute infection. Br. J. Exp. Path. 52: 214, 1971.

86. Beeson, P.B. Medical education for the future. Montreal General Hospital 1921-1971. C.M.A. Journal 10.5: 1253, 1971.

87. Beeson, P.B. "Quality of Survival." Reprinted from Patient, Doctor, Society. Published for the Nuffield Provincial Hospitals Trust by the Oxford University Press, 1972.

88. Boyer, M.H., Spry, C.J.F., Beeson, P.B., and Sheldon, W.H. Mechanism of eosinophilia. IV. The pulmonary lesion resulting from intravenous injection of Trichinella spiralis. Yale J. Biol. Med., il: 351, 1971.

89. Durack, D.T., and Beeson, P.B. Experimental bacterial endocarditis. I. Colonization of a sterile vegetation. Brit. J. Exp. Path. 5.3: 44, 1972.

90. Durack, D.T., and Beeson, P.B. Experimental bacterial endocarditis. II Survival of bacteria in endocardial vegetations. Brit. J. Exp. Path. 5.3:50, 1972.

91. Walls, R.S. and Beeson, P.B. Mechanism of eosinophilia. VIII. Importance of local cellular reactions in stimulating eosinophil production. Clin. Exp. Immunol. 12: 111, 1972.

92. Walls, R.S., and Beeson, P.B. Mechanism of eosinophilia IX. Induction of eosinophilia in rats by certain forms of dextran. Proc. Soc. Exp. Biol. Med. 1A:0:689, 1972.

93. Durack, D.T. Beeson, P.B., and Petersdorf, R.G. Experimental bacterial endocarditis. III Production and progress of the disease in rabbits. Br. J. Exp. Path. 5A:142, 1973.

94. Durack, D. T., Petersdorf, R.G. and Beeson, P.B. Penicillin prophylaxis of experimental S. Viridans endocarditis. Reprinted from Transactions of the Association of American Physicians, Vol. 1, pg. 222, 1972.

95. Walls, R.S., Bass, D.A., and Beeson, P.B., Mechanism of eosinophilia. X. Evidence for immunologic specificity of the stimulus (37989). Proc. Soc. Exp. Biol. Med. Li.5: 1240, 1974.

96. Beeson, P.B. Some good features of the British National Health Service. J. Med. Ed. .49(1): 43-9, 1974.

97. Beeson, P.B., and McDermott, W. (editors) Textbook of Medicine, 14th Edition, Philadelphia, W.B., Saunders Col, 1975.

98. Gotch, F.M., Spry, C.J., Mowat, A.G., Beeson, P.B., Maclennan, I.C., Reversible granulocyte killing defect in anorexia nervosa. Clinical and Experimental Immunology. 21(2): 244-9, 1975.

99. Beeson, P.B., Presentation of the George M. Kober Medal to Walsh McDermott. Transactions of the Association of American Physicians. 88:35-9. 1975.

100. Beeson, P.B., McDermott, W., Letter: An error in recommended dose of gentamicin. Lancet. (2)7926): 190-1, 1975.

101. Beeson, P.B. The ways of academic clinical medicine in America since World War II. Man and Medicine 1:65, 1975.

102. Horstmann, D., and Beeson, P.B. John Rodman Paul. Biographical memoirs. Natl. Acad. Sci. (US). 41: 323, 1975.

103. Beeson, P.B. Infectious Diseases (Microbiology). In Advances in American Medicine. Essays at the Bicentennial. Eds: Bowers, J.A., and Purvell, E.F., Macy Foundation, New York, 1976.

104. Starkebaum, M., Durack, D., and Beeson, P.B. The "Incubation Period" of subacute bacterial endocarditis. Yale J. Biol. Med. 5.0: 49, 1977.

105. Beeson, P.B. Role of the Eosinophil. In immunology of the Gut. (Ciba Foundation Symposium 46 – new series). Elsevier Excerpta Medica, North-Holland, pg. 203, 1977.

106. Beeson, P.B. The development of clinical knowledge. JAMA. 2.3.I:2209, 1977.

107. Durack, D.T., and Beeson, P.B. Protective role of complement in experimental Escherichia coli endocarditis. Infect. Immun. 16:213, 1977.

108. Beeson, P.B., and Bass, D.A., The Eosinophil. W.B. Saunders Co, Philadelphia, 1977.

109. Beeson, P.B., McKeown's The Role of Medicine: A Clinician's Reaction. Milbank Memorial Fund Quarterly. 1971, Pg. 365.Durack, D.T., and Beeson, P.B. Pathogenesis of Infective Endocarditis. In Infective Endocarditis. Ed: Rahimtoola, S.H., Grune & Stratton , New

York,)978.

110. Durack, D.T., and Beeson, P.B. Pathogenesis of Infective Endocarditis. In Infective Endocarditis. Ed: Rahimtoola, S.H., Grune & Stratton, New York, 978.

111. Beeson, P.B. Training doctors to care for old people. Ann. Int. Med . .20:262, 1979.

112. Beeson, P.B. The growth of knowledge about a disease: hepatitis. Am. J. Med . .61:366, 1979.

113. Beeson, P.B., and McDermott, w. (editors) Textbook of Medicine, 15th Edition, Philadelphia, W.B. Saunders Co., 1979.

114. Beeson, P.B. Book Review of "Infectious Diseases: Prevention and Treatment in the Nineteenth and Twentieth Centuries", by Wesley W. Spink. J. Hist. Med . .3A:370, 1979.

115. Beeson, P.B. Changes in medical therapy during the past half century. Medicine .59.:79, 1980.

116. Beeson, P.B. How to foster the gain of knowledge about disease. Perspect. Biol. Med. 2.3.:59, 1980.

117. Beeson, P.B. Some diseases that have disappeared. Am. J. Med . .6.8.:806, 1980.

118. Beeson, P.B. The natural history of medical sub specialties. Ann. Int. Med . .9..3.:624, 1980.

119. Beeson, P.B. The Clinical Significance of Eosinophilia. In The Eosinophil in Health and Disease. Eds: Mahmoud, A.A.F., and Asten, K.F., Grune & Stratton, New York, 1980.

120. Beeson, P.B. Withering revisited. New Engl. J. Med. .3.0..3.: 1475, 1980.

121. Beeson, P.B. Priorities in medical education. Perspect. Biol. Med. 2.5.:673-687, 1982.

122. Root, R.K., Beeson, P.B., Genetic disorders of leukocyte function: what they tell us about normal antimicrobial mechanisms of human phagocytic cells. Klinische Wochenschrift, 60(14): 731-4, 1982.

123. Beeson, P.B., Consequences of nuclear warfare. Western Journal of Medicine. 138(2): 254-5, 1983.

124. Beeson, P.B., Cancer and eosinophilia. New England Journal of Medicine. 309(13): 792-3, 1983.

125. Beeson, P.B. Lessons learned from editing a geriatrics journal. J. Am.

Geriat. Soc. 3 2.:849, 1984.

126. Beeson, P.B. Geriatrics. J.A.M.A. 2.5.2.:2209, 1984.

127. Beeson, P.B. Alleged susceptibility of the elderly to infection. Yale J. Biol. Med . .5-8.:71, 1985.

128. Beeson, P.B., Retrospective commentary on the bacterial endocarditis study. Reviews of Infectious Diseases. 7(4): 574-6, 1985.

129. Beeson, P.B. The Institute of Medicine report on aging and medical education - 1984 update. Bull. N.Y. Acad. Med . .61:478, 1985.

130. Beeson, P.B. Classics in infectious diseases: Observations on the sites of removal of bacteria from the blood of patients with bacterial endocarditis . Retrospective commentary. Rev. Infect. Dis. 1_:574, 1985.

131. Beeson, P.B., Retrospective commentary on the bacterial endocarditis study. Reviews of Infectious Diseases. 7(4): 574-6, 1985.

132. Beeson, P.B. One hundred years of American internal medicine. Ann. Int. Med . .10.5.:436 , 1986.

133. Beeson, P.B. The changing role model, and the shift in power. Daedalus 115: 83, 1986.

134. Beeson, P.B. Making medicine a more attractive profession. J. Med. Education 62: 116, 1987.

135. Beeson, P.B. Animal experimentation: context of a quote. Science. 245(4925): 1437, 1989.

136. Beeson, P.B., Animals in research: a quote out of context. JAMA, 264(9): 1105, 1990.

137. Beeson, P.B. Walsh McDermott: October 14, 1909-October 17, 1981 In Biographical Memoirs. Natl. Acad. Sci., 59:283-307, 1990.

138. Beeson, P.B. Too many specialists, too few generalists. Daedalus, pg. 2-6, Spring, 1991.

139. Beeson, P.B., Fashions in pathogenetic concepts during the present century: autointoxication, focal infection, psychosomatic disease, and autoimmunity. [Review] [23 refs] Perspectives in Biology and Medicine. 26(1): 13-23, 1992.

140. Beeson, P.B., An early call for health care reform: the committee of 430 physicians. [Erratum appears in Pharos 1993 Spring: 56(2): 29] Pharos of Alpha Omega Honor Medical Society. 56(1): 22-4, 1993.

141. Beeson, P.B., Age and sex association of 40 autoimmune diseases.

American Journal of Medicine. 96(5): 457-62. 1994.

142. Beeson, P.B., Effects of iodides on inflammatory processes [Review] [37 refs] Perspectives in Biology and Medicine. 37(2): 173-81, 1994.

143. Beeson, P.B., Hepatitis as a complication of blood transfusion. Haemophilia. 1(1): 70-3, 1995.

144. Glaser, R.J., Beeson, P.B., Career tracks of Kaiser scholars in general medicine. Transactions of the American Clinical and Climatological Association. 106: 222-6, 1995.

Index